Essentials of Business Conflict Resolution

Conflict is inevitable in today's business environment, but it can be managed constructively. This book offers a comprehensive exploration of the fundamental mechanics of negotiation and mediation, equipping readers with the tools to navigate and resolve conflict effectively.

Blending theory with practical applications, *Essentials of Business Conflict Resolution* demonstrates how successful organizations address internal and external conflicts to encourage growth, collaboration, and resilience. Adopting a problem-solving approach, the book explores the behaviors and skills essential for conflict resolution, including communication, decisiveness, and active listening. It examines how organizational structures influence conflict management and highlights strategies to streamline resolution processes, prevent crises, and create positive cultural change. Readers will gain insights into the stages of leadership, the role of peer review committees, and the critical functions of crisis managers and ombudspersons. Key features include clear and accessible explanations of negotiation, mediation, and conflict resolution techniques, designed for readers with no prior knowledge; real-world business examples that bring theoretical concepts to life, offering practical applications for students and professionals alike; and interactive exercises and group discussions in the appendix, encouraging readers to engage deeply with the material and apply it to real-world scenarios.

Whether preparing for a career in leadership or seeking to enhance team effectiveness, *Essentials of Business Conflict Resolution* teaches readers to recognize the root causes of conflict, apply constructive communication strategies, and develop actionable plans to address workplace challenges.

Sam Blank is an adjunct professor at the Gabelli School of Business, Fordham University, Lincoln Center, teaching graduate courses in negotiation and cross-cultural communication in the Executive MBA program.

Essentials of Business Conflict Resolution

Proficiency, Management and Structure for Organizational Leadership

Sam Blank

Routledge
Taylor & Francis Group
NEW YORK AND LONDON

Designed cover image: Getty Images. Tug of War Rope Pulling Business People Concept—stock illustration @ChrisGorgio

First published 2027
by Routledge
605 Third Avenue, New York, NY 10158

and by Routledge
4 Park Square, Milton Park, Abingdon, Oxon, OX14 4RN

Routledge is an imprint of the Taylor & Francis Group, an informa business

Library of Congress Cataloging-in-Publication Data
Names: Blank, Sam, 1947– author
Title: Essentials of business conflict resolution : proficiency, management & structure for organizational leadership / Sam Blank.
Description: New York, NY : Routledge, 2027. | Includes bibliographical references and index.
Identifiers: LCCN 2026022039 | ISBN 9781041359777 hardback | ISBN 9781041359753 paperback | ISBN 9781042000258 ebook
Subjects: LCSH: Conflict management | Work environment
Classification: LCC HD42 .B5825 2027
LC record available at https://lccn.loc.gov/2026022039

ISBN: 978-1-041-35977-7 (hbk)
ISBN: 978-1-041-35975-3 (pbk)
ISBN: 978-1-042-00025-8 (ebk)

DOI: 10.4324/9781042000258

Typeset in Sabon
by Apex CoVantage, LLC

Contents

About the Author

Sam Blank is an adjunct professor at the Gabelli School of Business, Fordham University, Lincoln Center, teaching graduate courses in negotiation and cross-cultural communication in the Executive MBA program. He has served as an adjunct professor at Pace University's Graduate School of Educational Leadership and an adjunct instructor at the City University of New York-Manhattan CC. He is the author of a professional textbook *Managing Organizational Conflict*, published by McFarland, and has co-authored a text *Stand & Deliver: High-Impact Presentations*, published by Pearson. He was an educational consultant to Heartland Media for a ten-part video series "Peace Talks," which aired on PBS.

He is certified as a mediation specialist by both the International Center for Cooperation and Conflict Resolution at Teachers College and the State of New York and has served as Director of Conflict Resolution Centers and Director of School Leadership Teams for the NYC Department of Education. He coordinated the relief efforts for the schools at Ground Zero following the September 11 terrorist assault and led various groups to Germany for a program underwritten by President George W. Bush and Chancellor Gerhard Schroëder.

He has taught "Negotiating to Win" seminars for the American Management Association and has delivered several speeches, conference keynote addresses and workshops, and trainings on safe and caring workplaces, crisis management, and international friendship.

Acknowledgments

In writing this book, I have many people to thank. I would like to express gratitude to my colleagues and good friends who encouraged me along the way and who have shared with me their experiences and taught me meaningful lessons: Dr. Bozena Mierzejewska and Dr. Francis Petit from Fordham University, Dr. Tzu-Wen Cheng from CUNY, Richard Bradley from the American Management Association, and Michael Pritchard. A special thanks to Dr. Joseph A. DeVito from Hunter College who stood as an outstanding role model of what a college professor ought to be.

Special acknowledgments must go to my students who over the past have provided the inspiration essential to this kind of task. I am indebted to my cadre of stellar graduate students at the Gabelli School of Business and my undergraduate communications students from the City University of New York—BMCC.

For tremendous love and support of all kinds, I thank my wife Ellen Afromsky and my family for keeping me humble, making me laugh, and challenging me to grow each day.

Introduction

At the beginning of chapter 6 in *Managing Organizational Conflict* (Blank, 2020), it is put forward that organizational conflicts can occur in a host of ways and when disagreements are allowed to fester, these can threaten company efficiency and impact productive pursuits. When business conflict arises, it is usually the result of interference between two or more interdependent groups of people who perceive incompatible goals, values, or expectations in attaining those ends; the incompatibility can result in the incapable role of existing harmoniously (Martin and Nakayama, 2022).

People are communal by nature, and we are often happiest and perform at our best when we are with others. But at times that social aspect can create discord—working in an office environment, or even working remotely as a team, creates situations where differing personality types may have to encounter one another to cooperate on shared tasks. And while opposing viewpoints have been shown to foster creativity and problem-solving, there are instances where clashes may arise due to incompatible values, approaches, or needs, leading to disruptive conflicts. And if left unaddressed, these conflicts can easily spiral out of control.

Organizational structures are essentially blueprints that disclose how companies are run and managed and how information is passed within the organization. An organizational structure is literally a chart or diagram that depicts the logistical organization of a company and may describe how they address conflict and crisis situations. Businesses of all sizes require an established, organized structure to drive business outcomes. Business managers must distinguish between task conflicts involving goals and priorities, relationship conflicts of trust, emotions, and identity, and structural conflicts that focus on authority, incentives, and resources.

However, not all companies operate best with a traditional, hierarchical organizational structure and a lack of organizational structure (or choosing the wrong type of structure) can lead to miscommunication, work delays, poor process flows, and other serious consequences that slow business growth. In contrast, a robust organizational structure enables employees to coordinate teamwork, understand their tasks and responsibilities, reduce conflicts, and

DOI: 10.4324/9781042000258-1

boost productivity. Streamlining an enterprise's strategy for addressing conflicts, disputes, and disagreements serves the company in many ways.

A clear structure, which includes a peer review committee, allows every team member to be involved in some way. When employees know what they're responsible for and who they report to, they are more likely to take ownership of their work and that has a positive value to the organization. Having a documented organizational structure in place enables employees to improve efficiency and provides clarity for each individual employee and business unit. With this clarity, departments, especially human resources, can become more focused on how their actions and goals drive business outcomes.

The formation of the peer review process must accommodate two functions. The first, called the evaluation function, is the familiar process of evaluating the disputing parties' issues, wants, needs, and performance. The second, called the oversight function, is less familiar. It involves all the actions necessary to oversee the process to ensure that the conflict is addressed through the facilitative method of mediation and/or negotiation. These different functions use different sets of structural models and due to the complex structure and stakeholder relationships within company conflicts, the management of conflicts in programs therein proves more challenging than with single projects.

The internal conflict of a program affects the functioning of work teams and individuals. A peer review committee program that utilizes a conflict management model can be developed for the effective management of program conflicts. The model will usually provide a systematic view of the learning cycle of program conflict management, including conflict identification, resolution, feedback, and prevention, of which many patterns are found distinct from project conflict management. A clear structure, which includes a peer review committee, allows every team member to be involved. When employees know what they're responsible for and who they report to—which isn't the case in many fast-growing companies—they're more likely to shoulder ownership of their work.

Peer mediation in an organization is a voluntary process in which an individual is trained as a neutral third party that assists other colleagues in conflict to obtain a clear picture about their concerns, to better understand one another, and come to a mutual agreement about how they want to handle their conflict issues.

Peer negotiation is perhaps best considered as "do-it-yourself peer mediation." In other words, instead of having trained mediators, everyone is responsible for their own mediation and conflict resolution. In addition, peer negotiation can be described as an extension of peer mediation, a technique used in several institutions and similar settings to help people to resolve conflicts and problems without resorting to "authority."

Undoubtedly, negotiation is stressful and impacts money, opportunity, time, relationships, and reputations. Often that brings out the worst in people as they attempt to take advantage of the other side or try to look robust.

Most companies would be better off if there was a way to treat individuals equitably in a negotiation and get treated fairly in return.

Workplace conflict reportedly costs companies $359 billion a year, so it's not surprising that employers are always looking for ways to minimize that conflict. Conflict resolution processes are a traditional way to deal with work-related conflicts, but they often rely on face-to-face interactions. As more and more of our lives occur in online spaces, employers are turning to technology to find solutions for conflict when face-to-face resolution isn't possible.

However, employers should be cautious about removing the human element from conflict resolution since the process is inherently about interpersonal interactions and relationships, and it can be difficult to replicate that dynamic in an online environment (Avgar, 2022).

Restructuring negotiation can encompass using basic strategies to improve the process and reach a resolution more efficiently. Some strategies include the following: (1) Active listening: focus on the other party's perspective and avoid formulating your next argument while they are speaking; (2) Communicate: ask questions and get relevant information to set realistic goals and evaluate the other side's goals; (3) Cooperate: work together to find a solution that is a win for both parties; (4) Compromise: be willing to give and take to reach an agreement; (5) Stay composed: Remain calm and embrace change; and (6) Sum up: restate what you heard to ensure both sides understand the point.

The fundamental core of this book is to describe the rudimentary mechanics of both negotiation and mediation and how they affect the structure, configuration, and action of successful organizations that face internal and external conflicts. The examination of these concepts will be rooted in problem identification and problem solving and will highlight a collection of behaviors that include communication, decisiveness, and conflict management. The chapter breakdowns will concentrate on:

- Organizational Conflict and Crisis Management
- Conflict Resolution
- Fundamental Conflict Resolution Theory
- Technological Issues
- Internal and External Negotiation Contexts
- Cross-Cultural Business Negotiation and Behavior
- International Negotiation
- The Mediation Process and Strategic Management
- Strategies for Crisis Intervention
- Risk Management Strategies
- Business Risk Management
- Compliance Staff
- Conflict Management
- Integrative Problem-Solving and Salience
- Organizational Tension/Conflict

- Relational Identity Concepts
- Power and Conflict Issues
- Leverage in Negotiations
- Dispute Resolution Reporting Forms
- Crisis Preparedness
- Business Ethical Considerations
- Enterprise Reinvented
- PowerPoint Images/Media Presentations
- Appendix: Sample Enterprise Exercises
  Cited Enterprise Examples
  Key Terminology
  About the Author

Proactive approaches that enterprise incorporate highlight and benchmark internal negotiation and mediation strategies that move to conflict management without becoming crisis management. The area of crisis management and communication is divided into three areas:

(a) coping with the crisis; (b) adjusting information that affects the psychological crisis; and (c) reputation repair to ameliorate the damage a crisis inflicts on an organization (Sturges, 1994).

The theories and principles of negotiation and mediation can be used individually or in combination with one another. The applications depend upon the nature of the organizational crisis and what appears to be the critical factors in the crisis. Clearly, the hierarchical loyalty to the organization has been replaced in recent years by a sense of mutual commitment to a time-limited contract or task-oriented project and while technology has increased the ability to communicate, we might question whether it has increased or diminished our capacity to connect with co-workers in the workplace (Lewis, 2006). Transforming conflict at the workplace calls us to engage when we often feel compelled to attack or to avoid. We need to accept responsibility for the conflicts around us, and this will require mettle, stamina, and fortitude.

Ensuring that enterprise conflict resolution aims at creating win–win performance agreements may require a paradigm shift. The major focus is on results and not methods. Developing such win–win performance agreements is the central activity of management. When positive agreements are in place, employees can manage themselves within the framework of the agreement (Covey, 2004). Management can control outcomes, results, and agreements and the enterprise that endeavors to move in this direction will be successful. Workplace conflict is a warning sign and not a threat. It often indicates misaligned expectations, unspoken assumptions, and gaps in business procedures.

Throughout this book, the following theories and concepts are addressed:

Proficiency: what leaders and managers must personally be good at. Demonstration of core leadership capabilities that undertake interest-based negotiations.

Power and authority: awareness that can distinguish formal authority from informal influence and recognize various powers and leverage.
Cultural conflict competence: enterprise leaders demonstrating fluency in how conflict is shaped by national and organizational culture and be able to diagnose hierarchy expectations, confrontation versus harmony norms, and various decision authorities.
Emotional parameters: ability to de-escalate conflicts under pressure and reframe crisis into joint problem solving.
Management classification: directly addressing how conflict is handled operationally inside the enterprise.
Uniform resolution dialogs: targeted to undertaking the conflict resolution process that includes issue framing, facing constraints, and non-negotiables.
Organizational construct: developing how the enterprise is designed to support conflict resolution.
Internal resolution roles: designating facilitators, peer reviewers, mediators.

Proficiency in conflict resolution in contemporary organizations is not merely a soft skill. It is a strategic competency that protects value, accelerates execution, and strengthens culture. Effective leaders use conflict as a diagnostic signal of misalignment, resource tension, or structural gaps, as well as a device for innovation, surfacing conflicting assumptions and hidden risks. It presents a trust-building opportunity, demonstrating fairness, transparency, and accountability and organizations that master conflict resolution outperform because they reduce friction, increase psychological safety, and maintain operational drive.

My colleague Paul (Sloane, 2023) once wrote that we all have our strengths and weaknesses; people do, countries do, companies do. Individuals with closed minds can be oblivious to their failings, but open-minded thinkers can measure their weaknesses. When we apply the strengths of negotiation and mediation to address conflict issues, we change the rules and conventions that underpin how companies address conflict resolution. Although workplace conflict is an uncomfortable situation that can quickly escalate to major problems if left unaddressed, the major premise of this book is to postulate that company negotiation and mediation programs can help resolve and manage them effectively. Establishing conflict management processes in an organization is necessary and vital.

> *We are continually faced with opportunities which are brilliantly disguised as unsolvable problems.*
>
> ~ Margaret Mead

References

Avgar, A. (2022). *Streamlining Conflict Resolution Through Technology*. Alexandria, VA: HRCI.

Covey, S. (2004). *The 7 Habits of Highly Effective People*. New York: Simon & Schuster.

Lewis, G. (2006). *Organizational Crisis Management: The Human Factor*. Boca Raton, FL: Auerbach Publications.
Martin, J. N., and Nakayama, T. K. (2022). *Intercultural Communication in Contexts*. New York: McGraw Hill.
Sloane, P. (2023). *Lateral Thinking for Every Day: Extraordinary Solutions to Ordinary Problems*. London: Kogan Page Limited.
Sturges, D. L. (1994). Communicating through a crisis: A strategy for organizational survival. *Management Communication Quarterly*, 7(3), 297–316.

1 Organizational Conflict and Crisis Management

Solid negotiation and mediation skills are essential to be an effective leader in the workplace. Effective workplace leaders excel in communication, motivation, and strategic thinking. They foster trust, drive results, and build resilient teams through emotional intelligence and clear vision. They can help resolve tense situations and assist colleagues in getting along with one another. By implementing ways to manage workplace conflict, one can be a part of fostering a more positive company culture. Organizations seek leaders who can inspire, communicate, and adapt to the dynamic demands of modern workplaces.

Organizational conflict is an internal or external misunderstanding or disagreement that can occur between colleagues or leaders. These classes of disagreements can lead to a lack of cohesion and collaboration in the workplace. When employees don't get along with each other or disagree, it can make it challenging to get everyone aligned with the company's goals. A successful leader doesn't wait for things to happen; they're proactive and they anticipate desired results. They identify threats and take action against them. They're constantly thinking of ways to improve and do better. Whether that goal is business-related or personal, they always strive to seek good outcomes and agreements.

While some business conflicts are small and can be resolved quickly, other workplace disagreements can turn into something bigger. No organization is immune to workplace disagreements. However, not all conflicts hurt businesses. Some conflicts can help to bring positive changes to the workplace, which can ultimately result in improved employee performance, increased productivity, and increased revenue. To repeat, conflict is not always bad. In fact, conflict can often be a healthy and productive force when managed effectively. By encouraging constructive conflict, organizations can harness the diversity of perspectives, skills, and experiences of their employees to drive innovation and creativity, and effective conflict management can also help to build trust, strengthen relationships, and improve teamwork, communication, and decision-making.

DOI: 10.4324/9781042000258-2

Addressing Conflict in the Workplace

Organizational conflict management can be labeled as the prevention, management, and resolution of conflicts in organizations. How leaders and employees handle conflict is dependent on the kinds of systems organizations put into place. Setting employee expectations, implementing conflict-related policies and procedures, providing conflict resolution training, and other factors influence how and whether conflicts can be resolved in a satisfactory way. While addressing conflict in the workplace isn't always straightforward, it can be an opportunity for learning, growth, and innovation and is an essential opening for long-term organizational health.

While crises may be unavoidable, how an enterprise prepares for and responds to them can make all the difference. That is where crisis managers come in. These individuals work behind the scenes to anticipate and mitigate risks, lead their organizations through the storm when crises hit, and help them emerge stronger and more resilient on the other side. Workplace conflict is normal and unavoidable, but if unmanaged, it will drain productivity, damage morale, and fuel turnover.

Costly errors, such as incorrect orders, missed deadlines, and ineffective resource allocation, can lead to financial losses for the organization. These result in wasted time, resources, and potential loss of customers or opportunities. It can also lead to additional expenses and damage reputation affecting a businesses' long-term profitability. When communication breaks down in a business setting, it has harmful effects on workflow.

When conflicts occur, trust and confidence can be battered, leading to damaged relationships and dissatisfaction among the work force. The awkward relationships can have long-lasting effects on the company's reputation. Workplace conflict usually refers to tensions between employees or work teams, often stemming from:

- Contradictory values, priorities, or communication styles
- Role uncertainty or overlapping accountabilities
- Competition for resources or credit
- Personality battles or unanswered emotional dynamics

In *Managing Differences* by Daniel Dana (2006), the author outlines two fundamental rules that hold the threat of conflict at bay: don't coerce, and don't distance. These represent what not to do, but what then are the next steps? Experience indicates that without a plan, conflict escalates and quickly spins out of control. Some simple tips to help move us through conflict and develop conflict management skills are:

- Offer Something:

  Be the individual to initiate, in some way show that you have moved toward seeking restoration and harmony. Apologize, own up to your part, express regret about how things are, or say something nice to the other person to demonstrate that you are wanting a change.

- Make Time:

  Give the conversation priority. Agree on a time that is suitable for all parties.

- Focus on the Issue:

  Identify the issue or problem in as few words as possible. Focus on observable facts; explain what was said or done in concrete terms.

- Listen:

  Give the other party the chance to respond first. Listening, much like distancing and coercing, does not come naturally.

- Craft a Solution:

  Explore options together. Look for solutions and ways to move forward that all parties agree on.

All crisis managers possess a set of pivotable responsibilities that encompasses a thorough crisis cycle:

- Handle risk assessments: Managers work proactively to identify and prioritize potential threats to the organization, from natural disasters to cyber-attack risks.
- Develop crisis management plans: The crisis managers create comprehensive plans outlining roles, responsibilities, and step-by-step response procedures for various crisis situations.
- Reframe the narrative and turn "us vs. them" into "we vs. the problem."
- Focus on a positive workplace environment: A job site where conflict is handled constructively to promote a company culture of trust.
- Assemble/train a crisis response team: After identifying and preparing a of internal experts who will move into action when a crisis hits, they conduct training sessions that usually include crisis simulations and drills.
- Monitor for warning signs: Managers watch for early warning systems to detect potential crises before they escalate.
- Use third-party facilitation, especially when trust is low or stakes are high.
- Construct and foster stakeholder relationships: They proactively develop relationships with key stakeholders who will be crucial during a crisis.
- Assist in the enhancement of worker relationships: Properly addressing the conflict that will cultivate respect and understanding among employees.

Relational conflicts, task conflicts and principle conflicts are three categories of workplace conflict. Differences in employee personalities and conflict styles are part of relational conflicts. An organization's strategic direction, the assignment of projects, and the methods by which work is accomplished are part of task conflicts. When employees have contradictory views about the way to solve work issues (what is right and wrong), their differing perspectives comprise principle (values) conflicts. Despite good intentions, when stakes are great and emotions are deeply rooted, workplace conflicts can still develop. These conflicts can show up in different ways. Some are fueled by strong, impassioned emotions, while others involve aloofness; people withdraw, appear emotionless, and avoid contact with other workmates however possible.

For example, two steadfast team members find themselves arguing over a project timeline. As deadlines loom and tensions escalate, the once-cohesive partnership begins to break down under the weight of clashing viewpoints. Within this mayhem, complaints to other team colleagues intensify the situation, underscoring the urgency of effective conflict resolution. These workplace dynamics do not necessarily indicate a deterioration of workplace collaboration but can serve as catalysts for further understanding and improved teamwork.

Workplace conflict should be addressed using strategic thinking and emotional intelligence. An easy model that targets this conflict area focuses on the following aspects: (1) clarify the specific issue by using probing questions; (2) actively listen with empathy; (3) discover all possible options with the disputants; (4) connect with clear actionable steps; (5) reinforce any trust issues; and (6) build in flexibility for future renegotiation.

Crisis Management

Crisis management is an organization's process and strategy-based methodology for identifying and responding to a critical event. A critical event can be defined as any threat, unanticipated incident, or negative disruption with the potential to impact an organization's people, property, or business processes. Business leaders who take the front burden of addressing company crisis issues can formulate the backbone of robust strategies that include the five principles of crisis management: (1) comprehension; (2) clarity; (3) consistency; (4) credibility; and (5) contingency. Additionally, those business leaders understand that the vital stages of a crisis plan involve identifying potential vulnerabilities and implementing measures to prevent the crisis from occurring, developing a crisis plan; responding and activating a crisis management plan; conducting a post-crisis evaluation to learn from the experience to improve future responses.

Any business, large or small, may run into problems that negatively impact its normal operations. Crisis management is about identifying potential threats to a company and preparing effective responses to minimize damage.

A crisis can stem from internal actions or external events, such as natural disasters or data breaches. Proactive planning, such as business continuity plans, helps mitigate the impact when crises occur, maintaining business operations and reputation. Effective crisis management includes steps like detecting early warning signs, containing damage, and learning from the crisis to improve future responses. A first step in the management of a crisis is to recognize what type it is: (1) process conflict of disagreements about roles and responsibilities; (2) task conflict about how work should be approached and done; and (3) personal conflict that speaks to relationship tensions and trust issues.

It is important to discern the ways in which we respond to conflict. Of note, it is recognized that these ways are not totally constructive.

- *Avoidance.* Either out of fear of confrontation or as a means of controlling the situation, we avoid and evade conflict.
- *Accommodation.* We concede issues to the other side as a means of smoothing over the relationship, often at the expense of satisfying our owns needs and concerns.
- *Contest.* We move to achieve our own goals at the expense of keeping or having a positive relationship with the other side.
- *Conciliate.* We settle to compromise on a solution or agreement even though the needs and the wants of both parties are only partly met.

At the workplace, these responses will not really ameliorate the issues of the conflict. The above responses indicate the natural tendency to view conflict negatively. A fifth and more constructive response is to *collaborate*. Truly collaborative strategies are bound to realize improved communication and understanding, more creative solutions, increased enterprise productivity, and healthier relationships (Griffith and Goodwin, 2016).

Crisis management is best achieved when critical reasoning is utilized. When business leaders engage in crisis management, they absorb a great deal of information, interpret its meaning and relevance to the situation, assess the merits of possible resolutions, and determine the best solutions. Critical reasoning is vital to enable leaders to assess whether discussed solutions are fair, feasible, and satisfactory, Critical reasoning denotes that one is analytical rational, objective, consistent, and prudent.

Unresolved conflict can lead to lower morale and productivity and increased turnover and absenteeism. A larger problem for businesses is damaged trust and loss of work collaborations. Recent studies indicate that US businesses lost an estimated $359 billion annually due to unresolved conflicts (Picinu, 2019).

Integral to most business conflict management programs is the perception of how employees view and experience conflict.

Constructive conflict	*Destructive conflict*
Open and clarify issues (focus on understanding)	Divert energy making it hard to get work done
Help resolve the problem and gain closure	Destroy individual and/or company morale
Release new information and perspectives	Polarize work teams (win–lose mindset)
Help employees share information	Deepen and harden differences
Affirm direction and priorities (shared goals)	Produce irresponsible interpersonal behaviors
Promote growth of individuals and work teams	Undermine team spirit and cohesiveness
Result in breakthroughs and creativity	Suppress open communication and listening

Constructive conflict is the mainstay of wholesome debate in high-performing teams. Imagine a strategy meeting where diverse views are welcomed, challenged respectfully, and synthesized into a better plan. Destructive conflict often emerges in crisis or high-stress environments when psychological safety is faint—for example, a compliance failure followed by finger-pointing and heaped-up blame that spirals into organizational chaos and dysfunction.

Work-Related Conflicts

Each member of an organization contributes to the culture, engagement, and overall performance. Many serious problems can arise when workplace conflicts go unresolved. Proactive communication is the key to resolving and preventing conflict. In a diverse workforce, the ability to resolve conflict in a timely and effective manner can prevent escalation. Training managers and supervisors can aid employees in identifying the most common causes of conflict in the organization, provide techniques for managing workplace conflict, and identify the negative effects of unresolved conflict so employees understand the importance of immediately resolving their problems with coworkers and management (Blank, 2020).

Four examples of work conflicts involving different approaches to a project are as follows:

- Team members argue over whether to prioritize speed or thoroughness in completing a client project or insisting on extensive quality checks.
- Employees clash over a short-term project where one is direct and blunt while the other is more subtle and looks for collaborative discussions.
- Two managers are assigned to oversee similar parts of a production process, causing confusion among staff on who to follow. The work conflict centers around employees receiving clashing instructions which slows progress.

- Two departments, public relations and IT, both request funding for significant projects, but the company budget can only cover one and each department holds that their initiative is more critical.

Below are two instances of a work-related conflicts and possible solutions:

Conflict A: You're on a *design team* planning four new boutique coffee houses. You're thrilled to have this opportunity, and you are working with other people on the interior architectural elements, such as the final build's color schemes, menu board, and furnishings. While you're worried about the overall aesthetic appeal for the coffee franchise company, your workmates only seem to care about functionality. You feel like they're dismissing your ideas without even considering them, and it's causing friction between the team.

Resolution A: Resolve creative differences using your inventive outlooks to generate innovative solutions. Work together with the team to incorporate ideas from all sides, compromising where necessary to highlight the most promising aspects from each perspective. Reframe your opposing creative mindsets as a challenge to further your creativity and critical thinking skills.

Conflict B: You're in your *weekly team meeting*, deciding which marketing strategy to take on an updated company internet website project. You and your colleague disagree about which is the best route. You think your solution offers the most significant benefits to your company, while your colleagues feel other solutions are best suited for the upgrade. The discussion becomes intense, and you feel irritated. Try finding a resolution that encompasses all the points.

Resolution B: As a first measure, it's helpful to step back from the issue to stay calm and gain perspective. You can suggest to your colleagues that you return to this at the end of the meeting or take a 15-minute break to allow everyone time to think. Use this time to breathe and center yourself. This step benefits both parties by creating space and time to return to the problem with a fresh outlook. You can suggest a third neutral party from the IT division joining in to prevent this conflict from escalating. The desire is to confront it early.

Dispute System Design

Intervening quickly in cases of conflict can dramatically reduce the costs and time associated with dispute resolution. Many organizations lack an integrated system for business conflict management, leading to low morale and high turnover. One effective way to address such human resources problems is to follow the principles of *dispute system design* (DSD). DSD is the process of diagnosing, designing, implementing, and evaluating an effective method for business conflict management. DSD is typically grounded in conflict-solving strategies such as interest-based negotiation, in which parties share the interests that underlie their grievances and try to jointly negotiate a solution that satisfies all parties. Although outside mediators are sometimes enlisted to help parties involved in business conflict management, just about anyone in an organization who has experience in basic dispute-resolution processes, such as problem solving, active listening, and other mediation skills, can be a "DSD architect."

DSD is a new field, emerging as a synthesis of ideas and skills from a number of professional fields. DSD applies to both the product design and the activity of designing a system for preventing, managing, and resolving conflicts and covers systems within all types of organizations: business firms, nonprofit organizations, international and transnational bodies, systems that entail conflict in governance, and public agencies or organizations. It also covers systems designed by groups of people who form social associations or organizations by reason of proximity, shared religion or ethnicity, professional affiliation, or other shared interests in community (Ansler, Martinez and Smith, 2020).

As our global society becomes increasingly connected, enterprise will face challenges that demand creativity and innovation, from access to justice in local courts to consumer recourse in an online market and from international trade policies to the management of environmental resources. Such challenges inevitably engender conflict as we seek to effectively interact in society and govern ourselves. We need systems that empower people to manage conflict in ways that enable them to tackle challenges together. How do we design systems for managing conflict? What is most fair? What provides meaningful justice? How do systems vary and why? What is most effective? These are the central problems that dispute system design seeks to address.

Stages for creating a successful dispute system design in organizations begin with diagnosing the company's dispute symptoms by examining several key factors such as the types of disputes the enterprise deals with who is involved, how disputes are currently handled, and the role power plays in the resolution of current conflicts, and then, the principles of DSD with the primary goal of minimizing cost and emphasizing less invasive approaches before exploring other methods. Implementing a dispute system must ensure that relevant stakeholders in the organization are on board. The last stage involves evaluating the DSD to ascertain if those individuals in conflict are more satisfied with the conclusion than they were in the past.

Business dispute resolvers need to understand the institutional context within which they work. These institutions will vary widely; analyzing them involves DSD. All stakeholders and participants in these systems are responsible for doing the work to understand the system, not just a single case within it. This means learning to take a system apart, critique it, and make the system accountable for its impacts. Some might argue this is a job for experts, not stakeholders and participants. That is not correct: these systems arise in the context of governance structures. Unless the system's impacts are transparent, those who operate and host it cannot be accountable. A culture of confidentiality arising from traditions and conventions in negotiation, mediation, and arbitration has built a significant, and needless, barrier to empirical research on these systems. Business organizations should identify and train company individuals in DSD, as well as mediation and negotiation methodology.

Crisis management is an organization's process and strategy-based approach for identifying and responding to a critical event. A critical event can be defined as any threat, unanticipated incident, or negative disruption with the potential to impact an organization's people, property, or business processes. Being prepared to respond to and recover from a critical event requires a sophisticated crisis management plan. Prioritizing crisis management also helps organizations mitigate the secondary consequences of critical events. Beyond any immediate threat to people, property, and processes, critical events often yield unpredictable and cascading effects on brand reputation, customer satisfaction, employee morale, and even the supply chain. Establishing a crisis management plan helps organizations move from a position of reactivity to proactively safeguarding against all the effects a critical event can have on an organization.

Effective planning to manage critical events includes establishing a crisis management team and developing a crisis management plan to keep people safe, maintain business continuity, enable rapid recovery, and protect assets before, during, and after an event occurs. Further, it is imperative that every organization validates and tests its crisis management plan regularly and deploys the right technology, such as critical event management platforms, to support effective response across the organization.

In any collaborative environment, differences in opinions, priorities, and objectives are inevitable, but these conflicts do not have to lead to workplace dysfunction. Effective conflict resolution can spark meaningful dialogue, foster deeper understanding, and ultimately strengthen teams. A crisis management team will often need to address and navigate difficult conversation, and the most effective teams are characterized by (1) a shared and meaningful purpose; (2) a set of specific and measurable goals; (3) collaborative approach to reaching fair resolutions; (4) well-defined responsibilities and roles; and (5) conviction and passion to complete the task.

Building the crisis management team involves nominating the appropriate internal resources. These teams regularly comprise higher-level representatives from operations, finance, human resources, communications, IT, and legal, with at least one member of the executive team included as well. Within this group, a crisis manager is selected to direct the execution of the crisis management plan, including the organization's public response to the event. It is helpful if organizations recruit crisis management team members who specialize in a specific component of the crisis management plan.

The crisis manager is responsible for guiding the crisis management team and executing the crisis management plan. This individual must possess strong leadership, communication, and decision-making skills. The crisis manager ensures that all aspects of the crisis management strategy are effectively implemented and coordinates the organization's response to critical events. The major responsibilities of a crisis manager include assessing the situation, activating the crisis management plan, coordinating with internal and external stakeholders, and managing the overall response and recovery efforts. They must be able to remain calm under pressure and make swift, informed decisions to minimize the impact of the crisis.

Effectively managing workplace conflicts is not just about resolving disputes but involves fostering settings of open communication, empathy, and respect. It is key to highlighting the importance of early intervention, effective conflict resolution strategies, and the role of organizational culture in maintaining a healthy workplace. For HR managers, team leaders, and managers, understanding these dynamics is critical for nurturing a positive work environment and ensuring high team morale and productivity. The ability to navigate and resolve conflicts skillfully is an asset in today's vibrant work environments.

Dynamic Skills of Managers

The most important qualities for a crisis manager can vary depending on the specific context and culture of their organization. The finest crisis managers are those who can balance strategic vision with tactical execution. They exhibit business acumen, project management, functional expertise, and industry knowledge and have firsthand experience responding to crisis and learning from both successes and failures. The company conflict manager has a multifaceted role that focuses on preventing and resolving disputes effectively. Their major responsibilities span several areas, from identifying conflicts early to implementing strategies for resolution and ensuring follow-up. Each aspect plays a crucial part in maintaining a harmonious environment.

As we know, conflict is one of the biggest drains on workplace performance and many managers are not trained to handle it effectively. Managers are expected to provide more constructive feedback, but many feel that the company's HR department has not adequately trained them to do so. Organizations that invest in leadership development to improve conflict resolution training see an 11% increase in profitability (Desimone, 2024)

Despite the clear impact on engagement, productivity, and retention, conflict resolution is rarely treated as a core leadership competency. Instead of providing structured training, most organizations expect managers to navigate difficult conversations on their own—leading to avoidance, frustration, and unnecessary turnover. Good management helps ensure an organization's success in several ways. These include planning feasible strategies to achieve company goals; organizing and allocating resources; and directing and motivating employees where in today's times, the only constant is change and the only certainty is uncertainty, crisis managers have never been more essential. The enterprise future might by enigmatic, but with experienced crisis managers at the controls, it can certainly be more manageable.

Table 1.1 Differences among workers, managers, and leaders

Workers	*Managers*	*Leaders*
Performs basic tasks	Controls things	Creates things
Needs and uses resources	Budgets, makes ends meet	Finds resources
Interacts with peers	Interacts internally	Interacts with outsiders
Responsible for own effort	Responsible for performance of organization	Responsible for overall outcome
Lacks overarching viewpoint	Creates structure, is risk averse	Creates mandates, is a risk taker
Takes direction from others	Uses authority and rules	Uses influence, convinces
Provides feedback to the organization	Monitors organizational culture	Monitors outside culture

Extensive sets of personal work habits and behaviors can often impede successful projects from reaching fruition. Conflict resolution skill differences can drive employees, managers and leaders to achieve varying organizational goals. Bruce Peltier (2010) has outlined the key differences among workers, managers, and leaders.

Colin Rule was running an online dispute resolution company in 2003 when **eBay** hired him to improve the resolution of disputes among the users of both eBay and **PayPal**. Over the years, Rule and his colleagues created a structure for eBay/PayPal users to negotiate differences. We think of what Rule did as designing. We refer to the structured negotiations and a new online jury trial that Rule established as new processes. Rule's coordinated series of processes formed what we call a dispute processing system. This is an example of a design of a processes and of a system for preventing and managing disputes. Two people can deal with the disputes arising between them in a number of familiar ways. They can enter into negotiations, go to mediation, agree to arbitrate, litigate, try to overpower each other, or separate. In these common situations, people do not need a designer to create new processes or systems (Rogers, Bordone, Sander and McEwen, 2019).

Sound design management helps ensure an organization's accomplishment in several ways. These include planning strategies to achieve business goals; organizing company resources; directing and motivating employees; and ensuring that employees can effectively accomplish tasks. Ways to develop excellent managerial skills involve seeking guidance from an experience colleague or mentor. Two other methods are to peruse literature about management theories and styles and attending industry-related training, conferences, and workshops. Managers who master the vital functions of leadership, organization, and planning are better equipped to drive their organizations forward. In the broadest sense, a manager's team building directive is to ensure that individuals work together harmoniously and productively to maximize goal achievement (Payne, 2001).

In early 2009 **Google** began "Project Oxygen," an internal study aimed at identifying the characteristics of the company's most successful managers. They analyzed performance reviews, employee feedback surveys and nominations for top manager awards to find out what makes the best managers (Bryant, 2011). The study yielded several habits of effective managers who were great leaders of work teams:

- Being a good coach and engage workers with them to solve problems/disputes
- Being empowering and not micromanaging
- Creating an inclusive work environment.
- Being productive and results oriented
- Listening and sharing information freely
- Having a clear vision and strategy for the work team
- Collaborating across the organization
- Being a strong decision-maker

While some businesses may want to empower employees to resolve their own conflicts, there are times when management must wield more influence. Several decision-making processes that can be used often depends upon the degree of influence management wishes to share with the work staff (Griffith and Goodwin, 2016).

Directive decision-making	Decisions made with little or no input or participation from others.
Consultative decision-making	Decisions made after inviting input from others and considering their suggestions and ideas.
Joint decision-making	Share equally in decision-making process with no greater input over the decision than any other participant.
Delegation	Grant authority and responsibility to others while specifying the degree to which you require them to consult management.

In summary, the fundamental dynamic skills of an enterprise manager are:

- Calculated thinking and decision-making: Anticipating market trends and adjusting strategies accordingly; making data-driven decisions under uncertainty.
- Adaptability and change management: Leading teams through organizational change.
- Interpersonal and leadership dexterity: Adapting leadership styles to different team dynamics; navigating cross-cultural and intergenerational teams.
- Communication and influence: Communicating intricate ideas clearly; managing workplace conflict.
- Problem-solving skills: Solving complex, ambiguous problems creatively.

Several conflict management guidelines for managers, administrators and team leaders are:

- Set transparent expectations quickly.
- Address Issues early when tension first appears.
- Listen to all sides and exhibit fairness.
- Align everyone to a common goal.
- Use structured conflict conversations to describe and explain the issue(s).
- Encourage direct communication aimed at resolving the issue(s).
- Document everything with notes on incidents, meetings and agreements.
- Acknowledge progress and resolution.

References

Ansler, L. B., Martinez, J. K., and Smith, S. E. (2020). *Dispute System Design: Preventing, Managing, and Resolving Conflict*. Menlo Park, CA: Stanford University Press.

Blank, S. (2020). *Managing Organizational Conflict*. Jefferson, NC: McFarland & Company.

Bryant, A. (2011). The quest to build a better boss. *The New York Times*, March 13.

Dana, D. (2006). *Managing Differences: How to Build Better Relationships at Home and Work*. St. Louis, MO: MTI Publications.

Desimone, R. (2024). *Improve Work Performance with a Focus on Employee Development*. Gallup Workplace.

Griffith, D. B., and Goodwin, C. (2016). *Conflict Survival Kit: Tools for Resolving Conflict at Work*. Boston, MA: Pearson.

Payne, V. (2001). *The Team-Building Workshop: A Trainer's Gude*. New York: Amacom.

Peltier, B. (2010). *The Psychology of Executive Coaching: Theory and Application* (2nd ed.). New York: Routledge.

Picinu, A. (2019). *The Effects of Workplace Conflict*. Bizfluent.com.

Rogers, N., Bordone, R., Sander, F., and McEwen, C. (2019). *Designing Systems and Processes for Managing Disputes*. New York: Wolters Kluwer.

2 Conflict Resolution

Conflict resolution and management is a learned skill and one that improves over time. It is the process of addressing and managing disagreements in a constructive way that satisfies all parties involved or at least prevents further escalation. It's not just about ending a conflict or disagreement; it's about understanding the underlying issues, navigating emotions, and finding a path forward that builds trust rather than erodes it. Is there a correct way to handle conflict? What are the effects of poor conflict management? Disagreements in the workplace are inevitable, as employees have different personalities, goals, and opinions. Being able to solve enterprise conflict in a beneficial and effective manner has incredible benefits, including stress reduction, retention improvement, and better work relationships.

Non-Toxic Workplace

Conflict can be stressful, and everyone manages it differently. Working while under any level of stress is going to impact employees and their well-being. Resolving conflict at work means all parties involved feel heard and accounted for and can work with ease. Supervisors and managers should create a safe workplace and environment for staff and employees. That includes dealing with conflict as it arises. A manager who has best interest in mind for creating a positive work environment—one that includes accepting differences in a healthy manner—is one that an employee will more likely want to stay with. There are different definitions of what makes a great workplace environment, which largely depend on the values of an individual company, and it makes sense that employees want to feel like they're a valued member of the business they work for.

A positive work environment will make employees feel good about coming to the office or settling down at their workspace for the day. They will feel engaged and motivated, which will be reflected in their output. While conflict is normal and is bound to occur, how it's handled is important for long-term success in the relationship. Dismissing conflict outright is grounds for one or both parties to feel ignored and even resentful. Having the right strategies in

DOI: 10.4324/9781042000258-3

place for resolving conflict can lead to better relationships because both parties have the tools to come to a resolution in a productive manner.

A conflict is more than just a disagreement. It is a situation in which one or both parties perceive a threat (whether the threat is real). Conflicts continue to fester when ignored. Because conflicts involve perceived threats to our well-being and survival, they stay with us until we face and resolve them. We often respond to conflicts based on our perceptions of the situation, not necessarily on an objective review of the facts. Our perceptions are influenced by our life experiences, culture, values, and beliefs and conflicts trigger strong emotions. Indeed, conflicts are an opportunity for growth. When you're able to resolve conflict in a relationship, it builds trust.

Finding Agreeable Solutions

Using conflict resolution in the workplace can avoid or resolve conflicts that could negatively influence a company's productivity. These six steps can help find an agreeable solution (Herrity, 2024):

- Acknowledge the conflict: No one enjoys conflict, so it may be tempting to pretend it doesn't exist or will resolve itself. While this may happen, trying to ignore a problem will often cause it to worsen. Ignored conflicts grow over time and reappear at inopportune times. As a manager, it is best to address conflicts when they occur to head off what might become a volatile situation
- Define the problem: Defining the cause of the conflict will help you to understand how the issue grew in the first place. You need both parties to agree on what the issue is and discuss needs that aren't met on both sides. Obtain as much information as possible on each side's outlook. Continue asking questions until you are confident that all the conflicting parties understand the issue. You should help the parties remain focused on the issue, avoiding personal emotions during the discussion. Talk through the problem professionally without attaching a particular person or group to it.
- Meet on neutral ground: Clarifying a problem or discussing a resolution should be carried out in an environment that feels safe and neutral for all parties. Such a place also enables all involved to have honest communication. Do not choose either party's office or nearby location since it may imply one side has more influence or power over the other
- Let everyone have a say: Let each party have an opportunity to express their views and perceptions regarding the issue. Give them equal time to have their say. Embrace a positive approach in the meeting, and if necessary, set ground rules. Encourage all involved to share thoughts openly, comprehend the cause of conflict, and begin to identify solutions. They may find it easier to interact if they understand a shared goal to meet company objectives.
- Agree on a solution: After listening to both parties, take time to investigate the case. Do not prejudge or come up with a final verdict based on what

was said. Dig deeper and find out more about the happenings, parties involved, the issues, and how people are feeling. Also, try finding any underlying conflict sources that may not be evident or noticeable at first. After visiting each possible option, determine which one will be most favorable to everyone involved. Each party should provide an acknowledgment that the proposed solution is the best one possible.

- Determine each side's role in the solution: By now, both sides have had a say in negotiating a reasonable solution. However, for it to be effective, each party must feel the solution is just and fair. Ideally, both sides will now understand the other's side. Oftentimes, the conflict can be resolved just through facilitated, open dialogue. This step requires some time and effort as both parties work to set aside their differences and preferences and find common ground to work toward a resolution. Then, work with both sides to come up with a list of steps to achieve the agreed-on resolution.

The core principles for reaching agreeable solutions are as follows:

- Mutual interests over positions
  Focus on why people want something; not just what they demand for this shifts the conversation from fixed outlooks to flexible problem-solving.
- Common gains attitude
  Look for solutions where both sides feel they have won something, because even small concessions can build goodwill.
- Transparency and trust
  Hidden agendas eat away at agreement. Clear communication about constraints, risks, and goals makes compromise simpler.
- Systematized discourse
  Use frameworks like interest-based negotiation to keep discussions organized and fair.

Finding agreeable solutions using conflict resolution techniques is important because it can disrupt negative cycles that could affect the environment of the workplace. Instead of avoiding conflict altogether, which is inevitable, conflict resolution aims to create understanding and discussions that turn conflict into a productive and empathetic experience for those involved. It promotes healthy and growing employee interactions and improves interpersonal work relationships. As employees continue to interact and reconcile their interests, one may see positive organizational improvements, such as a more accommodating workforce.

Evaluating the dimensions of an agreeable solution should take into account the following:

- The impact on stakeholders: How will the solution affect employees, customers, investors, regulators, and the public?
- Ethical alignment: Does it sustain fairness, transparency, and responsibility?

- Practicability: Can it be implemented quickly with available resources?
- Reputation jeopardy: Will it restore or damage trust externally?
- Enduring value: Does it strengthen resilience beyond the immediate crisis?

An example of an enterprise conflict: *Round Robin Gone Wrong*

Nick is the newest addition to a small sales team. His experience at the company has been in information technology, but he's impressed management with his ability to interact with clients. His enthusiasm in his new position and his drive to prove himself by striving above any quota has led him to make a few mistakes with his new team. While accounts are usually assigned through a specific company set, there's an implicit rule on the team about new accounts from specific industries going to certain reps. Nick, however, understands this to be more of a suggestion than a rule and doesn't hand over some leads to the appropriate teammate. As a result, the other team members start squirreling leads and cutting him out of the loop because they feel he's gone rogue.

Sourness and resentment build on all sides until four of the salespeople complain to the manager about what they see as Nick's "go-it-alone" behavior. When confronted with their complaints, Nick feels waylaid and smeared. He tells the manager that he was only trying to do his best. The dissention has everyone feeling unwelcome and anxious. The manager doesn't think he'll seem very objective since he's personally friends with some of the salespeople and appeals to the business's People Resources (PR) representative to find a solution to this conflict. The People Resources (PR) team should consider several questions:

- What is PR's role in facilitating healthy, effective conversations? How can PR support an effective resolution together with the employees and managers involved?
- What is the origin of this conflict? Is an individual's behavior at issue or are there problems on both sides that need to be addressed?
- Are there any policies that are relevant to the situation or need to be addressed?
- What would be an appropriate response or conflict resolution strategy?
- What can PR or management do to prevent this kind of conflict from arising in the first place?
- How can employees contribute to a more positive workplace? What aspects of company culture need to be tackled?

Another example of a business conflict: *Department Heads and Budget Allocation*

The public relations department head is proposing additional funding aimed at increasing marketing. The consumer parts department supervisor wants more resources for targeted product development. Both managers approach the COO with their ideas and requests.

Conflict resolution methodology would encompass clarifying each department's position(s); exploring communal ideas and goals for company revenue growth; the establishment of metrics to measure and evaluate the impact of a resolution; and developing a framework for a company budget design that would support both departments.

Interpersonal Conflict

Interpersonal conflict occurs when two or more individuals have opposing needs, goals, or viewpoints that clash. Whether it's a disagreement over how to complete a task or a personal misunderstanding, interpersonal conflict in the workplace is not unusual. When managed successfully, it may lead to improved communication and possibly stronger relationships. The key is recognizing when a conflict is brewing and managing it before it escalates into something more damaging. Interpersonal conflicts are often rooted in communication breakdowns, clashing values, or unmet expectations. Sometimes, it's as simple as a misunderstanding as one person can interpret a comment differently than the other intended. Other times, deeper issues such as power dynamics, tension, or competing priorities can fuel disagreements. Recognizing the underlying cause of conflict may help in achieving interpersonal conflict resolution and prevent it from escalating further (Birke, 2024).

How does a conflict resolution team in a business get involved in forging resolutions? It is essential to understand the difference between conflict and disagreement. Though disagreements are sure to surface in any business that has more than a single employee, these don't normally require intervention because they're a marker of collaboration and communication. People are still talking and willing to work together in a disagreement. However, when disputes go beyond professional opinions and involve personal attacks, or resentment (whether vented openly or passive aggressively), these step over the line of acceptable disagreements into unacceptable workplace conflicts. Conflict disorders enterprise progress and make collaboration difficult. A conflict does not have to be an all-out screaming match, either. Avoidance or silence, which leads to frustration and resentment, can also be a sign that there's something wrong and that it's time to step in with conflict management/resolution strategies.

Because conflicts involve individuals that does not mean everyone will react to conflict the same way. Each of us has developed strategies that work for us, and those strategies are the result of our experiences, culture, upbringing, and more. We often tend to repeat what's worked for us before and discard what's failed and broadly speaking, when confronted with conflict, some people become controlling, some accommodating, and some avoidant. Controllers like to take charge, and while that works in some situations, in others, it can lead to someone feeling steamrolled. Accommodators put the needs of others ahead of their own, often stifling their own good ideas and feeling that "I do everything for everyone, and no one looks out for me."

Avoiders seldom make conflict worse, but they can bury complications deep in the soil, only to find that the problem developed even deeper roots and has grown. It's useful to recognize your own conflict style and those of others.

Strategies for conflict resolution in business recognize that conflicts can arise in any environment where people interact. Businesses are no different. While conflict is largely inevitable, a leader's ability to resolve disagreements quickly and effectively can prevent those conflicts from damaging productivity and interpersonal relationships. When conflicts are resolved effectively, a business and its employees can grow stronger by learning from the experience, making conflict resolution an important skill for business professionals to have.

Defusing Interpersonal Conflicts

Avoiding conflict will delay resolution. Hoping problems will de-escalate on their own is typically not an effective strategy because problems can fester, leading to higher levels of resentment. Following are the five strategies for defusing interpersonal conflicts:

- Accommodation: On occasion, being flexible is the quickest way to address a grievance. Each situation needs to be evaluated on a case-by-case basis, but giving the other party what they want can lead to positive outcomes.
- Embracing conflict: Embracing conflict represents the opposite approach to avoiding it. Managers who use this strategy believe that conflict is a normal and expected aspect of group interactions. Dealing with issues immediately can have many positive outcomes because there is not enough time for them to escalate or for resentment to develop. Leaders who embrace conflict often have strong interdepartmental communication channels that allow others to understand what conflicts may be brewing.
- Collaboration: This is built on a spirit of compromise and teamwork. If an employee voices frustration with a certain aspect of work or business policy, a manager can pool ideas from several workers to find a solution that is acceptable to everyone. Collaboration requires a significant timetable and may not be appropriate for all situations. Collaboration does involve group buy-in, meaning that the strategy can improve morale among the workers involved.
- Afford guidance: Some conflicts develop out of misunderstanding. Managers can play an important role by not taking sides and helping employees work out their problems in a constructive manner. Guiding the conversation while providing relevant information can lead to positive outcomes for both parties.
- Compromise: This approach calls on both sides of the disagreement to give some concessions for the good of the organization. Compromise works best when both parties hold approximately equal power. This strategy is frequently employed in other aspects of business, so many employees will be familiar with this concept.

One example that serves as a demonstration to the power of compromise in action is the 1978, Camp David Accords. This demonstrated the power of compromise in international relations as Egyptian President Anwar Sadat and Israeli Prime Minister Menachem Begin, facilitated by US President Jimmy Carter, engaged in 13 days of intense negotiations. The result was a historic agreement that led to a peace treaty between Egypt and Israel. The key to success was each side's willingness to make significant concessions. Israel agreed to withdraw from the Sinai Peninsula, while Egypt recognized Israel's right to exist.

Facilitating conflict resolution should include meeting with all parties to explore options. A key factor involves reviewing the CR process—presenting the issues and exploring options for resolution or arrange, if necessary, a separate meeting to seek agreement. Also, the key is the development of specific ways to resolve or improve the situation. Once options are generated, prioritize and examine what might assist if the options do not work as planned.

Effective communication abilities, skills, techniques, and practices are especially important as our society becomes more and more attuned to problems such as inequality, gender definition, and ageism. The vocabulary has changed and so have the expectations. Emotional intelligence is vital in keeping the enterprise environment pleasant and the workforce satisfied.

Emotional Intelligence

How would individuals rate their emotional intelligence during difficult conversations? Do they try to see themselves in the employee's situation? Do they hold off making quick judgment calls and reacting to office gossip? Enterprise leaders must be above these things. They need to have empathy and self-awareness and be well-versed in company-approved language regarding DEIB (Diversity, Equity, Inclusion, and Belonging). But what about individual employees who have a knack for getting under people's skin? Many seem to have an innate knowledge of manipulating emotions, and nothing gives them more satisfaction than making one lose your cool. Training and education are vitally important when addressing this type of team member because losing emotional regulation and resorting to angry words or name-calling could get on in difficulty with the human resources department.

Emotional intelligence (EI) plays a crucial role in conflict resolution/management by equipping individuals with the ability to manage both their own emotions and the emotions of others effectively (May, 2024). EI is a cornerstone of effective conflict resolution. It equips individuals with the necessary skills to understand and manage emotions, foster empathy, and facilitate effective communication.

- Enhanced self-awareness: EI begins with self-awareness, recognizing one's own emotions and understanding how they affect thoughts and behaviors. In conflict resolution, self-awareness allows an individual to identify personal triggers and manage emotional reactions. This awareness prevents emotions from escalating the conflict and enables a more reasoned approach to problem-solving.

- Improved self-regulation: Self-regulation is another critical component of EI that involves managing one's emotions healthily and constructively. Individuals who can regulate their emotions can maintain a calm demeanor during heated discussions, reducing the likelihood of the conflict spiraling out of control. This ability also helps maintain a focus on the resolution rather than the conflict itself, facilitating a more effective negotiation and collaboration.
- Increased empathy: Empathy allows individuals to understand and share the feelings of others, a key element in resolving disputes. It is perhaps the most critical aspect of emotional understanding in dispute resolution. By empathizing with the emotional state of another person, parties in a conflict can gain a better understanding of each other's perspectives and motivations. This understanding can transform potential confrontations into opportunities for collaborative problem-solving, as it promotes a sense of shared concern rather than opposition.
- Effective communication: EI significantly enhances communication skills, which are vital in conflict resolution. Emotionally intelligent individuals can convey their thoughts and feelings clearly and listen actively to others. Effective communication reduces misunderstandings and builds trust, both essential for resolving conflicts and achieving mutually beneficial outcomes.
- Building and maintaining relationships: The social skills component of emotional intelligence involves managing relationships effectively. In the context of dispute resolution, these skills help maintain constructive relationships even when disagreements arise. Being able to handle interpersonal dynamics adeptly ensures that conflicts can be resolved in a way that strengthens relationships rather than damaging them.
- Promoting cooperation and resolution: Individuals with high emotional intelligence are typically seen as more trustworthy and fairer. This perception fosters a cooperative environment where all parties are more willing to share their views and work toward a common goal. EI thus not only helps in resolving the present conflict but also prevents future disputes by establishing a foundation of respect and understanding.

Overall, emotional intelligence is essential in conflict resolution as it enables better control over emotional responses, fosters empathy, enhances communication, and promotes cooperation. These capabilities are critical in negotiating solutions that are acceptable to all parties involved, ultimately leading to more stable and substantial resolutions. EI is a foundation of effective conflict resolution. It can equip mediators and peer review personnel with the necessary skills to manage emotions and facilitate effective communication. By focusing on enhancing these skills, disputants can substantially improve their ability to resolve disputes and achieve peaceful and productive

Table 2.1 Major models of emotional intelligence

Core components	*Indications*
Self-consciousness	Recognizing emotions, triggers, strengths, and limitations
Self-regulation	Managing impulses and choosing prudent responses
Motivation	Using energy to pursue goals with optimism and resilience
Understanding	Reading cues and needs of others to adjust own behaviors
Social skills	Building relationships free of conflict with clear communication

outcomes. As businesses become increasingly aware of the importance of emotional acumen, its integration into conflict resolution strategies will undoubtedly become more pronounced, paving the way for more harmonious interpersonal and professional relationships.

While some studies show that there is a correlation between high EI and positive workplace performance, there is no general consensus on the issue among psychologists, and no causal relationships have been shown. Emotional intelligence is typically associated with empathy, because it involves a person relating their personal experiences with those of others. Since its popularization in recent decades and links to workplace performance, methods of developing EI have become sought by people seeking to become more effective leaders.

Recent research has focused on emotion recognition, which refers to the attribution of emotional states based on observations of visual and auditory nonverbal cues.

Numerous steps to take when managing conflict using emotional intelligence include the following:

- *Create* a positive environment by ensuring that you address conflict calmly and in private, as this is the best way to help the parties involved practice active listening. Airing all a team's hidden agenda can be embarrassing for those involved, and it can also hurt morale and productivity. Maintaining a neutral, calm space will help those involved get back in control of their emotions so they're able to focus on trying to resolve the conflict.
- *Foster* good communication by making sure everyone involved practices active listening to fully understand the situation. Ensure that all parties know they're free to ask questions, request clarity.
- *Employ* self-regulation to remain calm and make certain that all non-verbal communication (i.e., posture is relaxed) so that one's body language doesn't encourage more conflict. Maintaining respect and authenticity will demonstrate integrity.

My hope was that organizations would start including this range of skills in their training programs—in other words, offer an adult education in social and emotional intelligence.

~ Daniel Goleman

The greatest ability in business is to get along with others and influence their actions.

~ John Hancock

EI and Conflict Analysis

Emotional intelligence (EI) plays an important role in conflict resolution, especially in high-stakes environments where trust, power, and psychological safety are on the line. In a real-world application, the breakdown results are as follows:

> **Situation**: One team member publicly criticizes the decision of the project manager of that team in a meeting.

Soft EI Response: Defensiveness, reprisal, or evading and shutting down.
Elevated EI Response: A self-awareness of rising frustration resulting in self-regulation.
Exhibition of Empathy: A response might be: "It sounds like you're troubled about the effect of my remarks, can you verbalize more about your concerns?"
Reframing Mode: Reframe the conversation toward possible agreement.
Incentive: Indicate willingness to work toward mutual resolution.

References

Birke, R. (2024). *Seven Tips for Interpersonal Conflict Resolution at Work*. Irvine, CA: Jams Pathways.
Herrity, J. (2024). *5 Conflict Resolution Strategies: Steps, Benefits and Tips*. New York: Indeed.
May, D. E. (2024). *The Role of Emotional Intelligence in Conflict Resolution*. Law Offices of Hayward, CA: Denise May.

3 Fundamental Conflict Resolution Theory

Conflict resolution is a skill that benefits professionals across all types of paths. What makes this true? Simply put, interpersonal conflict can occur in virtually any setting, from office jobs to in-field work and understanding how to deal with interpersonal conflict, reconciling emotions and reaching an understanding are valuable practices that boost well-being and productivity. The theory of conflict resolution is more than just a single technique for understanding the difference between mediation and arbitration. It involves more than just navigating difficult conversations.

Conflict resolution is the process of ending disputes and reaching an agreement that satisfies all parties involved. Since conflict is an essential part of being human, effective conflict resolution is not designed to avoid disagreements. Instead, conflict resolution skills are used to facilitate discussions, increase understanding and control emotional responses.

Common Cognitive Errors

Five of the most common cognitive errors that lead to unproductive or unresolved conflict include (1) self-serving fairness interpretations—refers to the process of one or more parties deciding what is "fair" from a biased point of view; (2) overconfidence—when arguing or disputing a matter this can lead to undesirable outcomes (while overconfidence in a personal disagreement may simply cause embarrassment, this cognitive error can be even more detrimental when dealing with legal issues, such as contracts); (3) escalation—the tactics can prolong a dispute for longer than necessary, thus making an agreement even more difficult to reach; (4) avoidance—the practice of circumventing conflict (examples of avoidance may include storing up emotions, changing the subject when an issue is brought up, or physically leaving the situation altogether); and (5) blaming—often refers to the tactic of one or more parties ridding themselves of responsibility for a disagreement. When blaming is used during a conflict, it can be difficult to get both parties to agree on how they played a role in the situation.

Conflict is a dispute in a situation defined by the parties' underlying goals and beliefs, mutual perception and communication, and the facts involved.

DOI: 10.4324/9781042000258-4

The conflict itself is a process of communication—an engagement of fields of expression. Passions and beliefs become evident, the nature and intensity of hidden interests surface. In the process of achieving a new structure of expectations, conflict integrates underlying goals and mutual perceptions into a balance among the central interests at stake, the resolution, and the ability of the parties to support them. The balancing process can be shortened, intensity reduced, antagonism lessened, and the resulting expectations made more realistic by clarifying the conflict situation. Four guidelines can help the parties.

- Uncover the underlying or hidden goals and beliefs. Look beneath the conflict. A dispute really may be about hidden, perhaps even unconscious, beliefs and values.
- Determine the facts. Fact finding is essential to resolving conflict, for often conflicts are generated by a misperception or misunderstanding of the facts involved.
- Be sensitive to the other's position and perspective. See the conflict through his eyes. Resolving conflict is partially empathizing with the other, understanding his frame of reference, and sensing this reading of one's field of expression.
- State the other's argument and demands. Miscommunication and misperception can play a large role in conflict. One way to reduce these problems is to seek mutual agreement on the issue, claims, and justifications.

These four rules—look underneath, look at the facts, look at oneself, and look at the other—alone will not achieve peace, but they help to focus on the real issues and reduce the emotional content (Rummel, 1981).

How does the business community view conflict? Conflict emerges and is experienced along cognitive (perception), emotional (feeling), and behavioral (action) dimensions. It is usually described primarily in behavioral terms, but this can oversimplify the nature of the experience. Taking a three-dimensional perspective can help one understand the complexities of conflict and conflict sometimes seems to proceed in contradictory directions. As a set of perceptions, conflict is the belief or understanding that our own needs, interests, wants, or values are incompatible and in determining the source of conflicts, there is a basic question one cannot dodge. Are conflicts, at all social levels, due to inherent human aggressiveness. Or are conflicts due to the emergence of inappropriate social institutions and norms that reasonably would seem to be well within human capacities to alter, to which the person has problems in adjustment?

Conflict Resolution

If inherent aggressiveness is the problem, then conflicts just must be lived with, while controlled as much as possible by police and deterrent strategies.

Conflict resolution, that is, getting to the source of the problem, becomes irrelevant: the source is known and cannot be altered. At best, there could be corrections of perceptions and adjustments of personal behavior in particular cases (Mayer, 2012). If social conditions are the problem, then conflict resolution and prevention would be possible by removing the sources of conflict: institutions and social norms would be adjusted to the needs of persons.

Conflict is also experienced as an emotional reaction to a situation or interaction. We often describe conflict in terms of how we are feeling; angry, upset, scared, hurt, bitter, hopeless, determined, or even excited. Sometimes a conflict does not manifest itself behaviorally but nevertheless generates considerable emotional intensity. Often a conflict exists because one individual feels upset, angry, or in some other way in emotional conflict with another, even though those feelings are not reciprocated by or even known to the other person. The behavioral component may be minimal, but the conflict is still very real to the person experiencing the feelings.

Conflict is also understood and experienced as the actions that people take to express their feelings, articulate their perceptions, and get their needs met, particularly when doing so has the potential for interfering with others' needs. This behavior may involve a direct attempt to make something happen at someone else's expense. It may be an exercise of power. It may be violent. It may be destructive. Conversely, this behavior may be conciliatory, constructive, and friendly. Whatever its tone, the purpose of the behavior is either to express the conflict or to meet one's needs.

Implied in conflict resolution, therefore, is the proposition that aggressions and conflicts are the direct result of some institutions and social norms being incompatible with inherent human needs. The argument is that aggression and anti-social behaviors are stimulated by social circumstances. There are human limits to abilities to conform to such institutions and norms: the person is not wholly malleable.

On the contrary, the needs that are frustrated by institutions and norms require satisfaction. They will be pursued in one way or another. These needs would seem to be even more fundamental than food and shelter—needs such as personal recognition and identity that are the basis of individual development and security in a society. Denial by society of recognition and identity would lead, at all social levels, to alternative behaviors designed to satisfy such needs, be it ethnic wars, street gangs, or domestic violence. Such a possibility has not been part of the thinking (Burton, 1998). Law has it that there is a right to expect obedience, and others have an obligation to obey. Illegality can therefore be defined. Sociologists have been greatly concerned with the socialization of the individual into the norms of society. Psychologists are concerned with the adjustment of the person to the social environment. Failure is an abnormality.

An overwhelming majority of employees, 85%—at all organizational levels—experience workplace conflict to some degree. This conflict can result in lost productivity that costs organizations billions of dollars a year.

When it comes to dealing with conflict, we often rely on the conflict style that we know best instead of the style that best fits the situation. Effective conflict management involves awareness of one's default conflict style and being able to use other styles when appropriate to achieve more positive outcomes. It requires understanding of the situation and the styles of others to identify the best path forward when conflict arises.

The *Thomas–Kilmann Conflict Mode Instrument* explores five different conflict-handling modes, their impact on interpersonal and group dynamics, and how to choose the best one for any situation (see chapter 4 in Blank). They include competing, collaborating, avoiding, accommodating, and compromising.

Strategic Decision-Making

Strategic adaptability involves being flexible and responsive to changing circumstances. Understanding and recognizing default conflict-handling modes can support strategic decision-making and change management when applied to the TK Conflict Model:

- *Recognizing Default Responses*: Knowing your own and your team members' default conflict-handling modes helps in anticipating reactions to change. This awareness allows for proactive management of potential conflicts and smoother transitions.
- *Tailored Approaches*: Different situations may trigger different default responses. By understanding these triggers, leaders can tailor their approach to manage change more effectively. For example, a team member who typically avoids conflict might need extra support during times of significant change.
- *Improved Communication*: When everyone understands the TKI Model, it creates a common language for discussing responses to change. This shared understanding can improve communication and facilitate more effective collaboration during transitions.

Conflict resolution strategies that are drawn from research on negotiation can encompass the notion that all of us may have biased fairness perceptions. Both parties to a conflict typically think they're right (and the other side is wrong) because they quite literally can't get out of our own heads. Our sense of what would constitute a fair conflict resolution is biased by *egocentrism* or the tendency to have difficulty seeing a situation from another person's perspective.

Deliberate Leader Proficiencies

Conflict resolution strategies can embrace the development of cognitive aptitudes. Capable business leaders need to understand the nature of conflict:

- Systems thinking: recognizing how incentives, structures, and interdependencies create predictable conflict patterns.
- Root-cause analysis: distinguishing between surface disputes and underlying drivers (identity, power, resources, and values).
- Cultural intelligence (CQ): understanding how norms, communication styles, and power distance shape conflict behavior.
- Negotiation literacy: knowing when to use interest-based negotiation, positional bargaining, or mediated processes.

Maintaining Relationships

An important aspect of conflict resolution is maintaining positive relationships after the conflict has been resolved. Conflict can be a source of stress, frustration, and resentment, but it can also be an opportunity for learning, growth, and collaboration. How can one ensure that relationships with team members and clients are not damaged by the conflict but rather strengthened by the resolution? What are several strategies to maintain positive connections with all parties after resolutions are achieved?

- Express appreciation and gratitude. After resolving a conflict, it is important to acknowledge the efforts and contributions of the other party. Expressing appreciation and gratitude can help to restore trust, respect, and goodwill.
- Offer positive feedback. Another way to maintain positive relationships after conflict resolution is to provide positive feedback to the other party. Positive feedback can help to reinforce the positive outcomes of the resolution, as well as to recognize the strengths and skills of the other party.
- Follow up on the agreed actions. A decisive step in maintaining positive relationships after conflict resolution is to follow up on the agreed actions. Following up on the agreed actions can help to ensure that the resolution is implemented effectively, as well as to show one's commitment and accountability.

When convivial relationships have been maintained, we may often tend to avoid escalating tensions with threats and provocative moves. When we feel we're being ignored or bullied, we often try to capture the other party's attention by making a threat, such as saying we'll take a dispute to court or try to ruin the other party's business reputation. There is a time and place for litigation, but threats and other attention-getting moves, such as take-it-or-leave-it offers, are often a mistake. Because of the common human tendency to treat others the way they're treated, people tend to respond to threats in kind, leading to an escalatory spiral and worsening conflict.

We should attempt to overcome an "us versus them" mentality. Group connections build loyalty and strong relationships, but they can also promote suspicion and hostility toward members of out-groups. As a result, groups in conflict tend to have an inaccurate understanding of each other's views and to see the other's positions as more extreme than they are.

> *Far too many people are looking for the right person, instead of trying to be the right person.*
>
> ~ Gloria Steinem

It is important to look beneath the surface to properly identify deeper issues. Our deepest disputes often seem to involve money: labor disputes over employee wages, family conflicts over assets, for example. Because money is a finite resource, these conflicts tend to be single-issue battles in which one party's gain will inevitably be the other party's loss. But disputes over money often involve much deeper causes of conflict, such as the feeling that one is being disrespected.

Once it is determined what the conflict is about, one can find how to choose where, when, and in what way to engage. Looking deeper into the conflict will raise questions like: (1) What is the goal or desired outcome in this interaction? (2) Given the conflict, is there enough time available to make headway? (3) Do the disputants have the cognitive resources to make this productive? (4) Are there specific strategies to manage this conflict that might work?

When business relationships are imbued with excessive or aggressive behaviors, two patterns of reaction can be identified (Knapp, Vangelisti and Caughlin, 2014). *Withdrawal* is a conflict pattern that arises when the disputants want to flee and rid themselves of the conflict. The parties desire relational peace and harmony. *Escalation* is the conflict pattern that develops when the disputants want to fight rather than flee. In contrast to those who want to avoid conflict, these individuals want to pursue it. The acts of withdrawal and pursuit are not, in and of themselves, bad for constructive conflict. Workers who engage in productive conflict will manifest withdrawal as well as a desire to fervently pursue a problematic issue.

When persistent conflict issues and problems afflict organizations, they usually stem from a combination of forces, not a single attitude, act, or outdated norm. As a result of that complexity, solutions can be elusive, and we often see intransigence even in places explicitly committed to change.

Within organizations where leadership is essentially monocultural, conflicts over individual and group differences are often suppressed, and leaders may be blind to the dominant power structures and stereotyping that exacerbate those differences. Even so, whenever people must compete for scarce resources and rewards (attention from senior leaders, project support, plum assignments, promotions, office space, and so on), the conflicts persist, bubbling under the surface if unacknowledged. Those in power, while often insulated by their privilege, might fail to recognize and respond to those concerns and feelings.

Conflict resolution research shows that workshops and training may fail to go deep enough to address the attitudes, incentives, and norms that perpetuate these systemic patterns. Sometimes they even make problems worse, escalating tensions by increasing awareness of injustice without offering a path toward resolution or simply raising defenses and rallying resistance to change. But many organizations don't know what the alternative to training is, so they keep at it, spinning their wheels, knowing they must do something (Coleman, Chen-Carrel and Regan, 2022). However, organizations that handle tensions and conflict constructively can create and sustain change.

The conflict resolution field is in continuing progression. The scope of interests considered continues to expand both in the range of conflict stages and in the variety of conflicts that are of interest. The field is necessarily becoming more differentiated, with workers in the field specializing in particular kinds and stages of conflicts and particular aspects and methods of conflict resolution. The conflict resolution field is likely to increase in size and societal penetration in the future. Intensifying business and world integration is a source of more and more potentially destructive conflicts, as well as a source of reasons to reduce and contain them. The cost of failing to prevent and stop destructive conflicts is rising and conflict resolution can help foster more constructive methods to wage and resolve conflicts. Traditional reliance on coercive impositions with little regard to possible mutual gains and reasonable regard for opponents' concerns is proving to be increasingly maladapted to contemporary global developments (Bercovitch, Kremenyuk and Zartman, 2009).

Constructive/Destructive Enterprise Conflicts

This is a comparison between destructive and constructive business conflicts:

Aspect	*Constructive conflict*	*Destructive conflict*
Emphasis	Solving problems, improving processes, producing new ideas	Blaming, personal attacks, winning at any cost
Result	Innovation, stronger teamwork, better decisions	Broken relationships, stalled projects, financial loss
Communication style	Respectful, fact-based discussions	Hostile, defensive, emotional, avoidance
Impression on morale	Boosts engagement, sense of inclusion	Causes stress and distrust
Collaboration	Encourages teamwork and sharing	Creates rivalry and damage
Long-term effect	Builds trust and organizational pliability	Damages reputation, increases turnover
Management role	Facilitates dialogue, ensures fairness	Intensifies tension, ignores or worsens issues

In the workplace, destructive conflict hinders work performance, because people refuse to speak to each other or they don't have civilized conversations. Destructive conflict between two people can bring down the morale of an entire department, thereby reducing productivity and efficiency. Constructive conflict, on the other hand, embraces differing ideas and worldviews, in an effort to move the company toward its goals and mission. This type of conflict increases productivity, rather than hampers it. Conflict should be seen as positive when it results in clarification of issues, results in people learning about each other, or results in people considering new ideas. Destructive conflict needs to be addressed as soon as it is identified or reported. Doing so prevents the situation from escalating, which would further bring down team morale and productivity (Leonard, 2025).

Promoting constructive conflict helps to open the eyes of team members to new views, opinions, and ways of doing things. Employees should be encouraged to offer opinions in team meetings and hold team-building exercises to help workers develop a real respect for each other.

References

Bercovitch, J., Kremenyuk, V., and Zartman, I. W. (2009). *The Sage Handbook of Conflict Resolution*. Thousand Oaks, CA: Sage.

Burton, J. (1998). Conflict resolution: The human dimensions. *The International Journal of Peace Studies*, *3*(1).

Coleman, P., Chen-Carrel, A., and Regan, B. (2022). A new conflict-resolution model to advance DEI. *MIT Sloan Management Review*, Winter 2023.

Knapp, M., Vangelisti, A., and Caughlin, J. (2014). *Interpersonal al Communication and Human Relationships*. Boston, MA: Pearson.

Leonard, K. (2025). *Differences Between Destructive & Constructive Conflict*. Houston. TX: Chron.

Mayer, B. (2012). *The Dynamics of Conflict: A Guide to Engagement and Intervention* (2nd ed.). San Francisco, CA: Jossey-Bass.

Rummel, R. J. (1981). *Understanding Conflict and War*. Beverly Hills, CA: Sage Publications.

4 Technology Issues

Technology is often presented as a tool with the potential to improve humanity. But when tech does the opposite, enterprises need to understand why it happened and to intervene if possible. Building purpose-led tech requires more than just mitigating potential issues. It necessitates implanting the foundational values of an organization in decision-making. This could involve using corporate values to drive the investments, explorations, and consumption of technologies. That requires aligning governance and executive stakeholder support with initiatives that historically might have been central only to the corporate social responsibility teams. It might also require making values a key part of the technological decision-making process. This quandary boils down to one question: How can organizations manage tech responsibly? The possible answer is: By intentionally considering the potential social impact of a specific technology when considering whether to invest. That incorporates assessing the technology's potential financial or operational impacts (Golbin, 2023).

While technology has increased the ability to communicate, one might question whether it has increased or diminished the capacity to connect with co-workers or others in the workplace. It is through feeling this connection that we derive our sense of team, community, attachment, and belonging. It is these core social and emotional elements that lubricate human beings and keep them going in times of difficulty, be it a personal or professional crisis (Lewis, 2006).

Technology has overhauled the way things were done. Its use in every sector is significant. Whether it's for business or social purposes, we no longer rely on traditional methods and means. Businesses have also adopted technology for their benefit. This is one of the reasons why tech companies like Apple, Microsoft, Samsung, etc. have become dominant drivers of economic growth. Interestingly, these companies also rely on technology to stay ahead.

Technology has become one of the most powerful forces reshaping business negotiations. It has exploded the power of information and has collapsed traditional information irregularities by:

- Allowing buyers to target prices instantly.
- Having sellers research many solution/agreements quickly.

DOI: 10.4324/9781042000258-5

- Having AI tools access and analyze BATNAs, reservation points, and likely concessions.

The many implications focus on power. Power will now come less from controlling information and more from interpreting it. Negotiators who can synthesize data into insight win. AI technology tools will be able to now:

✓ Draft negotiation drafts and counter offers
✓ Analyze tone and attitude in emails
✓ Predict concession patterns
✓ Identify cultural risk signals
✓ Surface hidden interests from communication patterns

However, AI cannot replace the human elements of trust, emotional intelligence, and reading the room. New technologies can remove geographic barriers but can also initiate many new cultural risks:

- Direct versus indirect communication styles become intensified in text.
- High-context cultures may find digital negotiation too blunt.
- Power distance norms shift when hierarchy is compressed in digital space.

Some recent research (Pinto, 2025) indicates that 85% of employees experience workplace conflict, with technology environments being particularly susceptible due to high-pressure deadlines and complex technical decisions. AI-powered conflict management tools are revolutionizing how technology leaders detect, analyze, and resolve workplace disputes before they escalate, and effective conflict management can improve team productivity by up to 30% while reducing employee turnover and fostering innovation in tech environments. Proven strategies exist, including proactive communication frameworks, data-driven resolution tracking, and hybrid resolution models, that are transforming how technology teams handle disputes

Enhanced team collaboration in technology organizations shows significant returns through reduced hiring costs and improved retention while remote work dynamics have created new conflict patterns that require specialized approaches and digital-first resolution strategies. Businesses that adapt to new technologies can realize lower costs and faster decisions and that they can frame a better customer experience.

Adaptability in business is more than just a reactive approach; it is a proactive mindset that fosters resilience and innovation. Companies that prioritize adaptability can rapidly pivot their strategies, reallocate resources, and embrace new opportunities. This agility allows them to stay ahead of competitors and respond effectively to challenges. In recent years, there have been new inventions and developments in the field of technology. Modern tools like artificial intelligence, the Internet of Things, big data, and cloud computing are some examples. These developments have transformed the traditional ways of doing things. Nowadays, everything is being brought to digital platforms. E-commerce, E-learning, remote working, and online banking, almost everything now require some sort of technology. According to the US Chamber of Commerce, 84% of small businesses are using at least one digital platform to share information with their audience. About 80% advertise products and services on social networks and 62% of small enterprises say that having strong digital and media skills is a key factor in the recruiting process (Pathak, 2020).

Adaptive Technology Needs

According to a recent study by Deloitte, 85% of businesses believe that technology is a key enabler of their business strategy (Smith, 2023). As new technologies continue to emerge at a rapid pace, businesses are under pressure to keep up to stay competitive. However, as businesses adopt new technologies, they need to consider the ethical implications of their decisions. In this blog post, we explore the technology ethics and what businesses need to consider when adopting new technologies.

The necessity of adaptability is critical when it comes to adopting new technology. The transformation of industries by artificial intelligence, blockchain technology, and automation requires entrepreneurs to constantly evaluate their technological foundations. Entrepreneurs should not blindly follow every emerging technology. However, they need to learn how to identify those which will truly strengthen their business offerings.

In just one example, independent bookstores have made adjustments to thrive alongside e-commerce competition such as Amazon. They have succeeded by adopting hybrid business models. These include online shopping platforms alongside personalized recommendation systems and community events that capitalize on their unique attributes while selling in a transformed market landscape (Economy, 2025). The adaptation process centered on enhancing these bookstores' foundational principles through careful technological integration.

The integration of technology into business practices can be transformational, but it is not without its pitfalls. While tech solutions have the potential to streamline operations, enhance productivity, and foster connectivity, there are circumstances when technology can actually hinder business progress. This blog takes a closer look at the ways in which reliance on or misuse of technology can become a stumbling block, rather than a steppingstone, for businesses.

One of the most significant benefits technology offers businesses is improved communication. Tools such as email, instant messaging, and video conferencing platforms facilitate instantaneous and clear communication between team members, regardless of their physical location. Additionally, technology enables efficient data management through sophisticated databases and cloud storage solutions, ensuring vital company information is organized, secure, and easily accessible. Furthermore, advanced analytics and business intelligence tools empower businesses with data-driven insights, enabling them to make informed decisions, understand customer behavior, and predict market trends effectively.

As businesses adopt new technologies, they open themselves up to a range of risks. For example, they can inadvertently collect and store personal data without the proper consent, leaving them vulnerable to data breaches and cyber-attacks. Technology sometimes has unintended consequences, such as the displacement of workers or the exacerbation of social inequalities. As such, it is important for businesses to carefully consider the ethical implications of their technological decisions.

Businesses are constantly on a hunt for the latest enterprise technology trends, and for a valid reason. While not all emerging technologies will end up being the drivers of progress, identifying the most promising ones has always been make or break for many companies. In 2024, in particular, enterprises face numerous needs to expand the processing power of their IT infrastructures and align services with new customer expectations. Along with growing security requirements and increasing costs, these demands can sometimes be virtually impossible to meet without tapping into the new available tools. In addition to learning about current enterprise tech trends, it's crucial for businesses across all sectors to implement them consciously to gain considerable results (Shalimov, 2024).

Recent Trends and Impact

Businesses need to consider the impact that their technological decisions have on society. For example, the adoption of automation technologies occasionally leads to job losses and wage stagnation, particularly in low-skilled industries. Similarly, the use of artificial intelligence (AI) and machine learning algorithms sometimes exacerbate existing biases and perpetuate discrimination, particularly against marginalized groups. As a result, it is imperative for corporations to think about how their technical options affect society as a whole and try to limit any unfavorable effects.

One key technological ethic for attention when adopting new technologies is informed consent. Informed consent refers to the practice of obtaining explicit consent from individuals before collecting, processing, or sharing their personal data. Altogether, it's particularly important in industries such as healthcare, where sensitive personal information is regularly collected and processed. Businesses must ensure that they are obtaining informed consent from individuals and that they disclose how their data will be used.

Transparency and culpability are also important ethical considerations when adopting new technologies. Businesses need to be transparent about how they are using data. They must be accountable for any negative impacts that may result from their technological decisions. This includes being transparent about the algorithms that are being used and how decisions are made, particularly in industries such as finance, where algorithmic decision-making is becoming increasingly common.

Certainly, regulation also plays a key role in ensuring that businesses are adopting technologies ethically. Governments around the world are increasingly implementing regulations to govern the use of new technologies, particularly in industries such as healthcare, finance, and transportation and it is vital for businesses to comply with these regulations and work to uphold ethical standards in their use of technology.

One of the ethical challenges involving technology is figuring out what the ethical position is. Ethics is a complicated topic that philosophers, religious leaders, and ordinary people have been debating for centuries. Digital piracy is an example: Some people who will never steal a physical copy of a book don't feel they're doing anything unethical if they pirate an e-book without paying the author. Differing ethics can also be an issue with monitoring social media. Some employees may feel they have a right to speak about politics or the wild party they went to last night. Their boss may think anything they say that doesn't enhance the company image is grounds for discipline.

The business owner, administrator, or supervisor is the ethical heart of the company. Thinking through and drawing up a clear policy on ethical technology lets everyone on work teams know where you stand. Then they have no justification for not living up the company standards.

Sustainability and resilience are mature management disciplines because much attention has been paid to developing strategies and implementing solutions to address them. Adaptive systems and resilient systems are often confused and thought of as interchangeable, but there's a vast difference between the two concepts. Whereas an adaptive system restructures or reconfigures itself to best operate in and optimize for the ambient conditions, a resilient system often simply has to restore or maintain an existing steady state.

Digital Transformations

Enterprises today are facing the transformative potential of generative AI. As businesses strive to improve efficiency and productivity, they also must navigate the complexities of responsible AI adoption and ensure ethical practices.

The varieties of complexities involving technology in business is astounding; however, there are many ways technology in businesses can benefit organizations to achieve success (Ugalde, 2023). One only needs to look at the proliferation of companies like **Netflix**, **Amazon**, and the countless manufacturers who have leveraged manufacturing automation to find examples of how useful different technologies can be. Technology is the future of businesses, although it presents new challenges. Businesses should learn what to expect to help them adopt workable technology solutions in advance. Businesses that leverage technology trend to stay ahead of the curve—inventory management, cloud-based resources, automation, data security, and management, and project management software.

Some examples of how digital transformations help businesses every day include the following:

- Cloud-based collaboration apps: Communication tools such as Zoom and Slack, as well as online document sharing solutions like Google Docs and Microsoft Teams, allow people to work together easily on important documents and projects despite being miles apart. There are industry-specific special sets of cloud platforms custom-made to distribute the diversified needs of distinct industries, including but not limited to healthcare, finance, and manufacturing. It provides dedicated and customized resources for improving efficiency and increasing compliance requirements with industry regulations for a business. This cloud saves a lot of time and provides customized solutions to the myriad problems that are prevailing in several sectors, including management and compliance.
- Inventory management solutions: Automated inventory tracking software helps businesses closely monitor their stock of important products or resources so they can maintain "just-in-time" supply chains that minimize costs without undue risk of running out of inventory.
- Customer-facing business apps: From digital storefronts to automated customer service solutions and other resources, customer-facing business applications—and particularly mobile applications—have helped businesses improve the way they interact with their customers to increase sales and customer retention.
- Data storage and retrieval: One of the biggest ways today's technologies helps businesses is in how modern companies can store and retrieve massive amounts of information at nearly any time from almost anywhere. Digital data storage has simplified the retrieval and transmission of important documents, reducing common data management tasks to mere seconds when they may have taken significantly longer using purely analog media.
- Project software: Project management software helps businesses track common project tasks and keep their project teams on track. With solutions such as Jira or Teamwork, project managers can assign specific tasks and monitor whether employees are on track to finish the project on time.

When leveraged effectively, technology can offer businesses across all industries a significant strategic and competitive edge. However, technology can also pose considerable challenges for businesses. There are common problems that often impede productivity and hinder business growth. From minor inconveniences to severe risks capable of permanently shuttering a business, the consequences of these challenges cross a wide spectrum.

Artificial intelligence (AI) and machine learning (ML) are rapidly transforming industries through automation in the areas of task, decision-making, and insights from data analysis. The AI markets are estimated to ascend to total market values of USD 190.61 billion by 2025, boosted by growing adoption across industry verticals, notably healthcare, finance, and retail. Helping that momentum are the increased uptake in deep learning, natural language processing, and computer vision. In more developed countries where businesses are adopting AI, with emerging markets catching up, the investment in digital infrastructure and technologies grows at a higher rate. Integrating AI into corporate business process cores is increasingly prevalent as companies seek means of boosting both efficiency and customer experience (Jain, 2025).

Lack of Strategic Planning

One of the biggest technological issues and challenges is when an organization has little or no strategic technology planning. In many corporations, technology is at the forefront of most business operations. Business executives who see the larger picture and have a vision for the business can make better-informed decisions when they involve IT professionals while trying to solve strategic business issues. IT professionals will be consultants that help to make long-term growth and scalability easier and more efficient. Common areas an IT team should help provide strategic direction are as follows: (1) optimizing business operations to streamline processes and improve productivity; (2) optimizing individual team members' productivity or department productivity; (3) selecting the best business management software applications and upgrading old or outdated hardware and software; (4) establishing cybersecurity best practices; and (5) creating a predictable IT budget plan so that expenses can be properly forecasted.

In the technological sector, cybercriminals develop new ways of infiltrating business networks, increasing the risk of cybercrime. This means that a business should be routinely upgrading its cybersecurity defenses. However, cybersecurity decisions should not be solely left to the IT department. These decisions impact on the entire business and need to be made with the buy-in of the leadership team. If leadership fails to recognize the risks and adequately address those risks and then becomes a victim of a cyber-attack, it will be to the detriment of the entire business (Adams, 2024). Working with an IT team to position a three-pronged approach that includes prevention, detection, and response is an important and needed step.

> *A vision without a strategy remains an illusion.*
>
> ~ Lee Bolman

Prevention—Are there right security tools in place, such as antivirus, anti-ransomware, firewalls, a VPN, MFA, Application Whitelisting, etc., to protect the organization from an attack? Are there regular training courses set up for employees on the latest threats and how to identify them?

Detection—This is a critical component of a quality security plan that many small businesses don't even know exists. Is there a way to know that the organization is under attack? If a hacker sneakily gained access to the network, would it go unnoticed until it became a bigger problem? The company's IT security team should be running regular scans, monitoring, and employing endpoint detection tools.

Response and recovery—Does a plan exist if the worst-case scenario happens? Would the workforce know what to do? The organization needs an IT team to identify and mitigate any issues quickly before the damage can be undone. Leaders in the organization should take this seriously. An organization technology assessment should endeavor to pose the following questions:

1. Are employees not fully productive due to underperforming technology?
2. Do operations fail to reach full potential due to roadblocks in technology?
3. Is the competition passing the company by due to limitations in your own technology?
4. Is the enterprise missing a budget for future technology expenses?
5. Is the company never entirely sure what's really going on with technology?
6. Is cybersecurity lacking and the company is unsure of how to improve it?

If you do not know where you are going, every road will get you nowhere.
~ Henry A. Kissinger

Continuity Planning

Business continuity planning is crucial and while each business's plan is unique to its needs, the foundation of the plan is generally the same for most organizations. The core goal is to document a company's risks and outline what is needed to avoid operational disruptions. Following are the several examples of business continuity plan components (Rock, 2025):

- Goal: Outline the key goals of the plan, especially as they relate to specific business units or systems.
- Contact information: Include communication information for the individuals responsible for overseeing continuity planning.
- Risk assessment: Shape the specific disaster scenarios that put the business at risk of an operational disruption.
- Business impact analysis: Document in clear terms how each type of disaster will affect the business, including impact on various operations, estimated recovery time, and associated financial losses.
- Preventative measures: Outline the procedures, plans, and systems that will help the company minimize the risk of various disasters from occurring.
- Disaster response plan: Document the specific protocols that should be followed immediately following a disruption to lessen the impact.

- Business continuity and disaster recovery systems: Outline the systems and procedures that should be used to maintain continuity or recover from an outage.
- Communication plan: Outline how the organization will distribute information to employees or between recovery teams if primary communication lines are unavailable.
- Plan review and update schedule: Create an agenda for reviewing and updating the business continuity plan to ensure the documentation remains accurate and relevant.

Miscalculations in Cybersecurity

In addition to creating and developing a technology assessment, it is more than prudent to review the top common cybersecurity errors. Relying on antivirus software alone is a mistake. Antivirus solutions have been the gold standard in cybersecurity for many years. This technology scans company files for known viruses, and some products feature malware threat response services and as cyber criminals' tactics have evolved, so have the technologies used to stop them (Mahna, 2024). While antivirus software is still helpful for modern businesses, an organization's cybersecurity strategy should not rely on it alone.

Organizations may think an IT breach will not happen to them. In fact, cyberattacks occur all the time and they may not even know that a hack has happened in their workplace until it is too late and that is why it is critical for organizations to understand the risk of breaches. A risk analysis can show where their IT security strategy is working and where it needs work. Understanding risk profiles can help organizations prepare for the unexpected. An independent third party is best for risk analysis. Organizations should select a reliable vendor who has extensive knowledge of audits and will perform an analysis that does not just follow a stated framework but personalizes it to the specific circumstances of the organization.

A vigorous cybersecurity system is an investment in an organization's future. However, many business owners and executives might see it more as a financial burden. With fines for breaches and public relations nightmares with customers, organizations need to realize that the benefits of a strong cybersecurity strategy far offset the costs. The organization will remain more competitive if customers know their information will be protected. Prospective employees will also prefer those firms. They will know their work is secure on a highly protected system.

Failing to update company systems and applications can increase the risk of a breach. Updates to systems help reduce errors by including new updates to close loopholes and protect from vulnerabilities and with frequent software updates, organizations can stay ahead of cybercriminals. Without them, they could be at risk for coordinated cyberattacks by criminals who target companies that do not update their products regularly.

Two-factor authentication, also known as 2FA or multi-factor authentication (MFA), is a security strategy used to log into systems. 2FA creates an extra layer of security over sensitive data. To do 2FA, organizations need a password and a second login method. Some systems may require them to log into a system using an authentication code sent to an employee's email or phone. Hackers cannot get the code needed to log in without access to an employee's email or phone. The more difficult corporations make for cybercriminals to get into their systems, the less likely they are to try.

Retail giant **Target** agreed in May 2013 to pay $18.5 million to settle claims by 47 states and the District of Columbia and resolve a multi-state investigation into a massive data breach. The investigation, which was led by the Attorneys General of Connecticut and Illinois, found that cyberattackers had accessed Target's gateway server through credentials stolen from a third-party vendor. The Target data breach was one of the biggest security breaches in history. During the Target breach, cybercriminals were able to steal 40 million credit and debit records and 70 million customer records. This occurred during the holiday season in 2013. While it wasn't the single largest security breach in history, it was one of the largest. And because there had been many other high-profile data breaches just before, customers were particularly wary.

Target's data breach highlights one of the major issues that occur after a breach. It isn't just a security disruption, and it isn't just the cost of the settlement: It's those customers who no longer had faith in their security. After the data breach, customers were worried that their data would be leaked, so they were hesitant to buy from Target.

The retailer handled the data breach very well, all things considered. It was able to notify customers about 20 days after the breach occurred, but only 4 days after they noticed it. In the wide spectrum of data breaches, this is very fast. The issue is that the data breach occurred at all. Target could, and should, have been more cautious about its third-party solutions and there were internal issues that needed to be resolved.

Following the data breach, Target did issue more secure chip-and-pin cards. They discovered that chips alone weren't enough to secure many of the cards that had been compromised, although consumers learned a lesson, too—credit cards are much more secure than debit cards. With credit cards, it's easier to overturn a transaction, and a fake transaction doesn't leave you without money. The estimated cost of Target data breach goes well beyond the $18 million settlement. In fact, it's estimated the company lost over $200 million. Retail data breaches are extraordinarily expensive, but no industry is safe.

Disaster Preparedness

Companies should have a disaster preparedness plan regarding security breaches. There should be a strategy in place for companies to restore customer faith and loyalty if the worst occurs. And there should be proactive solutions if a data breach occurs. It's always better to be proactive about company security.

As terrible as the Target cyber issue was, there was an even more horrific data breach several years after. In September 2017, **Equifax** announced a data breach that exposed the personal information of over 147 million people. The company has agreed to a global settlement with the Federal Trade Commission, the Consumer Financial Protection Bureau, and 50 US states and territories. The settlement includes up to $425 million to help people affected by the data breach.

Equifax, one of the three largest consumer credit reporting agencies in the United States, had been breached and the data breached included names, home addresses, phone numbers, dates of birth, social security numbers, and driver's license numbers. The credit card numbers of approximately 209,000 consumers were also breached. The Equifax breach is unprecedented in scope and severity. There have been larger security breaches by other companies in the past, but the sensitivity of the personal information held by Equifax and the scale of the problem makes this breach unprecedented.

In this breach, the US government indicted four members of China's military on charges of hacking Equifax to exploit the personal data of Americans. They allegedly conspired to hack into Equifax's computer networks, maintain unauthorized access to those computers, and steal sensitive, personally identifiable information of nearly half of all American citizens. EPIC President Marc Rotenberg (2018) testified before the House in 2018 and the Senate in 2017 about the breach. Rotenberg warned lawmakers and regulators that the failure of the US government to safeguard the personal data of Americans has placed American consumers at risk from foreign adversaries.

Isolation and Interconnected Complications

Technology has allowed many the opportunity to work from home in recent times. For many of the labor force, working from home has opened up greater flexibility to get the job done. While there are many positives, such as no commute, there are some situations that are made more difficult by the addition of technology in a conversation.

Identifying and resolving conflicts in the workplace has always been difficult. A great deal of managing human interactions is the ability to read the body language of an individual for context clues to how they truly feel about a situation. Now that we are separated by technology, we have added an extra layer that tends to blur how we interpret other peoples' actions and reactions. While speaking with someone in real life, in person, it is easier to assess how information is being received. If one feels it was not received correctly, one can take immediate steps to rectify the misunderstanding. However, when working remotely, we are now limited to email communication, telephone communication, or videoconferencing. In this time of amplified stress and worry for many, it is important to reduce the chances for conflict whenever possible.

Technology is largely transforming conflict resolution, shifting from isolated decision-making to interconnected, data-informed strategies. While historical strategies of conflict resolution were limited by geographical and communicative barriers, technological advancements like the internet and AI have broadened communication and understanding.

Digital Diplomacy

Digital diplomacy has seen a significant evolution with the integration of technology in mediating conflicts around the world. According to a research study by the Center for Strategic and International Studies (Laksmana, 2020), digital tools have become essential in promoting dialogue and peacebuilding. The report highlights that in 2020, digital platforms were utilized in over 70% of conflict mediation processes globally, showcasing a marked increase compared to previous years. This shift can be attributed to the accessibility and reach of technology, which has enabled diplomats and mediators to engage with a wider audience and facilitate discussions more effectively.

The future of conflict resolution can look promising with technologies enabling preventive strategies through predictive analytics and fostering empathy via immersive experiences and while technology offers immense potential in resolving and preventing conflicts, challenges such as privacy, and ethical considerations must be addressed.

References

Adams, B. (2024). *The Top 6 Tech Challenges Facing Business Today*. Mesa, AZ: AZComp Technologies.

Economy, P. (2025). *Adaptability Is the Key to Success in an Evolving Market*. New York: About Inc.com.

Golbin, I. (2023). *Best Practices to Achieve Purpose-led Tech*. New York: Price Waterhouse Coopers.

Jain, S. (2025). *Top 25 New Technology Trends in 2025*. Noida, Utter Pradesh: Geeks for Geeks.

Laksmana, E. A. (2020). *Global Expert Survey 2020: Global and Regional Dynamics After COVID-19*. Jakarta, Indonesia: Center for Strategic and International Studies.

Lewis, G. (2006). *Organizational Crisis Management: The Human Factor*. Boca Raton, FL: Auerbach Publications.

Mahna, R. (2024). *Top 10 Common Cybersecurity Mistakes to Avoid*. New York: Eisner Amper.

Pathak, R. (2020). *The Prophet's New Prediction*. Analytics Steps.

Pinto, P. (2025). *7 Powerful Conflict Management Strategies That Transform Technology Teams*. Miami, FL: Coachpedropinto.com.

Rock, T. (2025). *7 Real-Life Business Continuity Plan Examples You'll Want to Read*. Invenio IT.com.

Rotenberg, M. (2018). *Testimony before the House Committee on Financial Services, Hearing on Examining the Current Data Security and Breach Notification Regulatory Regime*, February 14.

Shalimov, A. (2024). *6 Tech Trends (and 4 Challenges) for Enterprises in 2024*. Herzliya, Israel: Eastern Peak.

Smith, B. (2023). *The Ethics of Technology: What Businesses Need to Consider When Adopting New Technologies*. Herdon, VA: Centurion Consulting Group.

Ugalde, J. (2023). *15 Technology Challenges Businesses May Face in 2023*. Chesterfield, MI: Systems X.

5 Internal and External Negotiation Contexts

In our culture, we reflexively tend to think of the term "conflict" in the negative. When we discuss conflict in the business world, we speak of it as a diminishing force on productivity, an ill that only compounds the difficulties of a job and an element that needs expunging if companies are to achieve their goals. Normally seen as the by-product of a "squeaky wheel" rather than a natural derivative of business itself, conflict is a force that causes short-term anxieties, and many view "fixing" ongoing conflict as synonymous with "eliminating" it.

Employees at all levels must learn to accept conflict as an inevitable part of their work environment. A recent study found that an overwhelming majority (85%) of employees at all levels experience conflict to some degree. Furthermore, US employees spend 2.8 hours per week dealing with conflict, equating to approximately $359 billion in paid hours in 2008. The question for management, therefore, is not whether it can be avoided or mitigated; the real concern is how conflict is dealt with, whether internally with the company or externally with outside partners. If managed improperly, businesses' productivity, operational effectiveness, and morale take a major hit, as evidenced in one finding that 27% of employees have witnessed conflict morph into a personal attack, while 25% say that the avoidance of conflict resulted in sickness or absence from work. On the other hand, when channeled through the right tools and expertise, conflict can lead to positive outcomes, such as a better understanding of others, improved solutions to problems or challenges, and major innovation. Roughly, three quarters of workers reported positive outcomes that resulted from conflict—results that likely would not have been produced if conflict was not initiated (Hayes, 2008).

Internal conflict is a type of conflict that can happen in a business or organization, and it can involve disputes between employees, management, partners, and shareholders. Unresolved internal conflict can have a significant cost, including (a) poor morale; (b) low productivity; (c) sickness and absenteeism; (d) disgruntled employees; and (e) lawsuits.

Individuals often bring many personal differences to the negotiation table. Expectations often vary depending upon the issues, people, timeframe,

DOI: 10.4324/9781042000258-6

conclusion impact, and other variables. The concept of internal negotiation within a company often speaks to a high level of expectation coupled with a personal commitment to performance that maintains an even level of communication, resolution and camaraderie. Underlying internal negotiations are four key elements: (1) a willingness to thoroughly prepare; (2) maintaining a high level of expectation; (3) developing the patience to keenly listen; and (4) harboring a deep commitment to personal integrity.

Negotiation Principles

Integral to nearly all internal negotiations are the "information-based-bargaining" approach. This involves solid planning and preparation, impactful bargaining style, solid goals and expectations, and resourceful pre-negotiation research. When negotiations take place within the organization, a win–win approach is especially vital. The issues being discussed aren't the only things at stake. If a negotiation sours a working relationship, it can lead to grudges, backbiting, and strained internal politics. When negotiating with colleagues and management in the organization, keep in mind that you are on the same team. Below are several principles to follow when the person on the other side of the negotiating table is a coworker:

- Remain unemotional: Feelings and emotions should never be brought to the negotiating table. It can be tempting to take an internal negotiation personally and make a mental "blacklist" of those who make your life difficult.
- Arrange to negotiate in person: Meeting in person is the best way to get a negotiation started on the right foot. Rather than dealing with your colleagues in an impersonal manner via e-mail or telephone, try to arrange a personal meeting first.
- Prepare and plan: Take the time to understand the other party's needs and concerns as well as how you may be able to meet those needs during a negotiation. Simply because you're dealing with a coworker does not negate the need to practice basic negotiation principles.
- Sidestep preconceived assumptions: Leave those notions about the other party away from the negotiating table. Test assumptions and try to uncover motivations behind requests or issues. Failing to test assumptions can lead to misunderstandings and lack of agreement.
- Remain ethical: Unethical tactics and dirty tricks can trip you up. Double-crossing your coworkers is often like playing with fire.

The final point of all negotiations is to finalize an agreement that benefits both parties. In addition to an amicable and fair agreement in many business negotiations is the notion that all parties will remain approachable enough to continue future interactions and business. Several important principles to keep in mind during enterprise negotiations (Gottlieb and Healy, 1998) include the following:

- The most important individual to know in the process is yourself.
- Each member of a negotiation team has power.
- Urgency often drives decisions.
- Agreement is the end; trading off is the means.
- Even when two sides are far apart on major issues, there are always things they can agree on.

Success with collaborative negotiation hinges on trust, shared interests, and creative problem-solving. The goal is a win–win outcome where both parties feel heard and valued. Researchers (Pruitt, 1981) have identified several keys to successful collaboration, and they are useful as a checklist for the strategic negotiator in planning and implementing a collaborative strategy.

- Create common goals or objectives.
- Maintain confidence in your own ability to solve problems.
- Value the other party's opinion.
- Share the motivation and commitment to working together.
- Begin and sustain trusting expectations.
- Develop a bedrock of clear and accurate communication.

Current research (Overvest, 2025) shows that the way one approaches a negotiation has a key role in the process of the negotiation. If you aim for a win–win outcome, the chances of this result will be significantly higher. To accomplish this, it's critical to put yourself in the shoes of the other party. What are their goals? Their interests? By doing this, you'll be able to turn win–lose situations into a win for both parties. This includes creating additional alternative solutions by giving something, which has little value to you, but great value to the other.

Key Terms and Concepts

Whether the negotiation is distributive or integrative, understanding key terms and concepts will greatly improve the process.

ASKING PRICE/VALUE: The asking price in negotiation is the initial figure one party proposes to set the tone and anchor the discussion. It's not just a number; it's a tactical signal.

ANCHORS: The first number made in a negotiation that usually stands to anchor against all subsequent offers that are rendered. The focus of this number can change while negotiations move forward. It is the cognitive bias where people rely heavily on the first piece of information offered when making decisions and it sets the tone and range for the discussion.

TARGET NUMBER: The target number is the best realistic outcome you hope to achieve. It's grounded in research, market data, and strategic positioning. This is the negotiator's end goal.

RESISTANCE POINT: The resistance point, also called the walkaway point, is the absolute limit beyond which a negotiator will not go. When the target number is the goal, the resistance point is the bottom line. For example, you are selling a warranty service, and your resistance point is $6,000; anything less isn't worth your time. The buyer's resistance point is $7,000 and they will not pay more. In this case, the Zone of Possible Agreement is $6,000–$7,000 where a deal is possible.

ZONE OF POSSIBLE AGREEMENT (ZOPA): The ZOPA stands as the negotiation range between each party's resistance points: buyer's resistance point is the highest they're willing to pay, and the seller's resistance point is the lowest they're willing to accept. If these intersect, a deal is possible. For example, the buyer's range is willing to pay $80–$100; the seller's range is willing to sell for $90–$110 and therefore the ZOPA is $90–$100. This is where agreement can happen. However, if the buyer won't go above $85 and the seller won't go below $90, there's no ZOPA, unless one party adjusts their expectations or determines new value.

The negotiation range is fundamental to each negotiation. The point of negotiating is to reach agreement. If one can't find the negotiation range, agreement is probably impossible and the negotiation fails. But an in-depth understanding of the negotiation range does more than improve the chances of reaching an agreement: it also helps one to achieve an outcome that goes beyond the bare minimum one would accept. Understanding the negotiation range enables the negotiator to assess their own bargaining position, planning your negotiation tactics accordingly.

Internal negotiations are when different parts of a company discuss and agree on what to include in a contract before they finalize it with another party outside the company. This step is central because it helps ensure that everyone in the company is on the same page and that the contract reflects the company's needs and goals. These discussions can cover everything from how much funding is allocated to how long a project should take, and what each team needs to do. When it comes to internal negotiations for contracts within a company, several critical roles are involved, each bringing unique perspectives and expertise to ensure the contract is comprehensive and serves the company's best interests.

> *Coming together is a beginning; keeping together is progress; working together is success.*
>
> ~ Henry Ford

Settlement Range

Every negotiation involves one or more issues. Successful negotiators plan a settlement range of acceptable outcomes for each issue. Less skillful negotiators will go in with just an opening position and any concession or movement from that position feels like a loss. Developing a settlement range is the best insurance against this feeling. Every negotiation involves one or more issues. Successful negotiators plan a settlement range of acceptable outcomes for each issue. Less skillful negotiators will go in with just an opening position and any concession or movement from that position feels like a loss. Developing a settlement range is the best insurance against this feeling. The settlement range, generally displayed on a continuum, consists of three main points (Gosselin, 2007):

- Desired settlement point (DSP) represents the point on the scale where you believe a "fair deal" can be executed. Ask, "Realistically, where are we likely to settle?" One can look at indices such as market conditions, precedents, comparables, previous deals, and so on. Always set this point first in developing your settlement range.
- Opening position (OP) is the point at or above your DSP that you believe meets two criteria: (1) high (but not excessive) and (2) defensible (i.e., can be argued by using objective criteria or independent sources of information).
- Walk-away (WA) point represents the point at which the other party's OP is unacceptable. Determining the WA is a critical part of your planning that prevents you from making a bad deal. Among successful negotiators, there is a saying, "No deal is better than a bad deal!"

The settlement range refers to the spectrum of acceptable outcomes that a party is willing to consider. It's a strategic tool that helps negotiators avoid feeling like any concession is a loss and instead frames movement as part of a planned resolution. Many negotiators simply plan their range of acceptability as below:

ABOVE GOAL
GOAL
BELOW GOAL

Before proceeding with the negotiation process, you really need to look at what point you want to settle. This puts a sense of control into the negotiation and enables you to know when you should stop or keep going. The settlement range can be formulated by means of a matrix, which allows you to sort out the issues that may become enmeshed with each other. This will help you to clearly assess the goals on each issue separately and to remain objective and focused on these goals throughout the negotiation. A clearer

Table 5.1 Negotiation settlement matrix

	Issue 1	*Issue 2*	*Issue 3*
Maximum supportable			
Really asking			
Least acceptable			
Deal breaker			

settlement range matrix than the one above can look like the one in Table 5.1 (Ré, 2003).

The *maximum supportable* is the most (or the highest) that you can ask from the other side without leaving the realm of reason. *Really asking* is what you really want to settle on. *Least acceptable* is the bottom line (lowest point) you would be willing to accept. The *deal breaker* is the point at which you would walk away and not conclude an agreement

Influences on the Process of Negotiation

Negotiation is a deliberative process between two or more actors that seek a solution to a common issue or who are bartering over an item of value. Negotiation skills include the range of negotiation techniques negotiators employ to create value and claim value in their dealmaking business negotiations and beyond. Negotiations are not just about persuasive arguments and strong communication; they are influenced by several factors that can significantly impact the outcome. It is shaped by a dynamic interplay of many factors.

Planning	Defining issues; setting targets; analyzing other side
Organization factors	Growing, stagnant, or shrinking; power and trust issues
Negotiation skills	Expertise in questioning; communication experience
Strategies and tactics	Content vs. relationship issues; managing emotions
Cultural and personal factors	Reputation of negotiators; differences in time and space
Legal factors	Codes for contracts and agreements; industry standards
The economy	Market conditions; issues of supply and demand

The preparation and strategy aspects should include thought and research about knowing negotiation priorities, walk-away points, and trade-offs that can enhance focus and adaptability. Additionally, pre-planning thoughts should consider how proposals will be presented (gain vs. loss framing) that may shift ongoing perceptions and openness.

Negotiation Format

If negotiators have the opportunity to select a negotiation format, an obvious choice is *in-person negotiation*. This format has substantial advantages; one can observe the other side's body language and there is a terrific opportunity to build a strong relationship with the other party. *Telephone negotiations* are a daily fact of life and they are challenging. Four key aspects of phone negotiations are: (1) prepare to do a large amount of listening; (2) take care notes to reconstruct the conversation; (3) do not feel pressure to offer an immediate yes or no answer; and (4) have a checklist at hand to give you an information advantage.

With the growth of virtual work teams and the cost of travel, *teleconference negotiations* have become more prevalent. Several guidelines for teleconference negotiations are as follows: (1) prepare an agenda that includes all participants' names; (2) questions and discussion of issues should be addressed to specific individuals; (3) ensure that no outsiders or people with no connections to the discussion are on the call; (4) try to limit the teleconference to four to six attendees; and (5) sensitive issues should be addressed offline in a forum that isn't so public.

Video conferencing (Zoom, Skype, FaceTime) has become a prevailing medium for negotiation, offering convenience and global reach but also introducing unique challenges such as reduced non-verbal cues, technical disruptions, and trust-building difficulties. Videoconferencing is widely perceived as a deep communication medium because it allows people to learn from each other's visual and verbal cues. Negotiators can build rapport and understanding by becoming involved with the verbal and nonverbal cues from the parties. In addition to allowing parties to communicate both verbally and nonverbally, video negotiation enables them to jointly view and discuss documents, slide shows, and videos.

Building trust in a virtual environment takes great effort and without the casual conversations that happen naturally in an office, negotiators must be intentional about nurturing relationships and uncertainty can be higher in remote negotiations, making credibility and transparency more important than ever. Globalization has further complicated virtual negotiations such as: (1) coordinating discussions across different time zones; (2) cross-cultural differences may demand sensitivity to diverse communication styles; and (3) negotiation expectations and the decision-making process may be more difficult. To succeed, negotiators must adapt their strategies to this digital environment with intentional preparation, clear communication, and sound relationship management.

The *use of email* in the negotiation process is increasingly commonplace in today's technology-driven business world. When used appropriately, it can be very effective and can be particularly beneficial in the fact-finding stage of negotiation. Since email is not a face-to-face communication, misjudgments can arise. To get the most out of e-negotiations, be knowledgeable about the following: (1) use and integrate email as one strategy channel of communication; (2) do not use email in a conflict situation; (3) do not forward anything without permission; and (4) assume that your email could be used in legal proceedings.

Negotiation Is Persuasion

All negotiators incorporate facts to persuade the other side to accept their points of view. However, facts only justify positions. Negotiation *includes* persuasion, but they are *not the same thing*. True persuasion involves a careful blend of facts and emotions. It involves the use of feelings, logic, values, and WIIFTs (what's in it for them). The negotiators persuasion combines three aspects.

- Appeal to emotion that opens the mind.
- Appeal to logic that justifies the proposed recommendations.
- Appeal to value that seals the agreement.

In a negotiation scenario, the three aspects can be fashioned this way.

- Appeal to emotion—stating a claim (unsubstantiated by fact).
- Appeal to logic—stating facts to support the claim (data that can be verified).
- Appeal to value—assigning a meaning/WIIFT (inherent benefit of the claim or fact).

For example, when negotiating with a home goods company for the sale of XYZ paint, the negotiator states:

CLAIM: *This is the best paint you can carry in your store.*
LOGIC: *This paint can cover the darkest colors in one coat and cleans up easily.*
VALUE: *Your customers can paint their room in just one day instead of spending the entire weekend painting.*

Failing to distinguish between negotiation and persuasion can lead to three significant mistakes:

- Persuading when negotiation is needed—trying to convince without compromise may alienate the other party.
- Negotiating when persuasion is required—offering concessions when clarity and influence are needed may weaken your position.
- Overusing one skill at the expense of the other—negotiators who only persuade can appear manipulative, while those who only negotiate can seem transactional and cold.

Persuasion is (1) one-way influence where you try to change the other party's beliefs, attitudes, or preferences; (2) a goal shift from their position toward yours; and (3) using tools of logic, emotion, credibility, framing, and evidence. *Negotiation* is (1) a two-way process where both sides adjust positions to reach agreement; (2) to create value and claim value; and

Table 5.2 Negotiation versus persuasion

Characteristic	*Persuasion*	*Negotiation*
Central goal	Influence behavior	Attain an equal settlement
Aim	Change minds	Balance interests
Tactics	Emotional appeal, logic	Concessions, BATNA
Result	Compliance	Resolution

(3) utilizing the tools of persuasion plus interests analysis, trade-offs, concessions, BATNA leverage, and offers/counteroffers.

> *One of the best ways to persuade others is by listening to them.*
>
> ~ Dean Rusk

Four aspects that link negotiation to persuasion are:

- Joint goals: Both involve influencing another party's thinking or behavior.
- Proof and sentiment: Persuasion blends logic (facts, data, precedents) with psychology (trust, credibility, emotion). Negotiation does the same, but within a bounded settlement range.
- Mutuality: Unlike one-way persuasion, negotiation is interactive; both sides persuade each other toward a mutually acceptable outcome.
- Framing: How one presents options (gain vs. loss, fairness vs. risk) shapes the other party's perception.

Framing

A key issue in perception and negotiation is framing. A frame is the subjective mechanism through which people evaluate and make sense out of situations, leading them to pursue or avoid subsequent actions. Framing is about focusing, shaping, and organizing the events and issues in a negotiation situation. Frames are important in negotiation because individuals encounter the same issues, events, and processes differently. The following are examples of frames that disputing parties use (Lewicki, Barry and Saunders, 2007):

- Substantive: what the conflict is about.
- Outcome: a party's disposition to achieving a specific result from the negotiation.
- Aspiration: a predisposition toward satisfying a broader set of needs.
- Process: how the disputant will go about resolving the issues.
- Identity: how the parties define who they are.
- Characterization: how the parties define the other side.
- Loss–gain: how the parties define the risk or reward associated with particular outcomes.

Framing an issue in negotiations means that one focuses attention on one aspect of an issue and leaving other aspects out. To understand why framing is so powerful, one needs to look at its psychological roots. People tend to weigh losses more heavily than gains, a concept known as loss aversion. A deal framed as avoiding a potential loss often carries more persuasive weight than one that simply highlights potential gains. Negotiators may elect to exclude some aspects of an issue from the frame because they're irrelevant, because they might distract from the main point, or because they don't advance interests. Framing is a way of calling attention to what one believes is the most important, or advantageous, aspect of the issue at hand. Negotiators can use more than one frame; however, mismatches between parties are sources of conflict. Certain types of frames may lead to particular types of agreements. Both parties have frames and they are controllable, at least to some degree. Conversations in the negotiation change and transform the frames in ways negotiators may not be able to predict but may be able to control.

To understand why framing is so powerful, one needs to look at its psychological roots. People tend to weigh losses more heavily than gains, a theory known as *loss aversion*. A deal framed as avoiding a potential loss often carries more persuasive weight than one that simply highlights potential gains. When an offer is framed as an industry standard, parties are more likely to accept it because they feel they are aligning with what others have already deemed acceptable.

Basically, framing works because the human brain doesn't process information in a vacuum. Every decision is filtered through cognitive biases, emotional responses, and mental shortcuts designed to simplify complex choices. Neuroscience has shown that the brain reacts differently to the same information depending on its presentation, even when the objective facts don't change. This is why a product described as having a 90% success rate sounds reassuring, while saying it has a 10% failure rate feels riskier, even though both are identical.

Daniel Kahneman and Amos Tversky's (1979) *Prospect Theory* reveals that people fear losses more than they desire gains, a bias that shapes nearly every negotiation. When an offer is framed as avoiding a loss, it triggers a stronger emotional response than when framed as an equivalent gain. The reason lies in our brain's amygdala, which processes fear and threat detection. A perceived loss activates this system, making the threat feel urgent and pushing decision-makers toward risk-averse choices. In contrast, framing something as a potential gain engages the brain's reward center, but with less intensity than a loss. This is why sellers often emphasize avoiding price increases rather than securing savings—it lands harder on the decision-maker's subconscious.

Beyond loss aversion, the prefrontal cortex plays a role in evaluating risks and rewards. However, under pressure, people rely more on heuristics than logical evaluation, meaning framing can override purely rational assessment.

A negotiator who understands this can shift the conversation simply by changing how options are presented, aligning their framing with how the human brain naturally perceives value.

Many negotiators use framing to emphasize the strengths of their position. Consider a circumstance where the objective is to sell a product at a premium price. Instead of fixating on the cost itself, one can highlight the product's superior quality and high demand. This approach elevates its perceived value and makes the offer much more attractive.

A conspicuous example of framing involved a yoghurt marketed in two different ways. One version displays "Yoghurt—30% Fat" while another boasts "Yoghurt—70% less fat." The second label shifts the focus away from what's there to what has been reduced, thereby changing consumer perception. Such intentional steering of information helps both sides see familiar details through a new lens, which can work wonders in negotiations.

Negotiation Managers and Negotiation Blunders

The legal team plays an essential role in internal contract negotiations, making sure everything is legally sound and beneficial for the organization. They help draft and review contracts to prevent future legal problems and ensure that the agreements comply with laws and regulations. These experts explain the complicated parts of contracts, making sure everyone understands their responsibilities and rights. They also negotiate to get the best terms possible and handle any issues that come up during discussions.

The finance team is crucial during internal contract negotiations because they handle all the money-related details to make sure the contracts make financial sense for the company. They look at the costs and potential earnings from the contract and evaluate any financial risks involved. This helps the company see how the contract might affect its financial health.

Additionally, they work with other departments to understand and manage the budget effectively. This includes making sure that the contract terms don't commit the company to spend more than it can afford.

Company project managers play a key role in contract negotiations by providing key information about the project. They explain what the project entails, what resources are required, and how long the tasks will take. Their experience allows them to identify and address potential issues early on, reducing the risk of future problems. They also collaborate with the legal and finance teams to ensure the contract aligns with the project's operational needs. Project managers advocate for terms that support the project's success, such as flexible provisions for managing changes, strategies for handling risks, and payment terms that reflect project milestones.

They also negotiate technical details with contractors and suppliers to ensure the contract meets the project's specific requirements. This requires effective communication and a deep understanding of the project's technical aspects. After the contract is signed, project managers oversee its implementation. They ensure everyone follows the contract, the project stays on schedule, and it stays within budget. If any issues arise, they address them to keep the project on track.

Negotiators' basic goal is to craft an agreement or settlement that is accepted by all. The choice is rather simple: accept a deal (perhaps, with some concessions) or accept no deal and walk away. Below are several common errors (Blank, 2020) that negotiators make that keep them from solving the right problems:

- Overlooking the other side's perspective: Of course, you need to understand your own needs and interests and your deal-breaker options, but it is important to understand TOS perspectives.
- Allowing costs and money to demolish other interests: Focusing exclusively on price can turn potentially cooperative deals into adversarial ones.
- Elevating positions to drive out interests: Three vital elements at play in a negotiation are the issues, the positions, and the interests. *Issues* are aboveboard for explicit agreement. *Positions* are one party's stands on those issues, and *interests* are the underlying concerns that would be impacted by the resolution. Positions on issues reflect underlying interests, but they need not be identical.
- Probing too hard for common ground: Common ground usually can overcome the differences that divide parties in a negotiation. Finding differences can often break open deadlocked deals.
- Neglecting BATNAs: The best alternative to a negotiated agreement may involve walking away, prolonging a stalemate, approaching another seller, forming a different alliance, and so on. A strong BATNA is an important negotiating tool.

Internal Negotiations

Finally, the procurement team is essential for the smooth operation of internal negotiations within a company. Their main job is to make sure the company gets the best deals possible when purchasing goods and services it needs to operate. They act as the go-between for the company and its suppliers, using their skills in finding sources, bargaining, and managing relationships to get the best results.

During internal negotiations, they work closely with different departments like finance, operations, and legal to make sure everyone's needs and goals are considered. They study market trends, supplier capabilities, and what the company needs to develop negotiation plans that fit the situation perfectly. When conflicts arise during negotiations, the procurement team steps in to smooth things over and find solutions (Carvajal, 2024).

Several common areas of company internal negotiations center around the following:

- Resource allocation—departments negotiating over budget, staff, or equipment.
- Workload distribution—team members negotiating who handles certain tasks.

- Project priorities—deciding which initiatives move forward first.
- Policy or process changes—employees and management discussing adjustments.
- Conflict resolution—negotiating solutions when disagreements arise.

The internal negotiations between company partners can be much more difficult and time-consuming than the ones with the client, who may be impatiently tapping their fingers and considering moving to another entity to negotiate. Internal interpersonal relationships can be broader than external interpersonal relationships. These interpersonal conflicts often revolve around emotions, impulses, and resources. The organization itself may contribute to some conflicts; these can evolve around struggles for promotion, battles over project funding, and debates about strategic directions (Folger, Poole and Stutman, 2013).

There are three main reasons internal negotiations are more difficult than external negotiations: (1) a failure to test assumptions people make about internal negotiations; (2) lack of preparation for internal negotiations; and (3) the lack of a common, internal process or negotiation infrastructure for conducting important negotiations.

- Failure to test assumptions: Assumptions are those things negotiators believe to be true without having tested their validity. Too often negotiators assume that because they work for the same organization, are "all on the same team," and have the same overall goals, internal negotiations will be easy. However, within a single department, let alone across an entire organization, there are likely to be conflicting goals, conflicting priorities, and conflicting ways of being rewarded. When that gets coupled with a lack of direct authority over many of the people one must negotiate with, internal negotiations can be quite challenging. Even if a department or individual within a company shares goals, they may not share priorities. Or if they share your goals and priorities, competing commitments may mean that he or she can't honor the schedule you want for the negotiations. A negotiator may assume that negotiation goals and strategy have been communicated, internally, when often they have not. A negotiator must see as his first task gaining and building internal alignment about the goals, strategy, and desired outcomes for any major negotiation by testing assumptions with key stakeholders.
- Lack of preparation: When negotiating with someone outside the company, organizations and individuals often spend a great deal of time preparing for those negotiations. A salesperson might spend weeks or months preparing to negotiate with a major customer. A union president will spend months mapping strategy for upcoming contract negotiations. When, however, an individual gets a call to meet with the boss to discuss upcoming negotiations, rarely will they see that meeting as a negotiation in and of itself. Therefore, they often walk in unprepared or prepared to sell their answer or strategy without understanding the boss's interests, concerns,

and goals. We would argue that before developing a strategy, an effective negotiator must identify the key internal and external stakeholders and begin the negotiation process by sitting down with them one-on-one or in small groups to ask, elicit their interests, and brainstorm possible options for the upcoming negotiations.

- Lack of a common process or negotiation infrastructure within the company: Many times the company has no negotiation infrastructure. There is no widespread process for how one goes about preparing for, conducting and reviewing negotiations. Too often, that is left to the initiative and skill of the individual who will be doing the negotiations; each person or department does its own thing. No organizational process or structure is in place to ensure thorough preparation for the negotiations or that a strategic review of the results occurs. There is no process to ensure that the company transfers the skills and tools of effective negotiation to its experienced or new employees. There is no common vocabulary or process for conducting negotiations.

External Negotiations

External negotiation occurs between an organization and outside parties such as customers, suppliers, specialty vendors, business partners, or even competitors. Some concrete examples of these negotiations usually involve pricing deals, contract agreements, sales deals, issues with labor relations and unions, and mergers and acquisitions. An excellent negotiation strategy is to create value for both sides through collaboration.

Some of the most common types of external negotiation are sales and client contracts, which address pricing and specific contract terms. Another type is supplier and vendor contracts, which includes costs and delivery schedules and timelines. A third and very important one involves external dispute settlements focused on resolving conflicts over performance, delays, or damages.

A real-world example of the above is demonstrated in the purchasing of a home. A house buyer discovers the roof of the home he wishes to purchase needs repairs and is able to negotiate a lower price. The seller counters by offering to fix the roof or cover closing costs, which demonstrates flexibility and creative problem-solving, which leads to win–win outcomes.

In 2013, **Disney** acquired **Lucasfilm** for $4.05 billion. The negotiation was built on trust and long-term relationship-building. Disney's CEO Robert Iger and George Lucas personally handled discussions over two years. Under the terms of the agreement and based on the closing price of Disney stock on October 26, 2012, the transaction value was $4.05 billion, with Disney paying approximately half of the consideration in cash and issuing approximately 40 million shares at closing. The final consideration was subject to customary post-closing balance sheet adjustments. In this external negotiation, this high-stakes deals benefitted from patience, personal rapport, and shared vision.

Rushing the negotiation process coupled with a lack of flexibility will deter any success in external negotiations. A common, but often huge error, is assuming a fixed pie by believing there is only one way to divide value, which limits creativity. A second error is facing extreme demands by the external partner, which may be followed up by small, slow concessions. To head off this tactic, it is important to have a clear sense of your own goals and the best alternative to a negotiated agreement (BATNA).

Internal and external negotiations are complex, multi-party deals and both negotiation types necessitate tangible resources, such as time, money, and people, and intangible resources, such as trust, honesty, and reputation. In addition, both involve complex working relationships that are perpetually evolving. Successful negotiators in external situations must not perceive the world with a win–lose mentality. The web of relationships necessitates conventional, adversarial negotiation be substituted with interest-based or principled negotiation. External negotiations need rapid, informed decisions, which in turn must have proactive internal negotiating so interests are apparent. Enterprises must take a win–win approach both externally and internally to increase and prolong value. While external compromises with others are necessary for collaboration and cohesion, there are certain principles and values within ourselves that we must hold sacred, without compromise. As individuals striving for personal growth and success, there are non-negotiable that we must adhere to (Mollah, 2024):

- Hard work: Committing to working hard and pushing ourselves to reach our goals, even in the face of adversity or challenges.
- Continuous improvement: Dedication to self-improvement, whether it's through education, training, or skill development, without becoming complacent or resting on previous accomplishments.
- Accountability: Taking ownership of our errors, confronting them head-on, and learning from them to become better versions of ourselves.
- Resolution: Facing our fears and challenges with resilience and determination, refusing to give up or give in to self-doubt.
- Self-discipline: Maintaining a strong sense of discipline and commitment to our values and objectives, even when tempted to stray from our path.

These internal principles will serve as a guiding light, shaping decisions and actions, and ultimately define who we are as individuals. They represent the unwavering foundation upon which we build our character and integrity. In the end, it's the ability to balance external compromises with internal steadfastness that leads to true fulfillment and success.

The differences between internal and external negotiations are summarized in Table 5.3.

In the Disney/Lucas Films example above, it was clear that the successful negotiation needed and valued trust. Great preparation, strategies, and tactics play a key role in negotiations, but one does not win successful outcomes

Table 5.3 Internal and external negotiation differences

Aspect	*Internal*	*External*
Parties involved	Between colleagues, teams, or departments within the same company	Between company and outside parties (clients, suppliers, partners, regulators)
Goal	Align internal priorities, distribute funds, resolve conflicts, improve collaboration	Secure favorable contracts, pricing, partnerships, or settlements with external stakeholders
Focus	Maintaining flowing working relationships inside the organization	Balancing profit, risk, and relationship management with outsiders
Approach	Collaborative (since both sides work toward the enterprise's success)	Competitive–collaborative fusion (both sides want the best deal, but long-term partnerships matter)
Results	Stronger teamwork, clearer roles, efficient operations	Revenue growth, cost savings, strategic advantage, risk reduction

without trust. Without trust, negotiations often spiral into competitive cycles where both parties withhold information, pushing them further into a win-lose situation and breaking this cycle requires trust. When a foundation of trust is created, one can focus on creating value for both sides.

Trust is critical in external negotiations because it can reduce risk perception. External parties often begin with skepticism and mutual trust lowers perceived risk and increases willingness to share information. It enables transparency for when trust is present, negotiators are more likely to disclose constraints, explore joint gains, and avoid zero-sum thinking. It also accelerates deal-making. Trust speeds up decision cycles by reducing the need for exhaustive verification and legal safeguards. Finally, in external negotiations, your reputation often precedes you. Trustworthiness becomes a form of social capital (Winkler, 2024).

Interest-Based Negotiation

When you know the areas of agreement where you and your counterpart are in alignment (and those areas on which you diverge), a skilled negotiator can craft an agreement that most closely approximates her own and her counterpart's needs while building a bargaining relationship with her counterpart. Rather than antagonistic, the negotiation process becomes a value-creating, integrative situation in which each side gets a "fair share" of the pool of resources. Interest-based solutions are usually more gratifying for all involved in negotiation, as the true needs and concerns of both sides will be met to some degree. It is a collaborative process and therefore the parties end up assisting each other. This prevents ongoing ill will after the negotiation concludes. Interest-based bargaining facilitates constructive, positive relationships between previous adversaries.

In interest-based negotiations, substance is important. However, interest-based negotiation also emphasizes the importance of relationships, especially if both parties work interdependently, they depend on each other to achieve a common goal or objective. In interest-based negotiations, the intent is to reach a mutually acceptable outcome, something that is mutually beneficial to both parties. The interests of both parties are being met. If a problem does emerge, the parties are hard on the problem and not on the person. And if they do yield, people yield to objective criteria, something that both parties can agree to as being legitimate and fair. The outcome of an interest-based negotiation is one where credibility is built between both parties as they develop a relationship of trust (Katz, 2006).

Negotiating for added opportunities with external stakeholders can be a challenging but rewarding skill for all negotiators. External stakeholders are those who have an interest or influence in your organization's activities but are not part of it. They can include customers, suppliers, partners, investors, competitors, media, and community groups. By building up trust, rapport, and value with them, you can magnify the network, enhance your reputation, and advance the vital aspects of external negotiations, which include (a) identifying your goals and interests; (b) researching the stakeholder's background and needs; (c) creating and communicating value; and (d) negotiating effectively and ethically.

On-going communication with external parties is critical. Businesses rely heavily on customers, so learning to listen to and learn from various stakeholders is crucial for successful projects. For organizing and planning communication with stakeholders, remember the communications process of receiving, interpreting, and sending information. Several ways of communicating with stakeholders can include the following:

- Email updates
- Recurrent progress reports
- Telephone meetings
- Focus groups
- Online web portals

An interesting case in point: Julia thought it would be easy to borrow three members of Don's team for a five-month project she'd been asked to undertake on behalf of the board. As senior managers of similar rank and responsibility, she thought he'd understand her resource constraints and the enormity of the project at hand. She'd also seen a lot more of Don in his office recently and put that down to him being less active than usual.

Julia gave Don a brief synopsis of the project before getting to the crux of the issue. But when she asked him if she could borrow his resources, she was surprised by his angered rejection. Don explained that he was struggling to complete multiple projects and refused to discuss it further. He'd been in his office more than usual because he was tied down managing multiple teams and delegating assignments so he could focus on reporting to the board. It was a firm "no" and Julia was back to the drawing board; the relationship slightly damaged from the interaction.

Internal negotiations, those between parties inside an organization, are often estimated to be easier than external ones but the reality is that they're often much more difficult. An internal negotiation has additional considerations and challenges that are underestimated. Colleagues are more likely to think their aims and objectives are similar, which will open doors for their internal negotiations.

Julia's internal negotiation did not work out because she made the first mistake of internal negotiations: underpreparing. She assumed that an informal meeting without much background research on Don's activities or challenges would suffice. She also assumed he was less busy than usual and failed to test this assumption. Julia should have considered potentially conflicting objectives. Another reason this situation did not work out was because of a failure to consider a stakeholder's unique and potentially conflicting interests. Most people assume or unconsciously hope that their teammate will naturally see how their request works for the greater good of the organization and quickly concede to their request. Internal negotiators often have conflicting views and perspectives on the organization and its direction and priorities.

Third, internal negotiators often smart from long-term assumptions, perceptions, and rumors about one another. When one has been in an organization for many years, it is natural to have some history with some of your colleagues or to have heard gossip about them. Such gossip or perceptions, grounded or not in facts, can create a rigid image of our colleagues in our minds. As a result, we have no incentive to properly invest in such relationships. We either give up on them or take them for granted.

Lastly, there is frequently a zero-sum mindset in internal negotiations that stems from parties perceiving that they are fighting internally for limited and thus zero-sum internal resources, such as status, money, and attention from management. With this mindset, it's easy to wind up in an "us vs. them" mentality, perceiving each other as enemies, believing value creation is not possible and adopting a win–lose attitude.

While in external negotiations, there are times that if one does not reach a deal, one can just move on to an alternative or the best alternative to a negotiated agreement (BATNA), but in internal negotiations, this is a much harder thing to do. This lack of alternatives can increase the internal negotiation tension and cause small cartels to emerge inside a firm. Not only do such cartels have a higher temptation to use their power, because the counterparty cannot walk away, they also have rules and regulations that diminish the incentives to find creative solutions.

It is easy to be lulled into thinking that consensus building among internal stakeholders would be easier when working at the same company (Falcao, 2017). It is important, therefore, to be aware of the internal negotiation pitfalls and devote the necessary resources to these meetings. Under-preparation, failure to consider stakeholders' interests, failure to reinvent relationships with your colleagues, falling prey to a zero-sum or monopoly mindset are all surmountable hurdles.

Organizational Structure

Organizations must build a negotiation infrastructure that creates a common language and process for negotiations and a common process and structure for conducting, reviewing, and learning from their negotiations. Otherwise, enormous amounts of time and money will be wasted, and valuable lessons and knowledge will go unshared.

Definitively, organizational culture plays a vital role in shaping internal negotiations. It can often be difficult to assess an organization's culture for many reasons; company culture may seem invisible. The health of an organization determines the success or failure of internal negotiations. Raines (2024) has developed sample questions that could determine the health of an organization's culture. The answers could range on a 5-point scale (i.e., strongly agree to strongly disagree.

- I am motivated by the mission of our organization.
- I am clear about my role in achieving the organization's mission.
- I like my coworkers.
- I trust my supervisor to make tough decisions when necessary.
- My supervisor treats me fairly.
- My input is valued.
- I would recommend this organization to a friend seeking work.
- My team members treat me with respect.
- Anyone can succeed here, regardless of race, gender, sexual orientation, or national origin.

External negotiations are those that take place between your company and your customers, suppliers, business partners, and other outside firms. Businesses must often respond to external political, economic, social, technological, environmental, and competitive factors.

> *It is unwise to do unto others as you would have them do unto you. Their tastes may not be the same.*
>
> ~ George Bernard Shaw

In negotiation, positions are the specific claims each party argues for, while interests are the fundamental needs or values that motivate those claims.

Positions are concrete and negotiable, while interests are abstract and non-negotiable. A position is a particular stance taken by one party in a negotiation. It typically outlines their preferred result. Interests, on the other hand, are the reasons behind the position. Interests define the problem.

When negotiating with external business partners, one of the key discoveries in dealing with solutions, resolutions, and outcomes is recognizing the vital differences between positions, interests, and needs. Clearly the key to successful external outcomes is to discard and move away from positions by uncovering the true interests and needs of the other side (TOS).

Take the following example as insight to positions, interests, and needs:

> *Ralphie is a sales executive in a software company that provides sales management solutions to the life insurance industry. A usual sale for Ralphie centers on a software license fee of $90,000, with an additional annual maintenance and support charge of $20,000, for a total purchase price of $110,000. Having competed effectively in a bid for a large insurance company, Ralphie was the preferred supplier. When it came to the negotiation, the buyer informed him that he needed him to rethink the numbers, as he was only prepared to pay $70,000 in total. Ralphie was surprised and dejected. He couldn't sell the software without maintenance, and there wasn't any way he could provide a full 25% discount. He tried everything to raise the buyer's offer. He offered free additional training programs and suggested that, if he could hold his price, he could add a second year's maintenance at a reduced rate. He even offered a dedicated support agent. Nothing worked. The customer held firm, stating that he could only pay $70,000. This customer had been reasonable to deal with; he provided information as requested and gave honest feedback on issues and progress. Ralphi was at an impasse. The customer wouldn't move from his $70,000 number! Finally, Ralphie just asked the customer, "What's so firm and magical about $70,000?"*

"It's all I have left in this year's budget." The customer's response opened the door to a creative solution.

Through Ralphie's pre-negotiation work and planning had revealed that an earlier project had been approved that took $50,000 from his buyer's coffers, leaving him with only $70,000. That left him $20,000 short, if he agreed to Ralphie's number. The buyer's issue wasn't value or price. It was that year's budget. His position stated that all he was prepared to pay was $70,000, while his interest, once uncovered, revealed that $70,000 was all he was prepared to pay in that financial year.

The problem was solved by selling a two-year maintenance contract and agreeing to a payment schedule that met his customer's requirements (Cullington, 2023). Successful negotiators probe beyond combative positions to uncover the shared interests that lie beneath. Arguing over positions is inefficient and frequently damages the relationship between the seller and the buyer. Too much emphasis on positions drives negotiation toward a risky, ritual dance that does not meet either party's fundamental concerns. Learning about and reconciling the full set of interests requires patience, researching the other side, asking many questions, and really listening. When shifting the discussions from positions to interests, the path to resolution becomes clearer. When the focus is on the buyer's interests, one can get to the heart of the matter more quickly, promote mutual understanding, and accelerate the search for a creative solution.

Following are several strategies for external negotiation, which are negotiations that take place between a company and outside firms, such as customers, suppliers, and business partners:

- Identify goals and interests: Know what you want to accomplish and what your interests are.
- Research the other party: Learn about the stakeholder's background and needs.
- Build rapport: Try to establish trust and rapport and share your own experiences.
- Communicate value: Create and communicate value.
- Practice active listening: Pay attention to what the other person is saying, ask questions, and repeat points to show you understand.
- Aim for a win–win: Try to shift the situation to a "win–win" outcome, even if it seems like a "win–lose" situation.
- Have a BATNA: Develop a Best Alternative to a Negotiated Agreement (BATNA), which is a plan for what you'll do if negotiations fail.

All negotiators have interests, priorities, and strategies. Interest-based negotiation, or integrative negotiation, involves exploring the deeper interests underlying parties' stated positions to identify potential tradeoffs and win–win opportunities across issues and interests. Negotiation ultimately involves a choice between the deal you've been offered and what you would get by walking away from the table. Thus, the negotiation process should involve a search for solutions that leave both parties better off than they would be if they reached an impasse and turned to their outside options.

> *People's greatest asset is not their money or power, it is their BATNA, which explains the cost of not making an agreement.*
>
> ~ Roger Fisher, William Ury & Bruce Patton

Interest-based negotiation has proven to be the most reliable way to create value and resolve conflicts. Interest-based negotiating often leads to win–win outcomes where each person gets their needs and desires met or their concerns and fears addressed. For example, if one person wants the air conditioner on and the other person doesn't, a positional negotiation might lead to the air-conditioner being on or off or perhaps with only the fan on. An interest-based negotiation might go as follows:

Why do you want the AC on? Because it is very warm here and I want some cool air.

Why do you want the AC off? Because I am battling a cold and don't want a draft.

A win–win solution might be to turn on the AC in an adjacent room to allow some cool air without creating any draft.

References

Blank, S. (2020). *Managing Organizational Conflict*. Jefferson, NC: McFarland & Company.

Carvajal, A. (2024). *How to Optimize the Internal Negotiation of Contracts*. Munich, Germany: Top Legal.

Cullington, N. (2023). *Not Just Another Vendor*. Cork, Ireland: Oak Tree Press.

Folger, J., Poole, M., and Stutman, R. (2013). *Working Through Conflict: Strategies for Relationships, Groups, and Organizations*. Boston: Pearson.

Gosselin, T. (2007). *Practical Negotiating: Tools, Tactics & Techniques*. Santa Rosa, CA: O'Reilly Media.

Gottlieb, M., and Healy, W. J. (1998). *Making Deals: The Business of Negotiating* (2nd ed.). Albuquerque: The Communication Project.

Hayes, J. (2008). *Workplace Conflict and How Businesses Can Harness It to Thrive*. CPP: Global Human Capital Report Workplace.

Kahneman, D., and Tversky, A. (1979). Prospect theory in psychology: Loss aversion bias. *Econometrica*, 47(2), 263–291.

Katz, N. H. (2006). Interest-based negotiation: Increasing satisfaction levels among critical stakeholders. *Government Finance Review*, 22.

Lewicki, R., Barry, B., and Saunders, D. (2007). *Essentials of Negotiation*. New York: McGraw-Hill.

Mollah, S. (2024). *The Art of Compromise: External Versus Internal Negotiation*. The Vex Mind.

Overvest, M. (2025). *13 Negotiation Principles: A Guide to Crush Your Next Deal*. Wichita, KS: Procurement Tactics.

Pruitt, D. G. (1981). *Strategic Choices in Negotiation. Negotiation Behavior*. New York: Academic Press.

Raines, S. (2024). *Conflict Management and Leadership for Managers*. Lanham, MD: Rowman and Littlefield Publishing.

Ré, E. (2003). *101 Secrets to Negotiating Success*. Albuquerque, NM: Canyon Crest Publishing.

Winkler, C. (2024). *Negotiation Skills: Building Trust in Negotiations and Why It's Important*. New York: The Negotiation Academy.

6 Cross-Cultural Business Negotiation and Behavior

Calculating how to negotiate in cross-cultural situations can seem like a daunting endeavor, and for good reason. Negotiating across the cultural divide adds an entire dimension to any negotiation, introducing language barriers, differences in body language and dress, and alternative ways of expressing pleasure or displeasure with the elements of a deal. As a result, many negotiators fear that they might accidentally scuttle an important deal or do something that causes lasting shame. A handful of fundamental negotiating skills can be put into practice easily in order to overcome these fears, redefine negotiation in an international context, and better understand how to negotiate in cross-cultural situations.

Getting accustomed to different processes in a negotiation can be challenging, but a willingness to embrace your counterpart's way of doing business can be essential. This is especially true when a negotiator is visiting their counterpart in their home country. While this can feel overwhelming, it is important to remember that we negotiate in cross-cultural situations all the time. For example, any businessperson who negotiates with another business has prepared for that negotiation by studying their counterpart's company "culture." That culture has the same set of rituals, preferences, priorities that can or cannot be negotiated.

Cultural Barriers

Culture has been defined in many ways—from a pattern of perceptions that influence communication to a place of contestation and conflict. The late British writer Raymond William (1983) wrote that culture "is one of the two or three most complicated words in the English language." How we think about culture frames our ideas and perceptions.

Understanding and respecting cultural differences in negotiation styles is crucial for successful international business dealings. By recognizing these cultural nuances and adapting one's approach, one can navigate cross-cultural negotiations more effectively, build stronger relationships, and achieve better results. Quite simply, cultural barriers are challenges that occur due to the many differences in cultures. We all might be human, but we have grown up

DOI: 10.4324/9781042000258-7

in vastly varying geographical locations with different formative experiences, and all of this shapes the way we see the world. Ethnologists have recorded over 3,800 distinct cultures around the world, and there are thought to be over 7,000 different languages (with 90% of these having less than 100,000 speakers!).

Culture encompasses the shared values, beliefs, and norms of a group of people. These elements shape individuals' behaviors, communication styles, and decision-making processes. In high-context cultures like Japan and China, communication tends to be indirect and nuanced, relying heavily on non-verbal cues and the context of the interaction. In contrast, low-context cultures such as the United States and Germany prefer direct and explicit communication. Behavioral differences are influenced by cultural norms and behavioral traits such as assertiveness, risk tolerance, and communication styles vary widely across cultures. For instance, in some Middle Eastern cultures, hospitality and building personal relationships are vital. Negotiators may spend considerable time engaging in social activities before discussing business. In contrast, Northern European cultures often prefer a more structured and formal approach, with clear agendas and minimal small talk (Newman, 2025).

English might be the most common business language, but that does not mean even all English speakers are alike. There are massive cultural differences between Americans, Brits, and Australians, even though many will claim English as their first or even only language. Even within the United Kingdom, cultural differences exist between English, Scottish, Welsh, and Northern Irish people. We can even zoom in further if you want to include the North/South divide in England alone! Even countries that share a geographical border, like France and Germany, will have several cross-cultural barriers that need to be overcome for successful discussions to take place. Cultural barriers can cause very real issues when they are allowed to take root (Scottwork, 2024).

Cultural norms and values can also lead to communication problems in business. Different cultures also have different ideas about what is considered to be polite behavior, how to treat positions of authority, and the appropriate conduct for business meetings.

For instance, in some cultures, it is perfectly appropriate to bargain over prices, while in others, this would be seen as very impolite. It's essential that businesses have a cohesive understanding of the values and expectations of their employees, clients, and suppliers to avoid any potential misunderstandings and ensure that negotiations are handled appropriately across different cultures. It's also important for businesses to account for a certain level of culture shock (a feeling of disorientation) in global projects. This culture shock may lead to communication problems as people may find it difficult to adjust to the new way of doing things.

Cultural values and behavioral traits play a significant role in shaping negotiation styles, tactics, and outcomes. Understanding these influences is vital for navigating cross-cultural negotiations effectively. Culture encompasses the shared values, beliefs, and norms of a group of people. These elements shape individuals' behaviors, communication styles, and decision-making processes. For instance, in high-context cultures like Japan and China, communication tends to be indirect and nuanced, relying heavily on non-verbal cues and the context of the interaction. In contrast, low-context cultures such as the United States and Germany prefer direct and explicit communication. Behavioral differences are influenced by cultural norms. Behavioral traits such as assertiveness, risk tolerance, and communication styles vary widely across cultures. For instance, in some Middle Eastern cultures, hospitality and building personal relationships are vital. Negotiators may spend considerable time engaging in social activities before discussing business. In contrast, Northern European cultures often prefer a more structured and formal approach, with clear agendas and minimal small talk (Pinger, 2025).

When parties from different backgrounds figure out how to communicate beyond their cultural differences in negotiation, they don't just reach agreements; they reach better ones than those from the same culture. It's all about bringing exceptional ideas to the table and seeing opportunities where others see barriers. Some resent research reveals that high "cultural intelligence"—the ability to adapt to different cultural contexts—boosts negotiation success. Those with higher scores are not only more cooperative but also more curious, leading to better outcomes than their less culturally skilled peers. But the benefits go beyond just those moments at the negotiation table. When one knows negotiating across cultures like the back of the hand, one can tap into new markets full of new customers. It also stands out when a business shows that it truly understands its diverse clientele and respects who they are. Not only will these international partners quickly notice and want to work with the company more, but the multicultural staff will also see and respect it.

> *Our cultural strength has always been derived from our diversity of understanding and experience.*
>
> ~ Yo-Yo Ma

Cultural variations shape every stage of a business negotiation—from how trust is built to how agreements are finalized. The biggest differences show up in communication style, attitudes toward time, decision-making norms, and the role of relationships. One general way to understand cultural variations in intercultural conflict resolution is to look at how cultural values influence conflict management. Face negotiation theory links cultural values to facework and conflict styles (Ting-Toomey, 2013). Facework refers to specific communication strategies we use to "save" our own or another person's face and is a universal concept. Studies have shown that individuals from individualistic societies tend to be more concerned with saving their own face than another person's, so they tend to use more direct conflict management styles. In contrast, people from collectivistic societies tend to be more concerned with preserving group harmony and with saving the other person's face (and dignity) during conflict. This leads them to use a more accommodating conflict style. How someone chooses to deal with conflict in any situation depends on the type of conflict and the relationship between the people.

The impact of international business in domestic markets compels us to ask a question: "How can we survive in this global playing field, and what can we do to run our businesses more effectively?" Nowadays, corporations of all sizes search for suppliers and customers on a global level. International competition, foreign clients, and suppliers may become a danger, but they may also generate huge opportunities to develop future business. The increasingly global business environment requires managers to approach the negotiation process from the global business person's point of view. This approach includes aspects that are usually unimportant in domestic negotiations. Some of the components of a cross-cultural negotiation process are more complex and difficult but will increase our success in avoiding barriers and failures in the international business arena.

When doing business internationally, one needs to consider the following (Salacuse, 1991):

- The negotiating environment
- Cultural and sub-cultural differences
- Ideological differences
- Foreign bureaucracy
- Foreign laws and governments
- Financial insecurity due to international monetary factors
- Political instability and economic changes

Culture and Negotiation

Being exposed to multiple cultures enriches our experiences in cross-cultural communication. How do we successfully negotiate with people? Whether they're business partners, clients, suppliers, or coworkers? When cultural differences add another layer of complexity? People do business with those they like. No matter where your counterpart is from. It is prudent to maintain a positive, respectful attitude, even if you don't fully understand someone's culture, politeness and respect go a long way. Research shows that individuals in a positive mood think 31% more efficiently and make better decisions (Cai, 2025).

The phenomenon of globalization has transformed the way businesses operate. In the past, technological advancements, particularly in communication and transportation, have blurred international boundaries, making it easier for startups to reach global markets. This shift has not only opened up new opportunities but also introduced a complex tapestry of cultural interactions. For a startup, this means that understanding different cultural norms and values is not just beneficial but essential for global success.

Preparing for a cross-cultural negotiation requires the same careful preparation, and done properly, preparation, and a willingness to adapt to new processes can help a negotiator get to the fundamental issues of a negotiation without obsessively thinking about the process. (PON, 2024).

Cross-cultural decision-making often hinges on behavior along with core beliefs, which means that cross-cultural agreements are frequently reached in vastly diverse ways. Cross-cultural negotiations are rampant with challenges as diverse groups come together to reach a mutually beneficial agreement.

These negotiations are complex and challenging. Cultural competency is becoming a must-have in the business world due to the intricacies involved such as the following:

- Country's culture
- Culture of the company/business
- Foreign currencies and volatilities
- Commercial risks
- Foreign laws
- Bureaucracy complications

Cross-cultural business negotiations are an important part of international business. Much business has been lost overseas due to miscalculations caused by cultural differences. Negotiating is a lengthy, difficult process by itself; but when one adds the cultural aspect, it becomes extremely intricate. Cross-cultural negotiation skills can be improved by adequate attention to details and a better understanding of the cultural heritage of the other side.

The consequences of neglecting cultural sensitivity can be harsh for any business striving to establish a brand. Instances of cultural insensitivity can lead to miscommunications, damaged relationships, and even public relations crises. For example, marketing campaigns that fail to consider cultural nuances can offend target audiences, resulting in brand damage and financial loss.

Moreover, in the internal business environment, a lack of cultural sensitivity can lead to a non-inclusive workplace, affecting employee morale and productivity. Understanding these risks underscores the importance of cultural sensitivity in every aspect of a startup's operations.

International business negotiations are made more difficult by problems of communications and culture. To conduct business outside of one's native culture, it is necessary to understand the style and intent of the business partners, and to learn to deal with culturally based differences. In addition, communications are conducted verbally and non-verbally; therefore, it is not just a problem of language barriers. All human interactions are, by definition, intercultural (Hendon, Hendon and Herbig, 1996).

Intercultural understanding combines personal, interpersonal, and social knowledge and skills. It involves learning to value and view critically their own cultural perspectives and practices and those of others through their interactions with people, texts, and contexts across the business spectrum. Working with the international community for economic survival means countries and cultures can no longer operate in a vacuum. Because of this, intercultural communication is no longer a choice but a *must*.

When dealing with partners from different backgrounds, what's said and heard can be worlds apart. Each culture has nuances in communication styles. Some are direct, while others are more subtle. Misunderstandings can spiral from something as simple as the tone of an email or the choice of words in a proposal. This lack of clarity isn't just unsatisfying; it can stall negotiations or send them off course.

The particulars of nonverbal communication can often complicate cross-cultural interactions even further. A friendly gesture in one culture can be a serious insult in another. For example, a thumbs-up is generally positive in the United States but offensive in parts of the Middle East. Eye contact, too, varies widely in meaning. While it might signify confidence and honesty in some Western cultures, some Asian cultures see too much eye contact as a challenge or a form of disrespect. Beyond these communication challenges, logistical issues like time zone differences can also disrupt the flow of negotiations. Trying to find a meeting time that works for parties on different continents means someone is always up too early or too late, which can strain the negotiation process. And with the rise of virtual meetings, maintaining rapport and reading the room becomes even harder, turning what should be simple conversations into potential misunderstandings.

In addition, misunderstandings resulting from a lack of familiarity with another culture are often embarrassing. Blunders like these can make it difficult, if not impossible, to reach an agreement with another country or close a business contract with a foreign partner. For travelers, a faux pas can also make interactions more awkward. In this article, we'll be discussing the importance of intercultural communication.

Bridging Culture Barriers

A framework that can help businesses bridge a cultural divide and foster a unified brand presence while considering the different ways they can build and sustain trust in new regions consists of three phases (Zaki, 2025):

- Awareness phase: Used before entering a new region to understand the cultural norms and ensure you implement the right trust-building mechanisms.
- Adaptation phase: During this phase, one tailors business strategies to align with the cultural insights gained during the awareness phase.
- Integration phase: This phase begins when the business has entered the region and established a foothold. At this stage, one needs to focus on consistency, identifying opportunities for collaboration and driving sustainable growth.

Intercultural communication competence is key to forging successful negotiation agreements and outcomes. There are many skills that are necessary for effective intercultural communication; some of them may be taught, while others are inherent and just require practice. Several crucial competencies include the following:

- Self-awareness: Recognizing how your personal views, behaviors, and possible prejudices could impact a conversation is a massive step in improving your ability to have meaningful interactions with others.
- Empathy: Intercultural communication relies heavily on empathizing with others and gaining insight into their varied experiences.
- Emotional intelligence: Learning to pick up on the subtleties of communication is essential when working with people from other cultures. Whether you get what is being communicated or not depends on how well you use your senses, how well you know yourself, and how well you can empathize with others.
- Patience: Effective communication across cultural boundaries doesn't happen instantly. That's why you need to have patience. Don't rush through the process of becoming well-versed in best practices; instead, take your time and make them part of your routine. Due to cultural differences, it may take more or less time than usual to absorb new information.
- Positivity: Sustaining an optimistic outlook when interacting with people of other cultures is fundamental. Misunderstandings occur all the time, and in most cases, it's not because someone was trying to be deliberately unclear. Those of us who aren't well-versed in other cultures often fail to grasp the intended meaning of a message. This is why it's essential to look at every intercultural exchange in a constructive light.

When preparing strategies for overcoming cultural barriers in negotiation, it is important to understand the numerous obstacles that may develop:

- Language and communication: Differences in language proficiency and communication styles can lead to misunderstandings and confusion during negotiations.
- Non-verbal communication: Gestures, body language, and facial expressions can vary greatly across cultures, leading to misinterpretations.
- Values and beliefs: Cultural values and beliefs shape individuals' perceptions and priorities, influencing negotiation strategies and outcomes.
- Etiquette and protocol: Different cultures have distinct rules and expectations regarding proper etiquette and protocol, which can impact the negotiation process.
- Attitude toward hierarchy: Hierarchy is viewed differently across cultures. In some cultures, hierarchy is highly valued, while in others, it is less important.
- Risk-taking: Risk is viewed differently across cultures. Some cultures are more risk-averse, while others are more comfortable with risk.
- Value of relationship: Relationships are viewed differently across cultures. In some cultures, building a relationship is essential before doing business, while in others, business comes first.

- Decision-making styles: Cultures may have different approaches to decision-making, with some valuing consensus while others prioritize hierarchy and authority (Mendiratta, 2024).

Incorporating cultural sensitivity in business plans involves market analysis and research on the cultural norms and values of a target market; product/service adaptation to tailor products or services to meet the specific cultural needs and preferences of different customer segments; and cultural risk assessment that identifies and plans for potential cultural misunderstandings or conflicts that may arise.

Work Issues

One of the most fascinating features of cross-cultural differences in the workplace is how team members from different cultures can work together effectively. With high cultural intelligence, team members from diverse cultures can find common ground and work together to achieve a common goal despite their different backgrounds. In many cases, cultural differences can be an asset in the workplace. Of course, cultural differences can also create challenges in the workplace. For example, team members from different cultures may have difficulty communicating with each other due to language barriers. They may also have different ideas about what is considered appropriate behavior in the workplace. However, these challenges can often be overcome with patience and understanding.

The challenges of cultural awareness involve recognizing and understanding the differences and similarities between cultures. It is the foundational step in cross-cultural communication. Consider a project team composed of members from the United States, Japan, and Germany. The American team members may value direct communication, while their Japanese counterparts might prefer a more indirect approach. Meanwhile, Germans might focus on specific and clear communication. A project administrator who is culturally aware and sensitive will recognize these preferences and adapt their communication style accordingly to ensure all team members feel respected and understood.

Understanding cultural differences is important in the workplace because it can help one avoid misunderstandings, be more productive, and build better relationships with work colleagues. Overall, taking the time to learn about the various cultures represented in the workplace can only benefit all employees. By developing a greater understanding of the people one works with, one can create a more positive and productive work environment for everyone involved.

There are many different types of cultural differences that can be found in the workplace.

✓ Language barriers can make communication difficult and lead to misunderstandings.

✓ Various customs and traditions can cause conflict or confusion.
✓ Different values and beliefs can create tension or disagreement.
✓ Different or alternative ways of doing things can lead to frustration or inefficiency.
✓ Different styles of dress or mannerisms can be distracting or off-putting.

In a globalized economy, cultural sensitivity is essential. Understanding and knowing about cultural differences is a key to successful cross-cultural negotiations. Understanding the language nuance, etiquette, and cultural time management differences can assist in the navigation of complex interactions (Blank, 2020). The goal is always to boost profitability with greater cultural fluency. This can be accomplished in three distinct ways:

- Understanding and utilizing various working styles
- Improving both internal and external efficiencies when working across borders
- Effectively communicating ideas and strategy across cultures

Clearly, the world is more globally allied than ever before. Effective cultural sensitivity policies target how workers interact within and outside the organization. Many of these policies can guide professional relationships between companies based in different places. When companies embrace these policies, they can reduce conflicts. Communication challenges will occur. But cultural sensitivity can help employees explore appropriate methods for solving those challenges.

The basis of a sound cultural sensitivity policy is to recognize the need for the policy. But seeing a need is only a start. Organizations must also understand that cultural sensitivity:

- Is an evolving process.
- May need regular training for new employees and existing employees.
- Works beneficially when supervisors actively promote the policies.
- Thrives when employees sense safety and value.
- Includes and listens to varied ideas and approaches for tasks and projects.

Cultural Sensitivity

Why is there a need for cultural sensitivity in business as part of a strategic management goal? Several key reasons underline its importance:

- *Building relationships*: Cultural sensitivity fosters positive relationships with clients, partners, and employees from diverse cultural backgrounds. Businesses can establish trust, rapport, and mutual respect by understanding and respecting cultural norms, values, and practices, leading to stronger connections and long-term partnerships.

- *Global market penetration*: In an increasingly globalized world, cultural sensitivity in the workplace allows businesses to penetrate new markets successfully. By understanding the target market's cultural nuances, preferences, and needs, businesses can tailor their products, services, marketing strategies, and customer experiences to resonate with local customers, gaining a competitive edge.
- *Reputation and brand image*: Demonstrating cultural sensitivity enhances a business's reputation and brand image. A company that values diversity, respects cultural differences, and promotes inclusivity is viewed positively by customers, employees, and the public. Conversely, cultural insensitivity or offensive behavior can lead to reputational damage, negative publicity, and loss of business opportunities. Cultural insensitivity in business can easily alienate customers, and fracture internal teams, especially in global or diverse markets.
- *Legal and ethical considerations*: Cultural sensitivity aligns with legal and ethical considerations in international business. Many countries have laws and regulations regarding discrimination, cultural respect, and fair treatment of employees and customers. By practicing cultural sensitivity, businesses ensure compliance with these laws and avoid legal consequences and ethical dilemmas (Bensla, 2023).

International business negotiations often involve crossing not just geographical borders but cultural ones as well. Culture profoundly influences how people think, communicate, and behave, which inevitably impacts the negotiation process. Acknowledging these cultural differences is vital for effective cross-cultural negotiations. Negotiators' personal styles, encompassing communication, titles, dress code, and interaction, are shaped by their culture. While some cultures prefer a formal approach, addressing counterparts by titles, others opt for informality. Being considerate of these cultural nuances fosters smoother negotiations. Cultural differences also affect communication styles. Some cultures favor direct, straightforward communication, while others rely on indirect methods, using non-verbal cues and context. Misinterpreting these signals can lead to misunderstandings during cross-cultural negotiations.

Negotiating processes can start from general principles and move to specifics or vice versa. This cultural preference impacts how negotiations unfold. Some cultures emphasize establishing a framework first, while others begin with specific details. Critical to win–win successes may rely on understanding how your counterpart's team is organized. Some cultures prioritize individual decision-makers, while others stress group consensus. Recognizing the structure can help navigate the negotiation process effectively.

Cultural differences can influence business negotiations in significant and unexpected ways, as many a hapless dealmaker has learned. In some cases, it's a matter of ignorance or blatant disrespect, as with the American salesman who presented a potential Saudi Arabian client with a multimillion-dollar proposal in a pigskin binder, considered vile in many Muslim cultures. He was unceremoniously tossed out and his company blacklisted from working with Saudi businesses. But the differences can be much more subtle, arising from deep-seated cultural tendencies that influence how people interact—everything from how people view the role of the individual versus the group to their attitudes, say, about the importance of time or relationships.

Cultural assumptions can sometimes make it very difficult to recognize or acknowledge who has formal decision rights. For example, when **Honda** invested heavily in an extensive relationship with British automaker **Rover,** workers and managers at the two companies developed very positive working relationships for more than a decade. Following are the main protagonists of this case study:

- Honda: A Japanese automaker that is one of the world's largest car manufacturers.
- Rover: A British automaker that was once one of the UK's largest car manufacturers.

The partnership intensified after the government sold Rover to **British Aerospace** (Bae), but as Rover continued to lose money, Bae decided to discard the relationship, abruptly selling Rover to **BMW** through a secretive deal that caught Honda completely unawares. The Japanese automaker considered its connection with Rover a long-term one, much like a marriage, and it had shared advanced product and process technology with Rover well beyond its effective contractual ability to protect these assets.

Honda's leaders were dumbfounded and outraged that Bae could sell—and to a competitor, no less. Yet while Honda's prized relationship was at the level of the *operating* company (Rover), the Japanese company had not taken seriously enough the fact that the decision rights over a Rover sale are vested at the *parent* (Bae) level. From a financial standpoint, the move made sense for Bae, and it was perfectly legal. Yet Honda's cultural blinders made the sale seem inconceivable, and its disproportionate investments in Rover in effect created a major economic opportunity for Bae. The bottom line: Understanding both formal decision rights and cultural assumptions in less familiar settings can be vital.

Finally, legal issues must be considered in cross-cultural negotiations. Where foreign law crops up as an issue, advice from counsel adept in the appropriate jurisdiction is a must. Parties will need to determine what law is to apply to any contract, both procedurally and substantively. Legislation in one or more countries may eclipse what is written in the contract if there is a conflict. As a result, it is imperative to have someone who knows the legal framework in the relevant jurisdictions. If contracts are drafted in more than one language, what will happen in the event of a conflict?

Additionally, what level of commitment is necessary to finalize an agreement? A written contract is the standard in most cultures, but the power of the handshake and verbal agreement varies from place to place and person to person. Ensure that all parties are on the same page about the level of commitment and have the appropriate protections in place to ensure compliance.

One of the primary tips for successful cross-cultural negotiations is to recognize the cultural differences between you and the other party. Cultural differences in negotiation can drastically affect communication and styles, attitudes toward time, hierarchy, and decision-making. Before entering into any negotiation, it is key to research and learn about the culture of the other party to understand their values, customs, and beliefs. To be effective in cross-cultural negotiation in international business, it is essential to research and learn about their culture. This can include understanding their communication styles, negotiating tactics, and business practices. By examining the other party's culture, you can anticipate their behavior, identify potential misunderstandings, and adjust your communication and negotiation approach accordingly.

Trust and Rapport

Building trust and rapport is a crucial component in successful cross-cultural negotiation. Everyone wants a positive relationship with the individuals they work with. However, building a healthy level of camaraderie, rapport, and comfortable conversations takes effort. Trust is often built on personal relationships, respect, and shared values. To establish trust and rapport, one should take the time to get to know the other party, show interest in their culture and background, and demonstrate a willingness to work together toward a mutually beneficial outcome. Assumptions and stereotypes can be a significant stumbling block to effective cross-cultural negotiation in international business. It is essential to avoid making assumptions about the other party's behavior or motives based on their cultural background. Similarly, stereotyping the other party can lead to misunderstandings and a breakdown in communication. Instead, approach the negotiation with an open mind and a willingness to learn about the other party's culture. Recognizing that cross-cultural negotiation can take longer than negotiations within the same culture, it is fundamental to practice patience and allow time for the other party to understand all positions fully.

A strong organizational culture that is deeply aligned with an organization's strategy, vision, and goals offers a variety of benefits.

- It assists with attracting and retaining top talent: Employees want to work for organizations with a vision that connects to their purpose.
- It increases employee engagement: Employees who feel connected to their organization are more likely to be motivated to perform at their best.
- It drives decision-making: Organizational culture shapes how employees behave and make decisions. When employees share a common set of values and beliefs, they're more likely to make decisions that align with the organization's strategic goals.

- It improves teamwork: Culture can build trust and accountability in teams. Employees who share common values and beliefs are more likely to communicate openly and work together more effectively.
- It enhances customer satisfaction: A strong culture can build a customer-centric mindset in employees.
- It drives innovation: A healthy workplace culture can foster creativity, which can lead to employees brainstorming new product and service ideas.
- It strengthens the organization's reputation: When the people in an organization reflect their values, it builds a positive image in the community and market. This image can differentiate the company from the competition and attract new customers and employees alike.

Rapport is the foundation of a meaningful relationship between individuals. When you're good at building rapport, you're practiced at establishing a connection between yourself and someone else. Good rapport can make the other party feel respected, heard, and seen. It's a great way to understand another person's needs and support them. Building rapport is about driving a meaningful connection between you and others. It isn't enough to feign interest; instead, practice openness and honesty in order to establish mutual trust (Martins, 2025).

- Tell team members the benefits of building rapport and connection in the workplace.
- Build mutual trust.
- Make team members feel more engaged.
- Expand constructive feedback sessions.
- Boost and enhance team loyalty.
- Build good group dynamics.
- Feel more "in sync" with the other person.
- Develop effective workplace communication.

Learning how to build rapport with someone is an important skill for everyone to have, regardless of your position in a company. It is an essential piece of networking and effective collaboration. It can also be crucial for customer-facing job functions, like sales and customer service, since it aids in understanding and empathizing with customers in an authentic way. Staying connected to others can lead to physical and mental health benefits of reduced stress, anxiety, and depression. Some examples of ways to establish rapport with workmates and others include the following (Miles, 2024):

- Inquire about someone's hobbies and interests.
- Volunteer to help a colleague, especially with a team project.
- Regularly share positive feedback and words of encouragement.
- Offer weekly check-ins and have some quality, no-pressure conversation time.

He who does not trust enough, will not be trusted.

~ Lao Tzu

Management of Opportunities

Building an organizational culture to effectively deal with confrontation and conflict is the goal of proactive, performance-driven, and relationship-oriented companies. Managing business opportunities cuts to the core of high-performance levels that help create and sustain an organization's vision and mission.

New and innovative business models are much different than a decade ago. The management of opportunities have changed as a result of the presence of dot-com mania, downsizing or rightsizing, reengineering, employment litigation, and virtual organizations (Levine, 2002). Add to these changes golden parachutes, sexual harassment issues, and project orientation, and companies must develop significant ways to deal with conflict and dissonance. Successful organizations understand that productivity, profits, and collaborations are functions of effective, explicit agreements.

Managing the many cultural differences that are the footings of many companies can sometimes test our own beliefs. It's central to remember that even if we cannot agree with another culture's ideals, it's not our place to challenge them. This all comes down to respect. To be successful, it is important to desist from directly opposing cultural norms. However, when the cultural practices of business partners clash with our own, things can and will get complicated.

A key aspect of the excellent management of opportunities is the building or relationships with individual team members which allows a department, team or company to better understand their needs from a cultural perspective. It also sets a precedent for future communication, which helps establish personal accountability for the enterprise's cross-cultural communications.

Making blunders in cross-cultural business interactions can hurt business. It is not easy, but the investment will pay dividends for many years to come. Clearly, cultural differences can influence how conflicts are perceived and resolved. Some cultures may encourage open confrontation, while others prefer to avoid direct conflict to maintain harmony.

In Western cultures, open and direct confrontation can be seen as a positive step toward resolving an issue. However, in many Asian cultures, such as in Japan or Thailand, maintaining harmony and avoiding direct conflict is preferred. Team leaders need to navigate these approaches carefully to resolve issues without causing further discord.

Using Time Effectively

Negotiations are dynamic interactions that require careful balance between assertiveness and flexibility. Time is a finite resource in these interactions.

The side that uses time most effectively usually wins. American negotiators are, in the eyes of foreigners, notoriously impatient and always seem to be in a rush. Many times, they are driven into an agreement they really did not plan for or want. It is therefore a good strategy not to let the other side know return plans. Plan for the long term and practice patience and try not to create self-imposed deadlines, as they may come back to haunt you later (Hendon, Hendon and Herbig, 1996).

An important aspect of time pressure in negotiation is the concept of time costs. Here, the negotiation is not a ticking time bomb, but a taximeter running up costs as time ticks away. Time costs do not impose a strict time limit but make the passage of time expensive. Time costs can be asymmetrical and when time pressure takes the form of time costs, some suggest that the optimal strategy isn't to disclose them, as with deadlines, but to keep them hidden. This is especially true when time pressure is uneven, and the parties face different time costs. While the party with higher time costs usually feels compelled to wrap up the negotiations as quickly as possible, potentially making rash concessions, the one with lower time costs could afford to be patient and use the threat of delays as a bargaining chip to gain more concessions.

Understanding the importance of time management in negotiations enables negotiation parties to:

- Improve clarity and focus: Apportioning sufficient time to discuss each point thoroughly ensures that both parties understand each other's positions clearly.
- Prevent escalation: Managing time well lessens the chances of frustration or fatigue that can escalate conflicts.
- Encourage thoughtful decision-making: Giving sufficient time helps avoid quick judgments and promotes rational choices.
- Improve relationship-building: Sufficient time allows for relationship development, trust-building, and rapport.
- Increase the likelihood of successful outcomes: Well-paced negotiations keep momentum while allowing room for creativity and compromise.

Time pressure exerts its influence in negotiations through two distinct facets: deadlines and time costs. Both have unique implications. Deadlines are the ticking clock in a high-stakes movie scene. The protagonist has limited time to accomplish a task, or else suffer the consequence. Similarly, in a negotiation, the final deadline imposes costs if an agreement isn't reached in time. And the costs can be symmetric: they may affect both parties, not just the one with the ticking clock.

A second aspect of time pressure is the concept of time costs. Here, the negotiation is not a ticking time bomb but a taximeter running up costs as time ticks away. Time costs do not impose a strict time limit but make the passage of time expensive. They encompass everything from the missed earnings of employees on strike to the mounting hourly rates of hired professional negotiators or even the opportunity costs of your own valuable time (Quoidbach, 2024).

Ultimately, efficient use of time not only improves immediate results but also builds trust and respect among all parties, laying the groundwork for future collaborations that are constructed on mutual understanding and professionalism. Developing strong time management skills is an invaluable investment in becoming a more effective negotiator across any context or industry.

References

Bensla, A. (2023). *Cultural Sensitivity in the Workplace*. Lewes, Delaware: Risely.

Blank, S. (2020). *Managing Organizational Conflict*. Jefferson, NC: McFarland & Company.

Cai, J. (2025). *How to Successfully Negotiate with People in Cross-Cultural Settings*. Las Vegas, Nevada: The Black Swan Group.

Hendon, D., Hendon, R., and Herbig, P. (1996). *Cross-Cultural Business Negotiations*. Westport, CT: Quorum Books.

Levine, S. (2002). *The Book of Agreement: 10 Essential Elements for Getting the Results You Want*. San Francisco: Berrett-Koehler Publishers.

Mendiratta, A. (2024). *Bridging the Gap: How to Overcome Cultural Barriers in Negotiation*. New York: Negotiation Academy.

Miles, M. (2024). *How to Build Rapport with Someone and Find Common Ground*. San Francisco, CA: Better Up.

Newman, S. (2025). *Embracing Cultural and Behavioral Differences for Global Negotiation Success*. Sydney, Australia: ENS.

Pinger, Y. (2025). *Embracing Cultural and Behavioral Differences for Global Negotiation Success*. Sydney, Australia: Negotiation Skills Training International.

PON Staff (2024). How to negotiate in cross-cultural situations. *Program on Negotiation at Harvard Law School*. Cambridge, MA: Harvard Negotiation Law Review.

Quoidbach, J. (2024). *Navigating Time Pressure in Negotiations: A Double-Edged Sword By*. Jersey City, NJ: Forbes.

Scottwork. (2024). *How to Overcome Cultural Barriers in Negotiation*. London: Scott Work Team.

Williams, R. (1983). *A Vocabulary of Culture and Society*. New York: Oxford University Press.

Ting-Toomey, S. (2013). Face negotiation conflict theory. In K. Keith (ed.), *The Encyclopedia of Cross-Cultural Psychology*. Hoboken, NJ: Wiley-Blackwell Publishers.

Zaki, M. (2025). *Breaking Cultural Barriers: A Guide to Building Trust Across Borders*. Jersey City, NJ: Forbes Media.

7 International Negotiations

International negotiations are discussions between parties from different countries to resolve disputes/conflicts or reach agreements. They are a central tool for international relations and can help build stability and confidence between states. These international negotiations endeavor to (a) identify areas of agreement; (b) narrow down options that are acceptable to all parties; and (c) formulate proposals to reach a specific agreement.

Because of the increasing complexity of issues and the fast pace of changes affecting both national and international interests, it has become essential for international agreements to contain sufficient flexibility in certain of their provisions to permit dealing with uncertainty and the needs of the parties to adapt to new and changing circumstances. In this sense, international negotiations and agreements must be not only reactive but also anticipatory.

There are four distinct layers of international negotiations: (1) strategic layer that includes interests and leverage; (2) cultural layer of communication and trust; (3) political layer that comprises many domestic pressures; and (4) psychological layer that often includes emotions.

Cultural Etiquette

The strategic layer that includes interests and leverage can create misunderstandings. Overlooking these customs can lead to unintended offenses, strained relationships, and even the collapse of business deals. For example, a seemingly innocent gesture or comment in one culture might be perceived as disrespectful or inappropriate in another, potentially jeopardizing a profitable partnership. Therefore, being well-versed in the local customs and traditions of a business counterparts is critical to fostering mutual respect and understanding. The importance of cultural etiquette in international business cannot be exaggerated. It serves as a bridge that connects diverse business environments and helps in mitigating misunderstandings. By appreciating and honoring the cultural differences of company partners, businesses can build strong, enduring relationships that are conducive to long-term success.

DOI: 10.4324/9781042000258-8

Cooperation is necessary for identification of an agreement on changes in options and constraints. International negotiations provide the means for developing innovative approaches for political, legal, institutional, technological, environmental, and economic issues and disputes.

Clear communication is harder in international negotiations when people have different expectations about tone, pace, and formality. Several simple adjustments can help with understanding and building trust (Mirra, 2024):

- Start slowly and take time to build rapport before diving into the agenda
- Avoid idioms, jargon, or sarcasm. Always use plain, direct language
- Check the meaning of key terms like *deadline*, *commitment*, or *pilot*
- Watch for silence or vague agreement and gently ask for clarification
- Use visual aids like diagrams or summaries to reinforce your message
- Match your counterpart's preferred communication style and platform
- Speak in short units if using an interpreter, and brief them ahead of time
- Recap key points and next steps in writing after each meeting
- Be mindful of tone and formality, especially in follow-up messages

Challenges to International Negotiation

Approaching a negotiation across cultures calls for more than just translating words. It means adjusting the process so that value isn't lost in miscommunication. The varied challenges of international negotiations include (a) cultural differences; (b) foreign bureaucracies; and (c) misunderstandings that can occur due to language barriers or cultural differences. International negotiations are important because they remain a key part of international business relations and can help maintain international stability and security while helping to build trust and confidence between states.

Individuals in businesses that negotiate internationally should obtain, invest, and demonstrate learned objectives that include the ability to:

1. Demonstrate an understanding of the cases, practices, successes, and challenges of conflict assessment and prevention.
2. Gain a deep understanding of the processes and outcomes of international negotiation.
3. Analyze international conflicts and negotiations in order to develop accurate policy recommendations, negotiation strategies, and tactical responses.
4. Examine and engage with some of the critical economic, legal, ethical, and political dilemmas that face nation-states and decision-makers in the aftermath of war.
5. Engage with and analyze trends, issues, debates, and dilemmas in post-conflict transition and reconstruction processes to grasp the challenges faced and lessons learned in specific cases of post-war transitions.

Commonly used tactics in international negotiation can include (Overvest, 2024):

Extreme demands that are followed by small concessions
A commonly used hard-bargaining tactic where negotiators start with unreasonable demands and make small, slow concessions. This strategy aims to delay reaching a deal and protect the negotiator from giving in too quickly. To counter this, know your goals, BATNA, and bottom line, and stay composed when facing an aggressive opponent.

Issuing threats and warnings
Recognize and respond to threats and indirect warnings strategically. Ignoring or directly addressing the threat can help defuse the situation.

Pressuring you to accede to their demands
The opponent keeps escalating demands to force you into conceding. Address this tactic directly, asserting your commitment to engage in fair and balanced offer exchanges.

Using personal attacks to unsettle you
Take a break if needed and communicate that insults and cheap strategies are unacceptable.

Bluffing or exaggerating
Misrepresenting facts to gain an advantage. Be cautious of claims that seem too good to be true and conduct thorough investigations.

Take-it-or-Leave-it offers
An inflexible approach where offers are presented as non-negotiable. To diffuse this tactic, focus on the offer's content and make a counter-offer that aligns with both parties' needs.

Undermining your options
Attempting to weaken your BATNA to influence your decisions. Remain firm and resilient, not letting the other party undermine your resolve.

Navigating the legal and regulatory landscape of different countries is a significant challenge in international negotiation for separate jurisdictions have their own set of laws, regulations, and contractual requirements, and failure to comply with these can result in legal complications. Strategies for addressing legal and regulatory differences include the following:

- Engage legal experts with expertise in international business law to navigate the legal complexities.
- Clearly outline the governing law and dispute resolution mechanisms in issues.
- Regularly update the contract to ensure compliance with changing laws and regulations.

Diplomatic Negotiation

Diplomatic negotiations are imperative in international relations as they serve as a primary mechanism for resolving conflicts, advocating peace, and fostering cooperation among nations. The importance of diplomatic negotiations in conflict resolution and peace building cannot be over stated, as they look to pursue mutually beneficial solutions to complex international disputes. At the heart of diplomatic negotiations is the ability to facilitate communication and understanding between conflicting parties. By engaging in dialogue and negotiation, nations can address their differences, find common ground, and work toward peaceful resolutions. Diplomatic negotiations play a vital role in preventing the escalation of conflicts in to full-blown wars, thereby contributing to global stability and security.

Following are several successful strategies (Mirra, 2024) that help one plan and settle with clarity and respect: (1) prepare with context and decision norms and to certain to learn how decisions are typically made in the counterpart's culture; (2) ask questions that open up the process; (3) present clear options that include multiple paths forward that allows the other side to choose without losing face; (4) use standards that feel familiar and support the proposals with benchmarks, norms, or examples that the other party already trusts; and (5) focus on real commitments, instead of vague agreement.

> *Diplomacy is the art of telling people to go to hell in such a way that they ask for directions.*
>
> ~ Winston Churchill

Diplomatic negotiations are instrumental in building trust and fostering relationships between nations. Through sustained dialogue and negotiation, countries can develop a deeper understanding of each other's perspectives, interests, and concerns, laying the groundwork for future cooperation and collaboration. This trust-building aspect of diplomatic negotiations is essential for maintaining peaceful relations and preventing the recurrence of conflicts. Diplomatic negotiations often involve the participation of international organizations and third-party mediators, enhancing the legitimacy and effectiveness of peace building efforts. The history of diplomatic negotiations is deeply intertwined with the evolution of international relations, reflecting the changing dynamics of global politics and the quest for peaceful resolution of conflicts (Turanevya, 2024).

Preparing a diagnostic outline for diplomatic negotiation readiness and leverage dynamics will help assess whether individuals are prepared to negotiate effectively. Several questions to pose are mentioned below:

- What is the strategic intent and goal?
- Are the objectives specific, prioritized, and aligned with long-term strategies?
- What concessions are acceptable?
- Is there internal support and stakeholder affiliation?
- Are there additional constraints?
- What is the skill level of the negotiators in terms of cross-cultural dialogue?
- Is there historical knowledge of past negotiations and successful outcomes?

Undoubtedly, global events, political changes, and economic instability can have a profound impact on international business relationships. Negotiators must assess and mitigate the risks associated with political and economic uncertainties to protect their interests. Strategies for dealing with political and economic instability include (1) checking geopolitical developments and assessing their potential impact on the business environment and (2) diversifying business operations and partnerships to lessen dependence on a single market.

Critical Role of Culture in Negotiation

The multicultural perspective in conflict resolution has important benefits for leaders and organizations. Groups, individuals, and businesses in conflict might otherwise be limiting themselves to those more familiar alternatives within their specific culture. Given an appreciation of multicultural complexity, they are less likely to accept quick and easy, but wrong answers by imposing their cultural perspective on others. By understanding a range of culturally different approaches to conflict resolution, their practical and theoretical options for resolving conflict are increased (Pederson, 2001).

Some cultural differences influence:

- Decision-making speed (are they quick and transactional or slow and relationship-based?)
- Risk tolerance (are they risk-seeking or risk-averse?)
- Communication style (are they direct or indirect?)
- Relationship versus task orientation (do they prioritize long-term trust or immediate deal-making?)
- Perception of time (are they strict about schedules or flexible?)
- Power dynamics (do they follow hierarchy or seek consensus?)

The substance of effective cross-cultural negotiation is cultural awareness: the ability to recognize and appreciate the differences and similarities between your own culture and that of your counterparts. Cultural awareness helps negotiators to avoid misinterpretations, adapt strategies to align with counterpart expectations, and foster respectful and productive dialogue.

Culture encompasses the shared values, beliefs, and norms of a group of people and these elements shape individuals' behaviors, communication styles, and decision-making processes. Behavioral traits such as assertiveness, risk tolerance, and communication styles vary widely across cultures. For instance, in some Middle Eastern cultures, hospitality and building personal relationships are vital. Negotiators may spend considerable time engaging in social activities before deliberating about business. In contrast, Northern European cultures often prefer a more structured and official approach, with clear agendas and minimal chitchat.

If one has experience negotiating across cultures, then it is apparent that misunderstandings and even conflict based on cultural differences can come up from time to time. Specifically, theory and research that categorize the world's cultures into three prototypes—"dignity," "face," and "honor" cultures—can help us address cultural barriers in negotiation. Cultural differences often spring from different histories, and two factors—population density and type of economy—determined whether a region developed a dignity, face, or honor culture. Recognizing and respecting these cultures can help when weighing how to deal with cultural differences in negotiation (Shonk, 2025).

Katie Shonk examined *dignity cultures*, which developed in societies built on agriculture with low population density where people strived to manage conflict rationally and directly while avoiding strong emotional reactions. *Face cultures* sprang up in agricultural regions with rapidly growing populations that required organized food production, a collective goal facilitated by cooperation and strong central governments. Face cultures have a reputation for social responsibility. Cultural norms encourage people to save face and preserve harmony by avoiding direct confrontation, suppressing negative emotions, and deferring to authority. *Honor cultures* sprang up in regions with herding economies and people became prevalent in these cultures to include a strong defense of oneself and one's family, reliance on a code of honor, and close family ties. Members tend to view insults and other conflicts as direct challenges to their status and to respond boldly and even aggressively to slights.

Successful Negotiation Tips

International business is expanding, and we are living in an increasingly globalized world with more companies engaged in cross-border transactions. Commercial agreements with businesses and organizations in other countries can be especially difficult to negotiate. Seven commonly used tactics in international negotiations are listed above; here are several tips to have successful cross-border negotiations (Marino, 2024):

- Develop comprehensive goals: This always begins with clearly defined, well-articulated goals that can signify what constitutes a positive outcome. Planning requires understanding not just the ultimate objectives, such as revenue targets and market expansion metrics, but also the subtleties of what success looks like in different contexts.
- Gather all applicable information: Organization is at the grounds of successful business negotiations and cross-border transactions are certainly no exception to the rule. Indeed, organization is key in any negotiation. It is especially critical when dealing with parties from different countries. The differences in legal systems, languages, and even time zones can all add serious complexity to the transactions.
- Identify regulatory barriers: One of the most significant challenges in cross-border negotiation is navigating the complex web of regulations and laws, as they can vary drastically from one country to another jurisdiction. Regulatory matters should not be overlooked. Early in the negotiation process,

one should proactively identify any potential legal and regulatory barriers that could impact the agreement and the business relationship more broadly. Among other things, this could include tariffs, trade agreements, local business practices, and other types of compliance requirements.

- Pursue professional guidance and support: Do not underestimate the value of seeking professional guidance and support. With so many potential legal, regulatory, and logistical issues, the right advocate on your side can make a dramatic difference. In the opportunities offered by cross-border transactions.

Even if you know who's playing, it's a failure to understand each player's role, and who owns which decisions, can be very costly.

To maximize the chances of success in the cross-cultural setting, one should consider several factors, including the following (Whitmore, 2024):

- Etiquette/protocol issues: Simple issues one takes for granted can make a difference in cross-cultural settings. How are the parties greeted and with what level of formality? Are there gender issues to consider that may impact on how to behave? Lack of understanding of etiquette can lead to tension, discomfort, and mistrust. Try to inform yourself and understand the protocol and etiquette norms in advance, but keep your senses open for any signs that you have stepped into inappropriate territory.
- Relationship issues: In many Western cultures, there may be varying degrees of comfort with personal relationships in a negotiation. Some people are inherently relationship builders by nature and want to get to know the other party before getting down to business. Others are more rational and cut to the chase by nature and may see personal relationships as external to or even dangerous in a business deal. Other cultures can approach relationships in different ways.
- Timing issues: Diverse cultures deal with time in very different ways. In Western cultures, punctuality is generally seen as a positive, though in the extreme, it can be seen as nitpicky behavior. Is timing a strategy or a cultural trait? One often infers negative intention from actions that have a negative impact on us, but we need to be careful about such knee jerk reactions. By clarifying the process in advance, we are less likely to be surprised in a negative way. It is worth investigating timing issues explicitly with all parties so everyone understands what is meant by a timetable.
- Trust issues: The approach to trust and information often varies with the parties' personalities and their relationship at the time, as well as other factors. The greater the level of trust, the more likely that fuller disclosure will occur. Other cultures may approach information and trust in different ways. Some cultures are more risk averse than others.
- Authority issues: Depending on the culture, true authority for decision-making may rest in various hands. There can be confusion and distrust

when authority is spread in a horizontal manner on one side of the table but hierarchically on the other. How can one deal with decision-making to make both sides comfortable? It is worth clarifying who has authority early on, modeling by one's own example.
- Procedural issues: When dealing with a foreign culture, one needs to be educated and aware of the political and practical realities of getting what one wants in the applicable environment. Are there channels that must be followed? If so, what are they, and what is the best route through them that is compatible with the ethical issues in both cultures?

Negotiation is a psychological investigation, and good initial preparation can save time and aid in the implementation of a deal (Voss, 2016). Several examples of cross-cultural communication norms in negotiation were addressed by Marc Mirra (2024). We all know that how we communicate is shaped by our cultural backgrounds and often differs greatly from one person to the next. Some concrete examples include the following:

- **Japan**: Communication tends to be reserved and indirect. Silence is often used strategically to convey thoughtfulness and consideration. Quick responses or overly assertive behavior may be perceived as disrespectful.
- **United States**: The communication style in the United States is typically direct and expressive. Business culture tends to be fast-paced and results-oriented, with an emphasis on clear, concise messaging.
- **Mexico**: In Mexican culture, physical contact like a handshake, a pat on the shoulder, or even a hug can be a sign of trust and friendship. Relationship-building often precedes formal negotiations.
- **India**: Speaking too loudly or forcefully in India can be perceived as aggressive or rude. Conversations are usually polite and respectful, with a strong emphasis on maintaining harmony and avoiding confrontation.

These examples highlight just how diverse communication norms can be and how it might go wrong. What an American might consider honest and open communication could easily be perceived as haughty and brash by their Japanese or Indian counterparties. Recognizing these nuances can help you interact more effectively with others and adjust your behavior accordingly when negotiating across cultures. Mirra also postulates that while cultural awareness is vital, it's important not to get too caught up in generalities. Remember, the other party may not adhere strictly to cultural "norms" and could even break from trends you've prepared for. At the end of the day, the negotiation is with people, not stereotypes.

Steps for International Negotiations

Awareness and cross-cultural understanding are critical for anyone looking to do business on a global scale. By recognizing how different cultures approach negotiation, one can learn to take advantage of the strengths each style offers.

It is important to be open to change and being flexible to adapt to different negotiation processes, especially in the international context. However, embracing the counterpart's business practices, especially when negotiating in their home country, is crucial. Like preparing for negotiations with a business, comprehending and respecting the cultural nuances of the counterpart's company is essential for success.

Effective preparation for international negotiations involves careful study and a willingness to adapt to new processes. By focusing on fundamental issues rather than fixating on the intricacies of the process, negotiators can navigate challenges successfully. A notable example is the 2015 Paris Climate talks, where negotiators, despite being unfamiliar with the South African process called *indaba*, reached an agreement by preparing with the core negotiation principles in mind.

For instance, the 21st Conference of Parties led to a new international climate agreement, the Paris Accord Agreement of 2015, which applies to every country. It aimed to limit global warming to 1.5–2°C compared to pre-industrial levels, in line with the recommendations of the Intergovernmental Panel on Climate Change (IPCC). Negotiators recognized the importance of addressing both political and technical issues. They decided to have experts handle the technical aspects separately, allowing for focused discussions on each issue. This careful approach prevented confusion and helped the negotiators concentrate on key elements, ultimately leading to more effective and successful outcomes. In cross-cultural negotiations, simplicity and respect will pave the way for better understanding and cooperation.

In cross-border negotiations, make friends, not just deals.

An important element common to cross-cultural business negotiations is the participation of governmental authorities. Governments often play a much larger role in foreign business than Americans are accustomed to. The presence of often extensive government bureaucracies can make international negotiation processes more rigid that is usual in the American private sector. Sovereign immunity can introduce legal complications into contracts. State-controlled businesses may have different goals from private companies. Whereas private firms are usually primarily concerned with profits, state entities may be willing to sacrifice some profitability for social or political ends such as greater employment.

Additionally international projects are vulnerable to sudden changes in their circumstances. Events such as war or revolution, changes in government, or currency devaluation have an impact on international businesses, which is much greater than the influence that the usual domestic changes have on national businesses. These risks require international business negotiator to have a breadth of knowledge and social insight that would not ordinarily be necessary in negotiating a US business arrangement. International businesses try to protect against these risks by employing political risk analysts, by foreign investment insurance, and by force majeure clauses, which allow for contract cancellation under certain conditions.

International business negotiators also encounter very different ideologies. Different countries may have very separate ideas about private investment, profit, and individual rights. Effective negotiators will be aware of ideological differences. They will present their proposals in ways that are ideologically acceptable to the other party, or that are at least ideologically neural.

Looking at a summary of global trends leads to indications of negotiation practices that take into effect marked situations, issues and inclinations (Blankenburgh, 2022). There are now more than 60,000 globally operating Multi-National Corporations (MNCs). These MNCs control more than 500,000 subsidiary companies. Their combined economic and financial power can influence national and international policy and since they control more than half of the international trade, they are a major talent magnet with a super diverse talent pool.

One cannot forget the ever-growing not-for-profit sector. Currently, there are more than 40,000 Internationally operating non-governmental Organizations (I-NGO's). The current I-NGO sector represents 4.5% of the global GDP—almost 5 trillion USD. When we look at people who live internationally or people who have exposure to multiple cultures, here are four important statistics that tell the story of how diverse our world is becoming:

- Close to 300 million people live outside the country of their passport.
- More than 220 million people are classified as Third Culture Kids (TCKs): people born into a multi-cultural family being raised in another country.
- We also have over 300 million Cross Cultural Kids (CCKs): people whose parents hold the same passport, but who were raised in another culture.
- And let's not forget one other significant trend: Of the 3.4 billion employees worldwide, about 1.3 billion connect interculturally on a regular basis through their work.

These statistics have forever changed the fabric of our working lives. We are in an interconnected world, and the above trends have led to unprecedented mobility (virtual or physical) of employment. In the past, only a few jobs were on the international job market. Today, most jobs are accessible on the international stage. Virtual work is here to stay, and this has led to anybody being able to work from anywhere, for anyone and with anyone. All the above is making the world of work more intercultural than ever before, and this has consequences for the skills and competencies needed today and in the near future.

If you want to communicate effectively, you have to know your audience.
~ Lee Iacocca

Faults in Cross-Cultural Negotiations

Cross-cultural negotiations are filled with opportunity but also troubled with potential missteps. Four aspects of common errors include the following:

- Assuming similar norms of negotiations
- Language fluency issues
- Unequal understanding of power and leverage
- Differences in time orientation

The international negotiation case study of **Microsoft**'s decision to purchase Finnish mobile phone company **Nokia**'s mobile device business for $7.2 billion was a deal, which closed in 2014 and quickly proved disastrous: Microsoft wrote off nearly all the deal's value and laid off thousands of workers in July 2015. Although there were many reasons the deal was a bad bet for Microsoft, a negotiating condition that Nokia set before agreeing to take part in serious negotiations may have offered one warning sign. Microsoft employees found Nokia's approach too passive and slow, leading to frustration and misunderstandings. Building trust between the two groups was another major hurdle. Many Nokia employees were skeptical about Microsoft's intentions and feared job losses. In 2015, Microsoft declared it was writing off $7.6 billion on the Phone Hardware division as goodwill and asset impairment charges, $400 million more than it had originally paid for the Finnish firm.

Making mistakes in cross-cultural negotiations will surely have an impact on the company's business. It can also directly hurt the reputation of the company, especially if it is known as an international enterprise doing business globally. Stakeholders who deal with international companies understandably assume that their representatives have the necessary experience and knowledge to carry out international transactions. Actions or omissions that prove this wrong will not reflect well in the company's status. This was the case in the Microsoft and Nokia deal.

Table 7.1 Major flaws in cross-cultural negotiations

Faults	*Reasoning*
Assuming a universal negotiation style	Projecting one's own cultural norms as standard
Misreading the communication style	Cultural variables in style, tone, and nonverbal areas
Misjudging hierarchy and decision authority	Cultural differences in broad participation
Overlooking rituals and protocols	Business etiquette varies widely
Language misunderstandings and translation missteps	Meanings, idioms, and nuances differ

Given all the best variations in how people deal with conflict, and the historical, political elements of intercultural conflict, what are the strategies for effective conflict management? Several strategies (Martin and Nakayama, 2022) for dealing with this are as follows:

- Stay centered and don't polarize.
- Maintain contact.
- Recognize the existence of different cultural styles.
- Identify your preferred style.
- Be creative and expand your style repertoire.
- Recognize the importance of conflict context.

When attempting to navigate negotiations across differing cultures, be mindful to research the cultural background of the counterparts to understand their negotiation style and expectations. It is also prudent to invest time in relationship-building, especially in high-context and collectivist cultures and adapt your communication style to match the cultural context of your counterparts with a focus on shared goals and mutual benefits to bridge cultural gaps.

One way to think about conflict across cultures is in terms of what is more or less successful conflict management or resolution (Augsburger, 1992). In productive conflict in individuals or groups, one should:

- Narrow the conflict to specifics in terms of definition scope and issues.
- Limit the conflict to the original issue.
- Trust leadership that stresses mutually satisfactory outcome.
- Promote cooperative processes: perceived similarity, trust, flexibility, and open communication.

In destructive conflict in individuals or groups, one should:

- Escalate and broaden the conflict from the original problem, bringing in unrelated issues.
- Polarize around leadership that is single-minded and militant.
- Encourage competitive atmosphere: coercion, deception, suspicion, and rigidity.

Where there is a history of extensive grievances on both sides, there is a call for more complex strategies such as mediation and peacebuilding. A peacebuilding approach is focused on listening and speaking, not to persuade but to clarify.

An example of a cultural grievance occurred in May 2001, when a class action lawsuit was filed against the world's largest fast-food chain **McDonald's**, in Seattle, USA. The lawsuit alleged that the company had, for over a decade, deceived vegetarian customers into eating French fries that contained beef extracts. The lawsuit followed a rash of media reports detailing how the French fries served at McDonald's were falsely promoted as being 100% vegetarian and although McDonald's initially declined to comment on the issue, the company issued a conditional apology, admitting to using beef flavoring in the fries. The furor over the matter seemed to be settling down, when to McDonald's horror, some of its restaurants in India were vandalized. Many activists of Hindu fundamentalist groups staged demonstrations in front of the McDonald's head office in Delhi protesting the alleged use of beef flavorings.

The Cultural Lens

A cultural lens is the interpretive framework through which individuals perceive and engage in negotiation. It influences what is considered fair or respectful and how trust is built. The cultural view on conflict drives many behaviors in conflict situations. The relationship group culture will focus on trying to dial down the conflict to protect people from getting into embarrassing situations and preserve the reputation of the group. The task-oriented culture sees disagreement as part of life and debate as an intellectual exercise to solve problems. It is the behavior of the individual and focuses more on the matter in dispute.

It is not easy to put on one's cultural lens when dealing with a conflict. It takes a conscious mind to remind oneself to apply cultural intelligence learning in the heat of things, literally. The overall advice for people in cultural camps is to come out of one's camp and move closer to the other side to reach out and build bridges of clarification and understanding. Here are some key principles for handling conflict in a cross-cultural context.

Key principles for handling conflict in a cross-cultural context include cultural awareness, empathy and perspective-taking, effective communication, respect and tolerance, and patience and flexibility. Building deep relationships across cultures requires ongoing effort and a commitment to understanding and respecting one another. By applying these principles, one will navigate conflicts in a cross-cultural context more effectively.

Additionally, the importance of clarifying misunderstandings and seeking feedback when interacting with people from different cultures cannot be overstated. Putting the other person's words in one's own words and repeating them can help confirm understanding. It is also possible to demonstrate a genuine interest in learning by asking questions and seeking clarification.

Cultural differences may have various bases such as geographical, educational, occupational, and historical backgrounds, and these bases have divided individuals into clans or groups. These factors can bring out many differences between cultures. One of the most important factors about culture is it doesn't remain the same. Every organization has its own culture and adaptability of both the organizations and acceptability to a particular adaptable culture becomes difficult for both the organizations and, therefore, results in failure of even a successfully running organization. To explain the impact of cultural conflict, an example of the merger of two successfully running organizations, **Chrysler**, an American automaker, and **Daimler**, a German unit, has been used, which merged with each other with an expectation to earn higher revenue and greater profit as well as expansion of their business (Sur and Anand, 2019).

Both organizations merged with the expectation of becoming each other's strengths. The shareholders of both the organizations effortlessly agreed to the merger, but the results were very different from the expected. The profit margin of the Chrysler unit started reducing. This was the result of cultural differences between both the organizations. The American work style was different from the German work culture and, even after being equally powerful and strong, still the companies could not retain their position after the merger. The American unit, Chrysler, followed a very lenient and free style of management whereas Daimler's style of management was very rigid and organized. As a result of the high stringency and rigidity, the Chrysler's employee could not adapt to Daimlers style, and this resulted in resignation of the highly abled executives and engineers. As a result, Chrysler faced a precipitous fall in terms of performance and profit as well. The dissatisfaction among the employees started increasing and their productivity started falling.

Cultural Conflicts

Cultural differences in the workplace consist of lots of factors such as individual upbringing, community, and history. There are lots of characteristics that can lead to cultural differences in the workplace. Diverse organizations consist of individuals from different economic backgrounds, age brackets, gender, religions, and much more. Some factors responsible for cultural differences include ethnicity, religion, level of education, and generational status.

According to an experiment done by Weber and Camerer (2003), it shows that the probability of failure of an organization due to cultural conflict and communication gap is often ignored and is also not considered to be an important issue, which later becomes a major reason for failure of an organization in the long run. They also draw the focus on the employees working for the organization and have been through the difficulties of communication barriers. It is usually assumed that these employees will be able to take care of the issues, but the organization does not realize the difference between the premerger and post-merger circumstances, which are even worse in terms of cultural adjustment.

Understand the differences, act on the commonalities.

When Rana Plaza, an eight-story factory collapsed in Bangladesh in 2013, killing an estimated 1,130 people, most of whom were low-wage garment workers manufacturing goods for foreign retailers, the Worker Rights

Consortium had already been working for years to press apparel brands to fundamentally change their approach to fire and building safety in order to bring about genuine safety improvements in their supplier factories there (Paton, 2021).

In this negotiation case, companies that outsourced their garment production faced public pressure to improve conditions for foreign workers. Labor unions focused their efforts on persuading the Swedish giant, H&M, to take the lead on safety improvements. The negotiation case highlighted the pros and cons of all-inclusive, diffuse agreements versus targeted, specific agreements. The negotiated accord was the first modern legally binding agreement between workers, factory managers, and apparel companies that require brands and retailers to:

- Open their supplier factories to fully independent inspections by qualified experts and engineers.
- Allow the results of these inspections to be reported publicly, in a searchable database.
- Help pay for essential safety renovations.
- Stop doing business with any factories that fail to make needed safety repairs.

Additionally, the negotiated accord outlined a complaint mechanism by which workers can anonymously report potential violations at their factory to the Accord. It also included an enforcement mechanism by which legal action can be brought against non-compliant signatories.

Intercultural differences in notions about friendships, both personal and business, involve ideas about identity and value. Marc Mancini (2003) has developed some interesting concepts about cultural variables in relationships.

CHINA: Face-saving is extremely important in China. They always avoid embarrassing situations and help one another save face and retain self-respect.
BRAZIL: To be invited to a Brazilian's home is an honor. Guests are expected to stay for many hours.
GERMANY: Germans tend to be formal. In business, they do not use first names unless they know the person very well.
FRANCE: When French greet people, they tend to be formal.

In general, most negotiators tend to act based on his or her own best interests, while keeping the bigger picture of the enterprise in mind. Different cultures arrive at the truth in different ways; they might be distilled into faith, facts, and feelings. Keeping in mind differing cultural notes when negotiating can lead to easier win–win agreements. Availing oneself of smart, authoritative sources of information about different cultures and countries before engaging in negotiations is outstanding. One key source of such information is *Kiss, Bow, or Shake Hands* (Morrison and Conaway, 2006). Several insights from the book are mentioned below:

INDIA: Indians appreciate punctuality but do now always practice it themselves. Request appointments as far ahead as possible. Go to the top of the company for major decisions. Expect delays in negotiations.
SOUTH KOREA: Age and rank are very important, and it is sometimes easier to establish a rapport with a businessperson your own age.
SWEDEN: Small talk is kept to a minimum at the start of business. They accept silence with ease. Do not rush to fill in pauses with conversation.
ISRAEL: Many Israelis have a confrontational negotiating style. The pace of business is slower, so be patient. Do not back up or shy away.
PERU: Be prepared to discuss all aspects of the negotiation concurrently rather than discussing it in a sequential manner. Include a variety of materials in your presentation (web-based communications, high-end graphics in printed format, etc.).

Understanding how to negotiate in cross-cultural situations requires continuous learning and respect, but the returns can be beyond measure. Perhaps the most challenging aspect to prepare for is how to master a negotiation where one does not reach an agreement. There is an added feeling of pressure to reach a deal when one goes to great efforts to reach out to counterparts. However, going into a negotiation with this in mind can be the most valuable asset, because a respectful "no" can become "we will revisit it later" and lead to unexpected agreements at another time.

References

Augsburger, D. (1992). *Conflict Mediation Across Cultures*. Louisville, KY: Westminster/John Knox Press.

Blankenburgh, M. (2022). *The Four Pillars of Successful International Negotiations: Best Practices*. Dubai, UAE: Knowledge Workx.

Mancini, M. (2003). *Selling Destinations: Geography for the Travel Professional* (4th ed.). Clifton Park, NY: Thomson Delmar Learning.

Marino, R. D. (2024). *Strategies for Successful Cross-Border Negotiation*. Bala Cywyd, PA: Global Link Law.

Mirra, M. (2024). *Understanding Cross-Cultural Communication and Negotiation Around the World*. Brooklyn, NY: Aligned.

Morrison, T., and Conaway, W. W. (2006). *Kiss, Bow, or Shake Hands*. Avon, MA: Adams Media.

Paton, E. (2021). Fears for Bangladesh garment workers as safety agreement nears an end. *The New York Times*, May 28.

Pederson, P. (2001). The cultural context of peacemaking. In D. J. Christie, R. V. Wagner and D. D. White (eds.), *Peace Conflict and Violence Peace Psychology for the 21st Century*. Upper Saddle River, NJ: Prentice Hall.

Shonk, K. (2025). *How to Deal with Cultural Differences in Negotiation*. Program on Negotiation. Harvard Law School.

Turanevya, K. M. (2024). *Diplomatic Negotiations and Conflict Resolution in International Relations*. Ethiopia: International Research Journal of Nature Science and Technology.

Voss, C. (2016). *Never Split the Difference: Negotiating as If Your Life Depends on It*. Harper Collins.
Weber, R. A., and Camerer, C. F. (2003). Cultural conflict and merger failure: An experimental approach. *Management Science*, *49*(4).
Whitmore, E. (2024). *Cross Cultural Negotiations*. North York, ON: Stitt Feld Handy Group.

8 The Mediation Process and Strategic Management

Clearly stated, business mediation is a structured, facilitated negotiation process where a neutral third party helps disputing parties move from positional conflict ("I want X") to underlying interests ("I need security, clarity, fairness, or recognition"). It's not therapeutic, not arbitration, and not a dominance play. It is designed as a problem-solving scheme designed to restore trust, clarify incentives, and create durable agreements.

Mediation is not a magic bullet for resolving any and all conflicts. Much of the scholarly research suggests that mediation is most apt to be successful in conflicts occupying a general middle range of difficulty. Six factors that mediation may produce agreement (Kressel, 1972). include (1) high levels of conflict; (2) low motivation to reach agreement; (3) low commitment to mediation; (4) shortage of resources; (5) disputes involving fundamental principles; and (6) parties of unequal power.

Flexible Dispute Resolution

The mediation process is a flexible dispute resolution method where a neutral third party, or mediator, helps parties in conflict find a mutually acceptable resolution. The process involves:

- Preparation: Parties may submit pre-mediation submissions.
- Selection of mediator: The parties select a mediator and schedule a date for the mediation.
- Mediation session: The parties, their counsel, and the mediator meet at a neutral location to discuss the dispute. The mediator may ask questions, reframe issues, and help the parties understand each other.
- Resolution: The mediator works with the parties to identify solutions and reach a resolution.
- Outcome: The mediator provides the outcome of the mediation.

The mediation process can involve several stages, including identification and listing of issues, multiparty exploratory discussion, private meetings, and combined negotiation. Mediation is usually faster than a hearing, which can

DOI: 10.4324/9781042000258-9

take a week or longer. Mediation sessions typically last four to six hours, but the length can vary depending on the complexity of the case. Mediation is free to attend both parties.

As a flexible dispute resolution process, an impartial third party facilitates negotiations between parties to help them devise their own acceptable solutions. Mediators will ask questions, reframe issues, assist the parties to understand each other, and help identify solutions. Mediators do not take sides, pass down decisions, offer legal advice, or reveal confidences.

Satisfaction with the mediation process tends to be significantly higher than with other forms of dispute resolution such as arbitration and court litigation. Many companies find that the process is fair, and the disputants are satisfied with the process and results (Bingham, Kim and Raines, 2002).

There are several kinds of discussions that parties can have in the context of mediation. Parties sometimes use their respective estimations of the likely outcome of litigation as a basis to trade offers, bargain, and compromise. At times, parties may engage in a collaborative process in which they work together to find solutions to problems relevant to their dispute. In cases where the parties have an ongoing relationship, parties may focus on their respective values and communication styles.

Mediators will work with the parties to determine what kinds of discussions appear to offer the best prospects for settlement. This process is flexible and relatively informal. It can take various forms, depending on the nature of the dispute, the approach of the mediator, and the needs of the parties. Unlike litigation or arbitration, the mediation process is not adversarial. It is not necessary to prove that one party is at fault. The most difficult part of the mediation process is to get individuals to accept that mediation can be an effective way to resolve their dispute.

Mediation Issue Example

An example of a mediation issue is:

> *Angela works in the Information Technology Department at Tech-Sense Inc. Paul is her supervisor. She has had difficulties arriving to work on time and is always apologetic, but Paul believes she is just making excuses. Anger and resentment build as the issue remains unresolved after several heated discussions. The two find it difficult to converse without arguing. Paul does not want to fire her—being a single mom Angela needs the job to support her children. Angela honestly tries to be at work on time but trying to get two young children ready for school can be difficult. Short of a formal disciplinary action, they elect to contact an alternative dispute resolution committee workmate.*

Mediation doesn't only have a place in conflicts; mediators can help families, organizations, and businesses find the best and most strategic way to move forward during a problem. For this type of mediation, the involved parties collaborate, share information, and work together to find the most suitable course of action.

Disputes are a distraction and highly disruptive to business plans if not resolved quickly.
Litigation can take years. Mediation can take days.

Organizations that can successfully resolve internal and external disputes quickly are poised to move forward from conflicts and focus on company business. Peer review and dispute resolution committees have a cadre of trained mediators and arbiters that:

- Receive complaints and for dispute/mediation resolution requests.
- Accept and review complaints for dispute/mediation resolution.
- Engage in fact-finding, rule or policy interpretation
- Compile and report the results of mediation and arbitration cases to the appropriate steering committee or individuals, while protecting confidentiality where appropriate.

Several of the key benefits of enterprise mediation are reflected in (1) cost-effectiveness that often avoids expensive litigation and minimizes disruption; (2) time-saving that is realized quicker than court proceedings, which allows managers to refocus on strategy; (3) relationship preservation by encouraging collaboration and empathy; and (4) flexibility in crafting solutions can are creative and tailored to enterprise needs.

Although there are many benefits to mediation, there are also frequent challenges. These can include (1) an imbalance of power that may involve executive leaders versus junior staff; (2) emotional passions where high-stakes decisions can trigger stress, anger, or fear; (3) cultural differences involving some misaligned values or communication styles across business sectors or teams; and (4) confrontations to settle as parties may stick to positions rather than focusing on interests.

Peer Review Committee

A peer review committee should comprise individuals that have completed educational and training requirements for mediators. They can, in many cases, be certified and receive continuing educational training of mediators. For example, in the state of New York, the New York State Dispute Resolution Association, Inc. (NYSDRA) is a not-for-profit membership organization committed to the promotion of quality conflict management and peaceful dispute resolution. Through leadership, education, promotion of professional standards, and training and development of innovative statewide programs, NYSDRA provides opportunities for people, communities, organizations, and businesses to effectively respond to conflict. NYSDRA manages several mediation and arbitration programs for state and federal agencies as well as provides training on various dispute resolution tactics. Customized services are provided through our statewide membership of individual practitioners and Community Dispute Resolution Centers (CDRCs). NYSDRA facilitates a 30-hour course that normally takes place over four days.

Two vital functions of the peer review committee process involve the evaluation function. This is the familiar process of evaluating employee and/or team performance. The second, called the oversight function, involves all the actions necessary to oversee the process to ensure that it is executed correctly.

Methods of becoming a trained peer review committee mediator usually involve an apprenticeship. This can involve observations; the goal with observations is to observe many different mediations sessions facilitated by as many different mediators as possible, so there is no fixed number of observations. At a minimum, an apprentice can be required to observe six or more mediations by several different mediators. Once the observation stage is completed, apprentice mediators co-mediate cases with certified mediators. Again, the number of co-mediations can vary per individual. The skills can come intuitively to some and are difficult to master for others.

Mediation training explores questions like below:

- What is mediation and how does it compare to other forms of alternative dispute resolution?
- What are the core skills I need to be an effective mediator?
- What are the foundational values of mediation?
- How can I identify and respond to power imbalances?
- How can I identify and respond to different values, cultural norms, and biases?
- What is my role as a mediator?
- What are the best practices for online mediation?
- What is successful mediation? What is not considered successful mediation?

There is no doubt that emotions can play a central role in conflict, mediation, and negotiation (Jones, 2001). The expression of emotions is usually culturally linked in that culture that defines what is emotionally important or relevant for involved parties. Strong negative feelings can drive negotiation parties apart and make agreement very difficult. Conversely, cultivating and enhancing positive emotions between parties can help them relate more positively toward each other and greatly facilitate arriving at mutually agreeable accords (Douglas, 1962).

Emotional Impact

Overlooking, ignoring, or minimizing an emotional component in mediation can certainly lead to an impasse. By framing the problem only as a substantive dispute, mediators may limit options for resolution. On the other hand, exploring possible emotional factors may provide real clues for avoiding or working through impasse. When confronted with an apparent impasse, how can emotional issues be brought to the surface? Some hints to look for include (1) obsession with position; (2) non-verbal signals; (3) cultural differences; (4) silence and withdrawal; (5) excessive aggression; and (6) defensiveness (Klapper, 2011).

If there's one thing mediators can rely on, it is that parties get emotional during conflict. One of a mediator's most important skills is the ability to set up a process to manage the inevitable emotions that the parties express, including anger, frustration, and fear. Managing the parties' emotions does not mean minimizing or dismissing them as problems to overcome. There is value in embracing them as part of the process and outcome, working to harness the constructive power of emotions to help the parties reach closure.

With the help of some mediation techniques, you can facilitate these situations and capitalize on strong emotions in ways that can benefit all parties involved. Following are a few mediation techniques for managing emotions during mediation:

- Cultivate an environment of safety and trust: begin by being sensitive to decisions like seating arrangements and create an environment focused on parties' needs, which encourages them to express their emotions in a more constructive way. By encouraging them to speak freely and confidentially in front of a neutral party, parties can let their guard down and express emotions more freely.
- Take a deep breath and sit back: one reason that people are uncomfortable with managing emotions is our cultural bias toward the "rational" and against the "emotional." However, this simplification of the way we think and express ourselves falls short when measured against our complex human experience.
- If it becomes destructive, return to the process: ask the parties how the conversation is going for them. This not only will allow the parties to regain control of the conversation but also gives them the responsibility and agency to decide whether the conversation is productive for them. You can also summarize what you've heard and seen so far to deescalate the tension, and you can name the source of their disagreement.
- Bring parties back into the present moment: parties in conflict are often stuck in the past. There is some pleasure gained by blaming someone else for all the wrongs that have been done to them. Often, parties will go back and forth throwing verbal punches at each other while a repeating trope of the past. A mediation technique for managing emotion in this situation is to be transparent and remind the parties of their goal: resolution.
- Recognize emotion as opportunity: strong emotions show that people are invested: they care about the issue before them. This could be a key to your movement forward. If a party expresses an emotion to you, stay with

them. Listen, reflect, and express empathy. If you sense that a party is unable to express themselves but is seeking a way to do so, there are ways to help them open (Doran, 2017).

Strategic Management

Strategic management evaluates and may reorganize company resources to achieve new goals and objectives. Strategic management looks at the competitive environment and internal organization, evaluates strategies, and ensures that management rolls out new approaches across a company.

Organizational leaders often focus on learning from past strategies and examining the current environment, especially after a series of unsuccessful mediations or business negotiations. Strategic management may include an analytic process, where all opportunities are accounted for and new guiding principles are created. The skills and competencies of employees, business culture, and company structure influence how an organization can achieve its objectives. Inflexible companies may find it difficult to succeed in a changing business environment. Creating a barrier between strategies and their implementation can make it difficult for managers to determine whether negotiation/mediation objectives have been efficiently met.

Managerial Roles

Henry Mintzberg's (1998) groundbreaking research identified 10 distinct managerial roles that capture the multifaceted nature of management work. These roles are organized into three primary categories, each representing a fundamental aspect of managerial responsibility: interpersonal interactions, information management, and strategic decision-making. This framework provides managers with a systematic understanding of their diverse responsibilities and offers a roadmap for professional development across all dimensions of leadership.

- Interpersonal roles: (1) Figurehead, (2) Leader, (3) Liaison
- Informational roles: (4) Monitor, (5) Disseminator, (6) Spokesperson
- Decisional roles: (7) Entrepreneur, (8) Disturbance Handler, (9) Resource Allocator, (10) Negotiator

A peer review committee may receive data or discover that an enterprise issue might need their scrutiny. For example, an area manager received and ignored an anonymous tip about possible unsafe working conditions that led to a minor accident, which led to a media/public scandal. Members of the committee would include (1) chair (facilitator); (2) ethics officer; (3) legal advisor; and (4) external observer (e.g., regulator or board member). Questions and issues that should be examined and discussed are as follows:

- Was the anonymous report accurate?
- Did the reported issue create what was alleged?

- Did the company follow up with integrity and transparency? How?
- How and why did the area manager not respond to the tip?
- How did the media learn of this issue? Effect of public scandal?
- How did the media/public scandal affect team trust, working conditions and morale? Company compliance policies?
- What recovery measures, if any, need to be addressed and taken?
- Does this tip reveal larger organizational vulnerabilities?
- What should the company embark on to prevent any reoccurrence?
- Does the company need to revisit whistleblower protection?

References

Bingham, L. B., Kim, K., and Raines, S. (2002). Exploring the role of representation in employment mediation. *Ohio State Journal of Dispute Resolution*, *17*, 341–378.

Doran, C. (2017). *Mediation Techniques for Managing Emotions*. Boston, MA: MWI.

Klapper, M. (2011). *Defensive Creative Impasse-Breaking Techniques in Mediation*. New York State Bar Association.

Mintzberg, H. (1998). *Strategy Safari: A Guided Tour Through the Wilds of Strategic Management*. Upper Saddle River, NJ: Prentice Hall.

9 Strategies for Crisis Intervention

Crisis intervention is a short-term management procedure designed to reduce potential permanent damage to an individual, group, or company affected by a crisis. A crisis is defined as an overwhelming event, which can include many variables. A "crisis" usually involves a disruption of an individual's or organization's normal or stable state. More specifically, a crisis occurs "when individuals face obstacles to important life goals that is, for a time, insurmountable through the utilization of their customary methods of problem solving" (Caplan, 1961).

On average, employees and leaders spend close to three hours per week dealing with workplace crisis or conflict. In business, every hour counts and over time, that can add up to hundreds of thousands of dollars in lost productivity. Workplace conflict between professionals, even between just two people, can feel impossible to navigate effectively. And if those two people are company leaders, that can impact the entire organization.

Stages of Crisis Management

Most crises involve *three* stages. Crisis communication is important in all of them. The stages include the following:

- Pre-crisis. Companies must always assume that a crisis is possible and plan for it ahead of time. That includes engaging in prevention measures to minimize risks and developing a business continuity plan to help ensure leaders can support business processes and customers as much as possible during a crisis and recover as quickly as possible after.
- Crisis response. This stage arises when the crisis is upon the organization. Consider the example of a power outage: Pre-crisis stages occur outside of electrical structures and during regular power situations when no threat is present. As soon as an outage is imminent for the organization, the crisis response stage begins. It lasts until after the dangers of the outage, including residual effects that have passed. During this time, the organization must put its crisis plan into action.

DOI: 10.4324/9781042000258-10

- Post-crisis. After the crisis, the organization begins to return to normal processes. Groups and teams might also consider what happened during the crisis and whether lessons can be learned to improve crisis plans and communication in the future.

Enterprise Survival

An organizational crisis can be defined as a disruption that threatens the survival of an organization and challenges the assumptions of its employees and managers. Crises can be caused by several factors, including mismanagement, poor products or services, and unrealistic market assessments. Some common types of organizational crises include the following:

Crisis of deception: When a company misrepresents information about its products or tampers with public data.
Crisis of management/misconduct: When management engages in illegal activities, such as selling fake products or confidential customer information.
Crisis of distorted management values: When management prioritizes short-term financial gains over the long-term interests of stakeholders.

> *Luck favors the prepared mind.*
>
> ~ Louis Pasteur

A business crisis occurs when an unexpected problem puts the stability of a company or organization at risk. These dilemmas can either originate internally or be brought on by external influences. The problem affecting the business escalates to the point where it's out of the company's control and they can't resolve it. If left unaddressed, this issue may permanently damage the business or cause it to fail (Griffith and Goodwin, 2016).

The simplest way to identify a business crisis is to assess the problem for three key elements.

- First, the problem must pose an imminent threat to the organization.
- Next, the situation must involve an element of surprise or shock.
- Finally, due to the gravity of the problem as well as its unexpected nature, the situation will place pressure on the business to make timely and effective decisions. Knowing the elements that make up a business crisis can be instrumental in identifying these problems before it's too late.

A steady flow of natural disasters throughout the world, together with the threat of viral pandemics, underscores how poorly prepared organizations are in the wake of crises. But although such catastrophes threaten the viability of organizations, it is more common for them to face crises that arise from organizational and market dynamics than from natural forces. After all, natural disasters such as earthquakes are acts of nature, over which humans have no control.

An organizational crisis is a low-probability, high-impact event that threatens the organization's survival and is characterized by ambiguity of cause, effect, and means of resolution, as well as by a belief that decisions must be made swiftly. Yet although events that precipitate crises are unexpected and their implications are ambiguous, organizational leaders are still expected to cultivate systems that can detect early warning signals, halt the development of emergent problems, contain them if their development cannot be halted, and then focus on bouncing back from the ensuing performance difficulties.

Crisis events are often critical turning points in a business's life. Whether such crises emerge from poor strategic positioning, managerial inertia, and organizational stagnation or, taking a population ecology perspective, from a chance misfit between a particular type of organization and its broader environment, such situations suddenly shine the spotlight on any major problem in the design and activities of an organizational system. To have and maintain an advantageous position in a complex and high-velocity environment, the top management team (TMT) needs to build up a repertoire of responses that will ensure the organization's viability under all plausible circumstances. For example, a TMT is expected to ensure effective management of the relationship with the organizational stakeholders in times of growth and stability but also during periods of decline and crisis (Carmeli and Schaubroeck, 2008).

Appropriate Communication Channels

Business crises are almost inevitable in a fast-paced, constantly changing social media world. When a business is in the midst of a crisis, it's essential to provide stakeholders, employees, and customers with a clear, heartfelt message. The speed and sincerity of the response can be the difference between the business moving forward and suffering irreparable damage.

Preplanning crisis communications can help any organization successfully navigate a public relations nightmare. Proactively preparing leadership teams and employees for any decline or downward spiral can decrease anxiety and foster confidence.

It can also be useful to use social media as a crisis communication tool. Social media platforms including X (formerly Twitter), LinkedIn, Facebook, Instagram, Pinterest, Snapchat, TikTok, and YouTube can be excellent crisis communication tools. During a crisis, these channels can help you provide timely updates and maintain an open line of communication with customers. A business blog is also a great communication tool in a crisis because it allows for more introspection and in-depth information.

Depending on the crisis, you may need to communicate changes in your business's operating hours, online options, available services, and more. To reach your customers, utilize multiple channels, including email, text, and social media.

Consider implementing a toll-free customer service phone number to provide frequent updates and assistance. Additionally, your business's voicemail is an effective way for customers to leave specific questions so you can respond as soon as possible. If you have a brick-and-mortar business, use door signage to share information with customers who visit you in person.

Monitor all available channels to ensure customers' needs are being addressed, and respond as best you can, even if your operations are temporarily closed (Thompson, 2025).

Using these appropriate communication channels will help improve reactions to the crisis issue. Most crisis intensity will typically diminish over time. When things have cooled off, take some time to evaluate your company's crisis response and ask the following questions:

- What strengths did we demonstrate?
- What weaknesses were uncovered?
- How is the company doing now?
- What could be done differently next time there's a crisis?

Enterprises often focus on lots of external communication during a crisis, addressing stakeholder and customer needs. However, it is vital to communicate with the business teams. Employees must be fully briefed on the situation to effectively communicate about the crisis. Additionally, be mindful that team members may experience heightened stress and pressure during a crisis. Supporting the workforce fosters a strong company culture and bolsters resilience, thus helping the business navigate and recover from the crisis more effectively.

Organization Values

An enterprise's organizational values deeply influence how messages are crafted and delivered. Following are the four steps to consider:

- Reflect on the company's core values. Are they focused on transparency, collaboration, or perhaps innovation?
- Think about how these values are mirrored in your communication. For instance, a focus on transparency might mean choosing channels that are open and accessible to all.
- Consider the team's preferences and habits. Do they prefer email, face-to-face meetings, or instant messaging?
- Align the communication channels with these reflections to ensure the messaging isn't just heard but also resonates.

Finally, depending on the crisis, one may have to deal with unhappy customers who feel they have been wronged. Their experience may lead them to leave bad customer reviews that, along with negative press, can hurt the business.

Identifying dissatisfied consumers, customers, vendors or employees early on in an interaction can help to manage or ameliorate the situation more effectively. Some cautionary signs can include the following:

- Verbal aggression—When they raise their voice, use threatening words or interrupts frequently.
- Indecision—When they hesitate, ask many questions and often change their mind, even when lengthy explanations are offered.
- Excessive demands—These often manifest themselves in repeated special requests and constant complaints, despite efforts to satisfy them.
- Distrust—It is also an important indicator and shows up when they ask for additional guarantees, demand detailed explanations, and remain skeptical despite assurances given.
- Impulsivity—It is another behavior to look out for, especially when they make hasty decisions without reflection, then abruptly change their mind.

While it's natural to feel defensive with the situations mentioned above, avoid the critical mistake of being less than truthful to protect your business's image. Don't lie, obfuscate, or shade the truth.

Customer Relations

Managing customer responses and word-of-mouth communication surrounding the crisis can be tricky. You want to prioritize the customer experience while accepting blame for the business's role in the crisis (if appropriate). To ensure the best possible outcome, don't play the blame game. Try to foster a supportive and collaborative attitude in all customer-facing interactions, including on the phone, social media platforms, the company blog, and the press (Thompson, 2025).

Depending on the crisis situation, the enterprise can use the following strategies to appease unhappy customers:

- Offer discounts for a future purchase of products or services.
- Contact the customer directly to apologize.
- Change the policy that caused the issue.
- Offer a refund.
- Communicate with the customers to determine what can make it right.

Prioritizing customers and accepting responsibility are key ways to reduce the situation's negative impact on your business and restore your brand image and when dealing with displeased customers and employees maintain professionalism. Following are some strategies to handle these situations effectively:

- Set clear standards: Establish clear policies and protocols to help individuals manage challenging situations with dignity and respect.

- Be an assertive communicator: Clearly express your opinion to maintain goodwill without alienating people.
- Identify the cause and timeline of the issue: Investigate the cause of the issue and its timeline to clarify whose fault it is. If they do not accept any wrongdoing, reevaluate the relationship.
- Empathy and active listening: Understand and relate to their feelings.

By implementing these strategies, businesses can improve stakeholder satisfaction.

Business Crisis Situations

Successful business crisis management is crucial for organizations and individuals alike. Throughout history, there have been several high-profile cases where crisis management efforts fell short, resulting in disastrous outcomes. The importance of effective crisis management strategies can provide valuable lessons that can be applied to any future crises. Missteps include poor decision-making and lack of preparedness and they will contribute to crisis management failures. Ineffective crisis communication and failed crisis planning leads to disastrous outcomes and public relations nightmares. Learning from these failures and implementing best practices is crucial for effective crisis response (Chaddock, 2023).

For example, **Starbucks**, the brand that popularized modern coffee culture and grew into the second-largest restaurant chain in the world (after McDonald's), found itself at a familiar crossroads, coping with a familiar boardroom melodrama. One crisis at Seattle-based Starbucks began with three consecutive quarters of disappointing results, including declining same-store sales and earnings in its two most recent quarters. The recent revenue misses are the first in about 15 years, when the 2007–2008 Great Recession was ravaging the economy.

A recent challenge is in part due to inflation; the company may be exploiting customers who no longer want to shell out high-priced coffee drinks. That's hardly unique to Starbucks. What is unique and much more difficult to address is that the once-consistent in-store experience has also deteriorated. The highlight of this organizational crisis involves knowing the customer. The product (coffee) matters 100% of the time, but what is also of paramount importance is maintaining an enduring brand that indicates a sense of understanding. This organization has become a store that sells fancy coffees that feel like an extravagance when consumers may be struggling to pay for the basics like rent, mortgages, car insurance, and groceries.

Adding to the crisis issue is that troubles in some of Starbucks' international markets have added to its financial woes. Starbucks is facing fierce competition from rival value chains in China, where same-store sales recently dropped over 10% late quarter.

Starbucks is also seeing economic volatility in the Middle East, where the Israeli Palestinian conflict is ongoing. Additionally, many customers have boycotted Starbucks since late 2023 after the company sued the Workers United union for trademark infringement over a now-deleted social media post expressing solidarity with Palestine.

A second organizational crisis example involves **Meta** (formerly Facebook), which faced a major public relations crisis when it was revealed that personal data of millions of users had been compromised due to a significant security breach. The key issue was data misuse, where the breach involved unauthorized access to sensitive personal information. The ensuing impact was that the scandal led to public outrage, regulatory scrutiny, and a decline in user trust. In the aftermath of this crisis, Meta had to implement enhanced security measures and faced substantial fines from data protection authorities.

How can enterprises efficiently manage a crisis? Both Starbucks and Meta addressed their issues in different ways. There are several conventional factors to initially consider: (a) identify risks, (b) define an action plan, (c) establish a crisis group, (d) designate and train a cadre of spokespersons, (e) define messages to put out, and (f) make space for crisis management.

Clearly, good crisis management starts with anticipation of risks that a company may face. Coordinating a brainstorming session and gathering representatives from all departments to create a complete list of all potential risks is an important first step. Once potential risks are identified, there is a need to define human and material resources to be put in place in order to respond effectively to every crisis situation. A crisis management plan takes into consideration all possible scenarios and provides for operational responses. It is central to be well prepared and to have a response plan ready before a crisis occurs. Why? As you are likely to react differently (less efficiently) under pressure when having to deal with a real crisis.

When a business crisis arises, the need to communicate is immediate. If company operations are disrupted, customers will want to know how they'll be impacted. Employees will be concerned and will want answers. The media will often be contacting the organization for comments. That is the reason you want a prepared and well-documented crisis communications plan. The company must be able to respond promptly, accurately, and confidently during a crisis in the hours and days that follow. Many different stakeholders must be reached with confirmed information specific to their needs and interests. The image of the business can be positively or negatively impacted by public perceptions of the handling of the incident.

Business image was impacted during the Chicago **Tylenol** murders; they were a series of poisoning deaths resulting from drug tampering in the Chicago metropolitan area in 1982. The victims consumed Tylenol-branded acetaminophen capsules that had been laced with potassium cyanide. Seven people died in the original poisonings, and there were several more deaths in subsequent copycat crimes. To reassure the public, **Johnson & Johnson**, the manufacturer of Tylenol, distributed warnings to hospitals and distributors and halted Tylenol production and advertising. The company also advertised in the national media for individuals not to consume any of its products that contained acetaminophen after it was determined that only these capsules had been tampered with. Johnson & Johnson also offered to exchange all Tylenol capsules already purchased by the public for solid tablets.

Johnson & Johnson received positive coverage for its handling of the crisis and in November, it reintroduced capsules in a new, triple-sealed package, coupled with heavy price promotions. Within several years, Tylenol regained the highest market share for the over-the-counter analgesic in the United States (Kleinfield, 1983).

An organization's crisis management plan outlines how the business will respond if a crisis occurs. Planning responses for each crisis will prepare teams and reduce the long-term damage done to an organization. Preserving a positive reputation is paramount. Effective crisis management helps mitigate the impact of negative incidents on brand image and public perception. By handling crises transparently and responsibly, companies can minimize reputational damage and maintain trust among stakeholders. Crises can be unpredictable and challenging to manage, and the crisis communication plan can provide a roadmap for handling the situation and mitigating its impact. By staying prepared and adopting a proactive approach to crisis management, organizations can emerge stronger and more resilient from even the most challenging situations.

Enhancing Creativity

By embracing productive conflict, one can come to recognize the value it brings to the creative process and help assist in the creation of a solid crisis management plan. In the absence of conflict, evaluating creative output can become an exercise in evaluating several iterations of a common idea. When one invites contrasting ideas, one can provide the business the opportunity to evaluate each one individually—and determine its merit as the single most resonating solution to the creative provocation. When one invites conflict into the creative process, one invites creative tension that must be explored, examined, and ultimately resolved. This process yields better, more refined creative output than one with a more harmonious beginning. Of course, it isn't simply enough to change the way you think about conflict—deliberate effort must be made across the organization to ensure that the people and processes are actively working in concert with this.

Business teams from various backgrounds, departments, and working styles can be challenging to navigate. However, if embraced and encouraged, most conflicts can improve creativity and innovation across the entire organization. By standing together, team members can gain new levels of trust in each other and their leaders. Conventional thinking reveals that conflict will be harmful for teamwork and should be kept out of the office, but putting individuals in a conflictual state of mind can enhance their creativity. The workplace can be full of conflict and groups of people, driven by different goals inevitably, find themselves at cross-purposes, and disagreements flare up, regardless of industry or country. Add personality clashes and different personal values into the mix and the firm can become a crucible of professional rivalry. For this very reason, managers are often instructed to downplay conflict as much as possible and to foster and facilitate team harmony because clashes are detrimental to trust, collaboration and creativity. However, what if such conflict could be harnessed by managers to enhance performance?

Most people want harmonious relationships with those around them and when obstacles to achieving that harmony appear, they can become more determined to overcome them. Many individuals define our "self" in relation to those around us. Some are more relational than others.

In a research paper titled *The Combined Effect of Relationship Conflict and the Relational Self on Creativity* (Lee, 2015), it was found that relationship conflict has the positive effect of boosting creativity for relational people, because it motivates them to think harder to find solutions for the conflict.

The researchers also investigated what sparked creativity in more independent individuals. What they found was that a process conflict (i.e., controversy in a group about how a task should be completed or how resources are allocated), rather than a relationship conflict, was equally effective at making them persistent and hence creative.

You cannot depend on your eyes when your imagination is out of focus.
~ Mark Twain

Creative Abilities

Resolving conflict demands creativity. Creativity requires the following abilities: openness, listening, acceptance, mutuality, risk-taking, trust, awareness, collaboration, and practice. These are the same skills required of an improviser. Improvisation requires one to be open to the ideas of others and accept what they offer. One approaches the situation without preconceived ideas. This is the foundation of creative problem solving. This openness allows one the opportunity to listen and "get out of your head" rather than focus on your position or pre-planned strategy. Disputants rarely enter a mediation or negotiation with this frame of reference. It is, therefore, even more important that the mediator enters the session open to possibility. Quieting one's mind so that one can hear the intuitive voice and be open to possibility is the first step in mediation.

Creativity also involves the concept of mutuality. Mutuality is a theory that is not well developed in conflict resolution training. It requires the participants in a session to join symbiotically. Through mutuality, synergy occurs. Synergy is the energy that will move ideas forward at rapid speed. As a mediator, synergy is witnessed when the impasse-dam breaks and the parties begin to talk rapidly, look for options, and make plans for resolving the problem. Mutuality is accomplished through agreement (Gerardi, 2001).

Creative problem solving applies human-centered design principles, practices, and tools to complex problems, enabling individuals, teams, and organizations to unlock innovation and navigate uncertainty in a rapidly changing world. It's all about tapping into the unknown to uncover brand new solutions, ones you've never thought of before or didn't know were possible.

The more complex a problem is, the more nuanced and layered the solution needs to be. Creative problem solving requires that one separate divergent thinking (idea generation and brainstorming) from convergent thinking (idea evaluation and decision-making) as opposed to trying to do both at once.

The ability to creatively problem solve involves gathering observations, asking questions, and considering a wide range of perspectives. It encourages better critical thinking, collaboration, communication, and last but certainly not least, creativity.

Creativity is more important than knowledge.

~ Albert Einstein

Image Repair and Restoration Theory

Johnson & Johnson utilized their crisis plan to respond to the horrific Tylenol crisis to repair their brand image. William Benoit (1995) created image retention theory (IRT) by integrating ideas from corporate apologies and account giving. Account giving is a concept that involves individuals supplying reasons for their actions, as evidenced by an attack or crisis on the organization's character. Image repair basically refers to the strategic communication process undertaken by organizations in response to a crisis or situation that threatens their reputation and public image. It involves the careful selection and implementation of verbal and non-verbal communication strategies aimed at repairing the damaged image, restoring trust, and mitigating the negative impact of the crisis.

The crisis response strategy used to defend and to repair the reputation can involve the following strategies:

- DENIAL: claim that the company was not involved and blame others.
- EVASION: reduce the organizational responsibility for the crisis.
- REDUCTION OF OFFENSIVENESS: endeavor to downplay the crisis.
- CORRECTIVE ACTION: restore or change the situation to pre-crisis state.
- ADMISSION ASK FOR REQUESTING FORGIVENESS: admit guilt, express concern, report corrective action.

When a crisis strikes, organizations can find themselves under extreme scrutiny from the public, stakeholders, and the media. The way they respond will have a substantial impact on its reputation, brand perception, customer loyalty, and long-term success. The enterprise will want to (1) protect its reputation by responding promptly and appropriately; (2) retain stakeholder support; (3) manage public perception by shaping the narrative, correct misinformation, and present their side of the story; (4) preserve customer trust by addressing the crisis openly, demonstrating empathy, and providing reassurance; and (5) consider legal and regulatory deliberations to demonstrate compliance, cooperation with authorities, and a commitment to rectifying any wrongdoing, potentially minimizing legal repercussions.

Another business crisis involved **Pepsi**. They faced significant backlash for its controversial ad campaign featuring Kendall Jenner. The advertisement received immediate negative responses from the public, accusing Pepsi of trivializing social justice movements. However, Pepsi responded swiftly to the crisis by pulling the ad, issuing a public apology, and pausing the campaign.

The brand's immediate and empathetic response helped to minimize the long-term effects of the crisis. By acknowledging their mistake and taking swift action, Pepsi demonstrated a commitment to addressing the concerns of their audience. This crisis management approach showed the importance of timely and sincere actions in mitigating the impact of a crisis.

Crisis management is not only about reacting to crises but also about continuous improvement. By learning from past mistakes, implementing preventive measures, and adapting to change, organizations can enhance their crisis management capabilities.

Often enterprise leaders may make errors in their crisis communication. Some mistakes to be watchful for include the following:

- Not being truthful and making situation go from bad to worse
- Having untrained leadership that cannot navigate the crisis
- Not listening to stakeholders' feedback
- Being inconsistent
- Not communicating and eroding trust

From preparation to response and transparency to evaluation, organizations and individuals must navigate crises with confidence to eventually come out stronger on the other side. This involves the dissemination of timely, accurate, and relevant information to stakeholders, including employees, customers, media, government entities, and the general public, in order to effectively respond to and mitigate the impact of the crisis. Accurate information enables organizations to have a comprehensive understanding of the crisis, make informed decisions, and communicate effectively so it is vital to determine reliable sources of information for gathering accurate and up-to-date data about the crisis. This can include internal sources, such as subject matter experts, operations teams, and relevant departments, as well as external sources like government agencies, emergency services, industry experts, and media outlets. Establishing an efficient system to monitor multiple channels for information related to the crisis is also important.

Fixing a business image matters because it affects: (1) customer trust; (2) market position; and (3) long-term success. Fixing a damaged brand image takes planning.

- Acknowledge the issue: Admit there's a problem. A real problem. This shows the company is responsible and willing to fix it.
- Take corrective action: Fix what went wrong. Bad product? Make it better. Poor service? Retrain staff. Change policies, even. All to stop it happening again.
- Transparent communication: Honesty matters. Talk to customers. Tell them what's being done to fix the problem. Keep them in the loop.

Finally, crisis communication is not a one-size-fits-all approach. It requires adaptability, empathy, and a commitment to transparency. Authentic language and tone, prompt and consistent communication, and the use of appropriate channels help build credibility and establish meaningful connections with stakeholders (Abbas, 2023). Straightforward steps to create a crisis plan are to (1) create a team; (2) evaluate any risk; (3) determine possible impact; (4) design a response; (5) solidify a plan; and (6) review and reevaluate.

References

Abbas, T. (2023). *12 Important Steps in Crisis Communication*. Change Management Insight. changemanagementinsight.com.

Benoit, W. L. (1995). *Accounts, Excuses and Apologies: A Theory of Image Restoration*. Albany, NY: State University of New York Press.

Caplan, G. (1961). *An Approach to Community Mental Health*. New York: Grune & Stratton.

Carmeli, A., and Schaubroeck, J. (2008). Organizational crisis-preparedness: The importance of learning from failures. *Long Range Planning*, *41*, 177–196.

Chaddock, L. (2023). *Bad Crisis Management Examples in Companies*. Salt Lake City, Utah: Sentiment.

Gerardi, D. (2001). Developing creativity and intuition for resolving conflicts: The magic of improvisation. *Mediate.com*.

Griffith, D., and Goodwin, C. (2016). *Conflict Survival Kit: Tools for Resolving Conflict at Work*. Upper Saddle River, NJ: Pearson.

Kleinfield, N. (1983). Tylenol's rapid comeback. *The New York Times*, *132*(45804).

Lee, S. (2015). Conflict is good for creativity. *INSEAD Knowledge*. Daejeon, South Korea Association to Advance Collegiate Schools of Business.

Thompson, J. (2025). *6 Effective Strategies for Communication in a Crisis*. Los Angeles, CA: Business.com.

10 Risk Management

Effective risk management takes a proactive and preventative stance to risk, aiming to identify and then determine the appropriate response to the business and facilitate better decision-making. Many approaches to risk management focus on risk reduction, but it's important to remember that risk management practices can also be applied to opportunities, assisting the organization with determining if that possibility is right for it.

Risk Defined

How is the concept of risk defined? Plainly put, risks are the things that could go wrong with a given initiative, function, process, project, and so on. There are potential risks everywhere. Companies should think about not seeking simply to avoid risks, but to integrate risk considerations into day-to-day decision-making.

- What are the opportunities available?
- What could be gained from those opportunities?
- What is the business's risk tolerance or risk appetite (i.e., how much risk is the company willing to take on)?
- How will this relate to or affect the organization's goals and objectives?
- Are these opportunities aligned with business goals and objectives?

Preliminary conversations about risks can develop by asking, "What could go wrong?" or "What if?" Within the business environment, identifying risks starts with key stakeholders and management, who first define the organization's objectives. Afterward, with a risk management program in place, those objectives can be scrutinized for the risks associated with achieving them. Although many organizations focus their risk analysis on financial risks and risks that can affect a business's bottom line, there are many types of risks that can affect an organization's operations, reputation, or other areas.

A substantial spectrum of skillfulness in risk management can be broadly described as a crisis management maturity model that ranges from reactive

DOI: 10.4324/9781042000258-11

to proactive—or even pre-emptive action (Marker, 2020). The different approaches along a crisis management maturity model, from most to least advanced, are as follows:

- Pre-emptive crisis management: This approach seeks to prevent or resolve a crisis at its earliest sign.
- Proactive crisis management: In this approach, organizations take initiative early in the crisis and seek to shape how events unfold.
- Responsive crisis management: This occurs when there is little warning of a crisis. However, thoughtful and quick analysis can lead to effective action that accounts for long and short-term results.
- Reactive crisis management: This is often a panic-driven or knee-jerk reaction. Emotions like fear play a leading role, and objective thinking is largely absent from the crisis response. The company faces crises defensively and, following the crisis, the business may experience problems, high turnover of senior leaders, or even business failure. Reactive communication is best exemplified in scenarios where an organization or individual responds to an unexpected crisis or event. A classic example is a company addressing a sudden public relations issue. The company may not have anticipated the crisis, but it quickly formulates a response to the emerging situation, often involving public statements, press releases, or social media engagement. This response is aimed at controlling damage, clarifying misunderstandings, and maintaining public trust.

Risk Control and Mitigation

Risk management as a discipline has evolved to the point that there are now common subsets and branches of risk management programs, from enterprise risk management (ERM) to cybersecurity risk management, to operational risk management (ORM), to supply chain risk management (SCRM). Supply chain risk management is the process of finding and addressing potential vulnerabilities in a company's supply chain. SCRM aims to minimize the impact of these risks on a company's operations, reputation, and financial performance. Supply chain management is essential to business operations. But amid globalization, supply chains have become increasingly complex and interconnected. Companies rely on a vast ecosystem of suppliers, manufacturers, distributors, and logistics professionals to deliver goods and services to customers around the world. Implementing a SCRM strategy is a way for companies to build the resilience to navigate uncertainty and ensure business continuity. With proactive preparedness, companies can avoid or minimize disruptions, reduce costs, improve quality, and enhance customer satisfaction. SCRM also assists companies to with regulations, protect their brand reputation and foster sustainability (McGrath and Jonker, 2025).

The key goals of risk management are to (1) protect assets and individuals; (2) safeguard business continuity; (3) comply with laws, guidelines, and regulations; and (4) preserve business reputation and stakeholder confidence.

Risk management is an integral component of any business strategy. It helps businesses and individuals protect against financial expenses, inefficiencies, reputational damage, and other potential losses. The root causes of risks are both internal (such as human error or system failures) and external circumstances (such as global crises, climate change, or technological advancements). When unforeseen events occur, organizations must bear the consequences.

The possible risks might be minor, such as a temporary cost increase. However, they could also be catastrophic and lead to serious ramifications, including major financial burdens, loss of reputation, or even business closure, and by adopting a comprehensive and proactive approach to risk management, businesses can protect themselves and respond when threats are present.

In essence, risk management is not just about preventing negative outcomes but also about enabling positive ones to support the overall success and sustainability of a business. Companies that adopt and continuously improve their risk management programs can reap the benefits of improved decision-making, a higher probability of reaching goals and business objectives, and an augmented security posture. But, with risks proliferating and the many types of risks that businesses face today, organizations should establish and optimize risk management processes (Villanueva, 2023). The risk control and mitigation process could be handled by:

- Avoidance—changing policies and plans to eliminate the risk.
- Reduction—implementing solid measures to lower the likelihood or impact.
- Transference—using insurance or contracts to shift responsibility.
- Acceptance—tolerating modest risks if the cost of control exceeds benefit.

Leadership Skills

According to Regina Phelps (2018), a noted expert in the field of emergency management and continuity planning, there are seven essential skills members of an organization's leadership team must possess and develop to navigate critical events effectively, protect their people, and maintain business continuity: situational awareness, improvisation, creativity and adaptability, decisiveness, action, communication, and reevaluation. At its straightforward definition, risk management is a systematic process for identifying, evaluating, and responding to potential threats to an organization. The goal is to reduce the likelihood of risks occurring and their potential impact. Risk management can help improve decision-making and reduce the quality of threats that organizations face. It can also help organizations balance the costs and benefits of different actions.

Business leadership can take many different forms. The goal of business leadership is to find the leadership model that works best for a particular company and its team of employees. One's leadership style becomes more evident within growth of the company and one's career, but typically leadership styles fall into three areas:

- Autocratic: Leaders and those in charge have final decision-making power. Feedback and solicitation from others are little to non-existent.
- Democratic: Everyone is given the same opportunity to contribute to the organization. Team members are encouraged to provide feedback.
- Unrestrictive: Under this leadership style, team members are encouraged to take control of their decision-making. Team members are responsible for managing themselves with little input from leadership directly.

Most leaders will fall into certain styles and being aware of your leadership style taps into your emotional awareness and allows you to better understand how your style impacts the workers around you.

Successful leadership crisis and risk management don't just happen by accident. Being ready to meet the moment requires three things from all of us in the fields of risk management, enterprise resiliency, and crisis management:

- Be in a constant state of readiness. Since you won't know the *precise nature* of the crisis in advance (timing, location, or specifics required at the time), people who may be managing a crisis must always be in a constant state of readiness, as near to instantaneous as possible.
- Have a wide range of contingencies at your disposal so you will be prepared for many possibilities.
- Be able to take initiative, which involves being able to complete tasks without asking for guidance or assistance.

Businesses can't operate without risk. Economic, technological, environmental, and competitive factors introduce obstacles that companies must not only manage but also overcome. According to some recent research, organizations that embrace strategic risk management are five times more likely to deliver stakeholder confidence and better business outcomes and two times more likely to expect faster revenue growth.

> *The first few hours after a crisis breaks are critical. The way in which a company responds can mean the difference between a quick recovery and a prolonged disaster.*
>
> ~ John D. Rockefeller

Risk management is about identifying, assessing, and taking steps to minimize or mitigate risks to ensure smooth sailing. Some key aspects of risk management include the following:

- Risk identification: Spotting potential risks that could affect the project or organization.
- Risk assessment: Evaluating the likelihood and impact of these risks.

- Risk mitigation: Planning and implementing actions to reduce the impact of risks. Risk mitigation involves identifying, analyzing, and acting to reduce or control risks, which can stem from a wide range of potential threats. Effective risk mitigation involves several strategies that can be applied to different risks. The primary aim is not to eliminate all risks but rather to minimize their potential impact on your organization or project.
- Monitoring and reviewing: Keeping an eye on identified risks and being alert for new ones.

In business, risk management covers areas like financial risks, operational risks, strategic risks, and compliance risks. It's a crucial part of ensuring long-term stability and success. In some cases, effective risk management proactively protects an organization from incidents that can affect its reputation. Business risk is especially pressing for those whose reputations depend on the trust of key constituents. For example, airlines are particularly susceptible to franchise risk because of unforeseen events, such as flight delays and cancellations caused by weather or mechanical failure. While such incidents are considered operational risks, they can be incredibly damaging. Some examples of internal and external risks that could disrupt business performance include the following:

- Financial: cash flow issues, market instabilities
- Operational: system failures, supply chain disruptions
- Strategic: poor decision-making, competition activities
- Compliance: legal or regulatory breaches
- Cybersecurity: data breaches, hack, cyberattacks

Operational Risks Instances

In 2016, **Delta Airlines** experienced a national computer outage, resulting in over 2,000 flight cancellations. Delta dealt with these serious computer troubles in 2016 caused by a power outage at its Atlanta hub. At that time, some 2,300 flights were canceled, and Delta was hit with a $150 million pre-tax charge. Delta also took a hit on its reputation as a reliable airline that prided itself on canceling cancellations. While Delta bounced back, the incident illustrates how mitigating operational errors can make or break an organization.

There are several different risk management practices that an organization can use, depending on its size and specific needs. Some standard examples include the following (Guevara, 2023):

✓ Compliance risks—Companies need to keep an eye on their compliance regularly. This means checking all their current processes, procedures, and technologies, and making sure they stay up to date. A risk management system can help with this.

✓ Safety risks—Risk management can also be best applied for safety risks inside the company. This way, any injuries or dangers can be prevented beforehand.
✓ Information security risk—Ever heard of a data breach? As technology begins to advance, more and more people find ways to hack into a company system to steal their cyber data. By using risk management, companies can carefully plan out how to enhance their information and cybersecurity networks.

All companies face risk; without risk, rewards are less likely. The flip side of this is that too much risk can lead to business failure. Risk management allows a balance to be struck between taking risks and reducing them. Effective risk management can add value to any organization. Companies operating in the investment industry rely heavily on risk management as the foundation that allows them to withstand market crashes. An effective Risk Management Framework seeks to protect an organization's capital base and earnings without hindering growth. Furthermore, investors are more willing to invest in companies with good risk management practices. This generally results in lower borrowing costs, easier access to capital for the firm, and improved long-term performance (Eichler, 2024).

A structured set of guidelines and best practices that help organizations identify, evaluate, and manage risks is labeled as Risk Management Framework (RMF). This framework will identify, evaluate, mitigate, and monitor risk. The RMF was initially designed for use by federal agencies but could be easily adopted by organizations operating in the private sector. Businesses cannot exist without exposing themselves to risks such as IT problems, litigation, and loss of capital. While it is impossible to eliminate all risks involved in running a business, they can be minimized.

A well-implemented Risk Management Framework can create more certainty to an organization's operations by providing a defined approach to risk identification and mitigation. The key benefits of an RMF include the following:

- Proactive threat detection: Helps anticipate notable threats. Spotting them early can reduce the chances of their unnoticed escalation and subsequent disruption to operations.
- Data-driven decision-making: Enables real-time visibility of crucial data, such as risk limits and real-time compliance posture, serving as a playbook for making informed decisions.
- Improved reputation: Customers and investors are more likely to choose organizations that maintain a robust RMF. A business also gets a blueprint to comply with industry standards and regulations more easily, which further strengthens its reputation.
- Better organizational resilience: Besides preventing risks, an RMF acts as a buffer during unfavorable events with built-in procedures to withstand and recover from active threats without too much disruption.

Table 10.1 Core components of risk management

Component	*Function*
Risk documentation	Find potential threats across all business operations
Risk assessment	Appraise impact of the risk(s)
Risk mitigation	Create strategies and actions to reduce risk(s)
Risk monitoring	Track and control risk(s)
Risk reportage	Ensure transparency and accountability for risk decisions

Five core components of a Risk Management Framework are included in Table 10.1.

On September 2, 2011, the Colorado Department of Public Health and Environment (CDPHE) notified CDC of seven cases of listeriosis reported since August 28. On average, Colorado reports two cases of listeriosis annually in August. By September 6, all seven Colorado patients interviewed reported eating cantaloupe in the month before illness began, and three reported eating cantaloupes marketed as "Rocky Ford." To manage this unforeseen and deadly risk, Jensen Farms issued a press release recalling it cantaloupe due to a potential link to a multi-state outbreak of listeriosis. The organization, as part of its risk management program, worked with the Food and Drug Administration (FDA) and the State of Colorado to remove the product from the marketplace.

The ensuing investigation revealed that water had pooled on Jensen's packing facility and was not easily cleaned or sanitized and the condensation promoted the growth of listeria monocytogenes. Eventually, Jensen Farms, a small, family-owned agricultural company, was closed and its crops destroyed. However, other cantaloupe growers suffered as well because the uncertainty created problems for them as consumers became fearful of the product and avoided all cantaloupe (Coombs, 2014).

Months before the outbreak, President Obama signed into law a food safety bill designed to shift the focus of federal regulators from responding to contamination to preventing it. The US Food and Drug Administration called the Colorado outbreak "the latest illustration of the continuing need for a strong food-safety program." Its investigation found multiple problems, and they also stated that the rare move to charge the Jensens was intended to send a message to food producers. They pleaded guilty to misdemeanor counts of introducing adulterated food into interstate commerce, which carried penalties of up to six years in prison and $1.5 million in fines. They pleaded not guilty to criminal charges and their attorneys argued in court filings that the case had already prompted a new awareness of food safety law, and the strict liability imposed on producers and food processors (Marklein, 2014).

As part of the risk management protocol in this case, an environmental assessment was completed by a multi-disciplinary team with expertise in produce safety, agriculture, veterinary medicine, epidemiology, microbiology, environmental health, and sanitation from FDA, the Colorado Department of Public Health and Environment, the Colorado Department of Agriculture, and Prowers County Department of Health. The team used Good Agricultural Practice (GAP) guidance and principles to develop hypotheses regarding potential routes for contamination of cantaloupes in the field. Areas of focus for the agricultural risk production operations include:

- Agricultural water
- Soil amendments
- Growing and harvesting practices
- Animal intrusion adjacent land use
- Employee health and hygiene practices

Much of the environmental risk assessment included in-depth interviews with Jensen Farms management regarding their food safety practices and procedures, as well as on-site visits to the farm, packing facility, and cold storage, and environmental and finished product sampling. Areas of vital focus pointed to facility and equipment sanitary design, cleaning and sanitizing practices, washing and drying of cantaloupes, cooling of cantaloupes, storage of cantaloupes, and transportation.

Managing Risk

Enterprise risk management is about assessing and prioritizing risks to minimize, monitor, and control the impact of unfortunate events or to maximize the realization of opportunities. Several core concepts of risk assessment are as follows:

- Qualitative assessment: Evaluating the severity and impact of risks in a more descriptive manner.
- Quantitative assessment: Using numerical methods to evaluate the likelihood and impact of risks.
- Risk matrix: A tool to prioritize risks based on their likelihood and impact.
- Risk appetite: Understanding the level of risk your organization is willing to accept.
- Avoidance: Eliminating a risk by not engaging in the activity that leads to it.
- Reduction: Implementing measures to reduce the impact or likelihood of the risk.
- Transfer: Outsourcing or insuring against the risk.
- Acceptance: Acknowledging the risk and preparing to deal with its consequences.

Effective risk management ensures that risks are adequately controlled and that the organization can continue to achieve its objectives even in the face of uncertainty. Managing business risk is crucial for maintaining a healthy and resilient organization. Steps that can effectively manage business risk include the following:

Step 1: SWOT

- SWOT analysis: Assess strengths, weaknesses, opportunities, and threats.
- Historical data review: Look at past incidents and near misses to identify recurring risks.
- Industry research: Remain updated with industry trends and potential risks.

Step 2: Risk analysis

- Qualitative analysis: Rank risks based on severity and likelihood using a risk matrix.
- Quantitative analysis: Use statistical methods to estimate the financial impact of risks.

Step 3: Mitigation strategies

- Avoidance: Adjust plans to avoid risky activities.
- Reduction: Employ controls and safeguards to minimize risk impact.
- Sharing: Transfer risks through insurance or partnerships.
- Retention: Accept minor risks and budget for potential impacts.

Step 4: Implementation controls

- Policies and procedures: Establish clear guidelines to manage identified risks.
- Training and awareness: Ensure employees are aware of risks and trained in mitigation strategies.
- Technology: Utilize software and tools for risk monitoring and management.

Step 5: Monitoring and reviewing

- Nonstop monitoring: Regularly track risk indicators and performance.
- Audits and inspections: Conduct periodic audits to ensure compliance with risk management plans.
- Feedback mechanisms: Collect feedback from employees to identify new risks and improvement areas.

Step 6: Crisis management

- Emergency response plan: Develop and communicate a plan for handling emergencies.
- Crisis communication: Establish clear communication channels for stakeholders during a crisis.

Strength, Weakness, Opportunity, and Threat

Using the template below can help to assess the strengths, weaknesses, opportunities, and threats of an organization, a specific product, service, project, or policy. Dividing the analysis into these four quadrants helps clarify the existing forces that will affect your organization's future. The analysis helps with strategic planning by providing valuable insights and helps teams make informed decisions, set realistic goals, and create effective strategies to achieve success.

Effectively managing business risk means being proactive and prepared, rather than reactive. It's about creating a culture of risk awareness and making it an integral part of the business strategy.

In many cases, risk is difficult to talk about. Multiple studies have found that people overestimate their ability to influence events that, in fact, are heavily determined by chance. We tend to be overconfident about the accuracy of our forecasts and risk assessments and far too narrow in our assessment of the range of outcomes that may occur (Kaplan and Mikes, 2012).

We also tend to anchor our estimates to readily available evidence despite the known danger of making linear extrapolations from recent history to a highly uncertain and variable future. We often compound this problem with a confirmation bias, which drives us to favor information that supports our positions, typically successes, and suppress information that contradicts them (typically failures). When events depart from our expectations, we tend to escalate commitment, irrationally directing even more resources to our failed course of action.

Organizational biases also impede our ability to discuss risk and failure. Teams facing uncertain conditions often engage in group thinking. Once a course of action has gathered support within a group, those not yet on board tend to suppress their objections, however valid, and fall in line. Groupthink is especially likely if the team is led by an overbearing or overconfident manager who wants to minimize conflict, delay, and challenges to his or her authority.

Collectively, these individual and organizational biases explain why so many companies overlook or misread ambiguous threats. Rather than mitigating risk, firms incubate risk through the normalization of deviance, as they learn to tolerate apparently minor failures and defects and treat early warning signals as false alarms rather than alerts to imminent danger.

References

Coombs, W. T. (2014). *Applied Crisis Communication and Crisis Management*. Thousand Oaks, CA: Sage.

Eichler, R. (2024). *Risk Management Framework (RMF): Definition and Components*. New York: Investopedia.

Kaplan, R., and Mikes, A. (2012). *Managing Risks: A New Framework*. Boston, MA: Harvard Business Review.

Marker, A. (2020). *Models and Theories to Improve Crisis Management*. Bellevue, WA: Smart Sheet.

Marklein, M. B. (2014). Cantaloupe farmers get no prison time in disease outbreak. *USA Today*, January 28.
McGrath, A., and Jonker, A. (2025). *What is SCRM*? Armonk, NY: IBM.
Phelps, R. (2018). *Crisis Management: How to Develop a Powerful Program*. San Fransico, CA: Chandi Media.
Villanueva, E. (2023). *Risk Management 101: Process, Examples, Strategies*. Cerritos, CA: Audit Board.

11 Business Risk Management and Compliance

Business risk management (BRM) is a methodology that looks at risk management strategically from the perspective of the entire firm or organization. It is a top-down strategy that aims to identify, assess, and prepare for potential losses, dangers, hazards, and other potentials for harm that may interfere with an organization's operations and objectives and/or lead to losses.

- Business risk management (BRM) is a firm-wide strategy to identify and prepare for hazards with a company's finances, operations, and objectives.
- BRM allows managers to shape the firm's overall risk position by mandating that certain business segments engage with or disengage from activities.
- Traditional risk management, which leaves decision-making in the hands of division heads, can lead to siloed evaluations that do not account for other divisions.
- Successful BRM strategies can mitigate operational, financial, security, compliance, legal, and many other types of risks.

Organization risk management takes a holistic approach and calls for management-level decision-making that may not necessarily make sense for an individual business unit or segment. Thus, instead of each business unit being responsible for its own risk management, firm-wide surveillance is given precedence.

It also often involves making the risk plan of action available to all stakeholders as part of an annual report. Industries as varied as aviation, construction, public health, international development, energy, finance, and insurance all have shifted to utilizing ERM.

BRM can work to minimize firm-wide risk as well as identify unique firm-wide opportunities. Communicating and coordinating between different business units are key for BRM to succeed, since the risk decision coming from top management may seem at odds with local assessments on the ground. Firms that utilize BRM will typically have a dedicated enterprise risk management team that oversees the workings of the firm.

BRM is a systematic approach to identifying risks associated with running a business, assessing their likelihood and potential impact, and developing

DOI: 10.4324/9781042000258-12

strategies to manage and mitigate them. Most businesses have some kind of risk management program in place. But in "traditional" risk management, the management is typically left in the hands of separate divisions or departments. By contrast, BRM is a holistic approach, requiring communication and coordination between business units to identify and manage risks across the entire organization. Many companies have established a BRM team that includes stakeholders from several key departments.

> *The point of enterprise risk management is not to create more bureaucracy, but to facilitate discussion on what the really big risks are.*
>
> ~ Thomas Stanton

Strategic Risks/BRM

The risks that business risk management (BRM) addresses cut across most departmental boundaries. These include strategic risks, which involve activities related to achieving business objectives. They also include financial risks that need to be resolved such as debt levels, cash flow shortfalls, or investments that could harm the business's bottom line. New technologies, notably generative AI technologies such as ChatGPT, could disrupt many companies' business models and open them up to possible compliance challenges. Insufficient cybersecurity can cause crucial company or customer data to fall into the hands of cybercriminals. There are legal risks that need to be managed such as lawsuits involving contracts or other business agreements. Then there are the risks associated with compliance—not meeting regulatory requirements such as Sarbanes–Oxley regarding financial reporting, for instance.

The Sarbanes–Oxley Act (sometimes referred to as the *SOA* or *SOX*) is a US law to protect investors by preventing fraudulent accounting and financial practices at publicly traded companies. Passed in 2002 in the wake of a series of corporate scandals and the bursting of the dot-com bubble, Sarbanes–Oxley imposed a number of reporting, accounting, and data retention mandates to ensure that business practices at big companies remain above board. The SOX Act is a product of a series of scandals that took place around the turn of the millennium. Several publicly traded companies—**Enron** and **WorldCom** were two of the most prominent—used accounting trickery, shell corporations, and other fraudulent techniques to hide business losses from the public and keep stock prices artificially high. Executives and board members used this deception to enrich themselves, cashing out and leaving investors (and, in Enron's case, employees who had been urged put their retirement into company stock) holding the bag when the deception could no longer be maintained and the stock price collapsed (Fruhlinger, 2020).

Business risk management also includes operational risk management (ORM), which focuses specifically on identifying, assessing, and managing risks related to the organization's day-to-day operations. These can include risks associated with technology, regulatory compliance, and onboarding vendors. Like BRM, ORM seeks to reduce risks. However, the risks ORM addresses are unintentional risks, such as employees who accidentally open up company data systems to cybercriminals. Besides managing all types of risk, BRM can also help an organization to optimize certain intentional strategic risks—those that could bring in new customers, new product lines, and new ways to reduce expenses and improve performance.

There are innumerable reasons why business risk management is essential. Most notably, it allows organizations to be proactive in identifying and monitoring potential internal and external risks rather than simply reacting to them after they occur. It also establishes protocols for mitigating those risks that an enterprise simply can't avoid. An additional key reason a business should establish a BRM program is to enhance its ability to operate more efficiently and profitably. By raising the profile of the potential dangers a company faces, BRM protocols can help inform strategic decision-making and implementation while also minimizing losses from potentially damaging risks.

By openly and transparently sharing information about risk and mitigation, a company-wide risk management initiative can keep all employees and other stakeholders aware of risks and risk management protocols. This can be beneficial when employees interact with customers about potential risks. That in turn can reassure all stakeholders about a company's resilience and durability.

Effective BRM starts with the risk management team having a deep understanding of the organization's internal and external risk profile, supported by risk assessments that gather insights from a wide set of stakeholders. Often supported by audit committees, risk managers must conduct ongoing assessments that incorporate input from across the organization. This threat detection process empowers the team to analyze and implement risk mitigation strategies that enable the organization to thrive.

It is essential that the risk management team work closely with the organization's board to ensure they are aware of the most consequential risks facing the organization, such as market trends, regulatory changes, and supply chain disruptions. Understanding the operational threats and overall risk landscape will help ensure the board is making well-informed decisions that enhance resilience.

Risk managers should also familiarize the board with the risk management strategies already in place. This awareness ensures that board actions and decisions support ongoing risk mitigation efforts and create opportunities to strengthen the risk management team (Rogula, 2025).

Risicum

In its broadest sense, risk means exposure to adversity. The Concise Oxford Dictionary defines risk to imply something bad, "the chance of bad consequence, loss, etc." Webster's defines risk in a similar manner to imply bad outcomes, "a measure of the possibility of loss, injury, disadvantage or destruction." Some believe that the origin of the word "risk" is either the Arabic word *risq* or the Latin word *risicum*. The Arabic *risq* has a positive connotation, signifying anything that has been given to a person and from which this person can draw profit or satisfaction. The Latin *risicum*, on the other hand, implies an unfavorable event, as it originally referred to the challenge that a barrier reef presents to a sailor. The Greek derivative of the Arabic *risq*, which was used in the twelfth century, relates to chance outcome in general. It may not be clear that what is given by God (according to the Arabic *risq*, which is always good) relates to risk, a situation that is typically understood to imply the potential of something bad (or something good) happening. However, what *risq* and risk have in common is uncertainty of the outcome. There is no guarantee that *risq* would come, and if it does, there is no guarantee how much it will be (Moosa, 2007).

Business is complex and regulations can be challenging. Too much risk is bad for business, and too much governance is bad for business, too. One can't achieve proper governance, risk management, and compliance unless one uses smart technologies and processes to manage complexity . . . easily and efficiently. Protect the business from the potentially devastating risks of noncompliance while reducing your costs in a very big way.

The major benefits of keeping risk and compliance in balance include the following:

- Taking a process-focused approach to risk and compliance management
- Managing compliance activities comprehensively, from testing to external audit
- Efficiently analyzing and evaluating compliance and operational risks
- Identifying risk-relevant processes and affected line items
- Automatically escalating issues for resolution
- Preparing, planning, executing, and reporting on your company's audits
- Updating management via an up-to-the-minute graphical dashboard
- Designing and implementing document controls, tests, and risk assessments
- Monitoring and retesting improvements in the shortest possible time
- Decreasing any risk of penalties

Risk compliance is the possible damage to an organization that can result from not following laws, regulations, or industry standards. This damage can be financial, legal, or reputational. Compliance risk can impact organizations of all sizes, from small businesses to large enterprises. For example, a small health clinic can face compliance risk if it doesn't meet HIPAA standards, just like a large hospital system.

To manage compliance risk, organizations can apply these six concepts:

- Identify applicable laws and regulations: Understand which laws, regulations, and standards apply to the organization.

- Find areas of non-compliance: Determine where the organization isn't meeting the required standards.
- Implement controls and procedures: Create processes to ensure compliance with the relevant laws and regulations.
- Stay up to date: Keep track of changes to the laws, regulations, and standards that affect the business.
- Monitor and report: Use a continuous monitoring process to track progress and report on compliance.
- Assess third-party risk: Build a process to assess the risk of non-compliance from third parties and vendors.

Compliance Risks

The best way to limit risk is to find potential soft links. Human error, server misconfigurations, and even an oversight in application logic are compliance risks. Though distinct, risk management and risk compliance are deeply interconnected. Risk management is proactive and strategic, while compliance is reactive and tactical. Together, they form a unified defense system. Several common compliance risks:

- Human error. Phishing and social engineering succeed because people make mistakes. If employees are not regularly trained on common cyber threats, data is at risk.
- Lack of monitoring. Compliance regulations often require data monitoring. With monitoring, administrators can identify active threats and get alerts when there's a data breach. Both of which can lessen the severity of a breach and subsequent fines.
- Improper storage. Sensitive data should be stored in encrypted form. Using clear text format puts your organization at greater risk if there's a data breach.
- Failure to audit access. Only authorized and authenticated users should have access to data. Every time someone accesses data it should be registered and recorded. These audit trails are useful in forensic analysis of data breaches.
- Misconfigurations. Simple misconfigurations can lead to severe data breaches. Before production, test configurations across the whole environment.

Compliance management is the process of ensuring an organization is always adhering to any regulatory or legal requirements and industry standards that it is required to comply with. Compliance management programs are critical for avoiding the legal and reputational consequences of non-compliance. It is vital to assess the compliance risk landscape by taking stock of all the regulations, laws, and compliance requirements the organization must operate under, then map any potential risks from a risk register that could compromise compliance. It is also important to use risk quantification methods to determine the financial impact of these risks.

A host of structured processes, policies, and monitoring mechanisms that companies deploy organization-wide to make sure perfect alignment is accomplished with pertinent laws, regulations, industry standards, and internal policies which are a part of business compliance activities. These regulatory compliance activities ensure the business stays on the right path by meeting current ethical expectations, mitigating risks, and maintaining transparency in operations.

Compliance Management

Compliance management is a systematic process organizations follow to ensure adherence to laws, regulations, standards, and ethics. It involves identifying requirements applicable to the industry, developing strategies that align with internal policies, implementing measures to meet goals, and continuous monitoring to address noncompliance. Compliance efforts should occur throughout the organization's lifespan and be regularly reviewed to remain up-to-date as regulations and standards evolve. Regulations and standards play a crucial role in protecting people and their environment. While some enterprises find these as impediments to their operations and profit, there is no denying their significance.

The foundation of compliance management involves outlining the rules, guidelines, and expectations so that employees can confirm lawful and ethical conduct. Policies provide clear instructions on compliance-related matters, including workplace safety, data privacy, and anti-corruption. Procedures detail the steps workers need to follow so they can abide by operational and ethical guidelines. Policies and procedures should be well-written and clearly defined as these standardize organizational behavior and provide a reference point for employees when navigating complex compliance issues. The key to success is collaborating with government agencies and industry leaders and creating compliance-related methodologies to abide by the rules that shape the business landscape (Caburao, 2025).

The main goals of investing time and resources in these compliance management activities ensure conformity with legal and regulatory requisites applicable to the sector and jurisdictions and mitigate and prevent financial, reputational, and operational risks triggered by non-compliance. Compliance risk comes in many forms, and the ones an organization faces will depend on the industry that it operates in and the types of data it handles. Some common types of compliance risk include the following:

Corruption, fraud, and illegal activity: Many countries have laws designed to prevent corruption, fraud, money laundering, bribery, and theft. Good examples of these types of regulations are the US Foreign Corrupt Practices

Act, the Dodd–Frank Wall Street Reform and Consumer Protection Act, and the Anti-Money Laundering Regulation (AML).

The Dodd–Frank Act was passed in 2010 and was dubbed *Wall Street reform* by supporters. The act introduced significant regulatory changes to the financial industry in response to the relaxed oversight of financial institutions that led to the burst of the housing bubble and the resulting financial crisis. The legislation is intended to increase transparency, accountability, and consumer protection in the financial industry.

This act was established under President Barack Obama, parts of it were rolled back under President Donald Trump, and portions have been strengthened under President Joseph Biden. The Dodd–Frank Act remains hotly debated, with detractors arguing that this legislation hinders the competitiveness of US financial firms and that it puts an extra burden on community banks and small financial institutions (Belczyk, 2023).

Data and privacy breaches: Cyber-attacks and other malicious activity very often targets the sensitive data that organizations use to fuel their products and operations, and all it takes to expose it is a misconfiguration or simple human error. This data can be of a deep personal nature, and there is a myriad of laws in place around the world designed to hold organizations accountable for the loss of any of it, including the General Data Privacy Regulation (GDPR).

Environmental protection: Any organization that produces material goods likely deals with waste products and the potential for pollution at some point. Even if an organization doesn't directly manufacture anything, there's a good chance that it's being done at some point in your supply chain. Most countries have laws and regulations designed to prevent pollution and environmental degradation. In the United States, the Environmental Protection Agency enforces most of these regulations, including the Clean Air and Clean Water Acts.

Workplace health and safety: Workplace health and safety regulations are designed to ensure worker safety and prevent accidents, injuries, and deaths on the job. In the United States, the Occupational Safety and Health Administration enforces these laws.

Regulatory changes: Regulations are constantly changing, and new ones are coming into force all the time. Failing to stay abreast of all these changes can put an organization at risk of non-compliance, even if one is not aware of the new requirements.

Business compliance and regulatory laws is a dynamic and ever-evolving field, driven by an intricate web of legislation. Business compliance authorities need to stay informed on key laws and regulations to adapt their companies' compliance programs accordingly.

References

Belczyk, J. (2023). *Corporate Compliance Laws and Regulations You Should Know*. PA: University of Pittsburgh School of Law.

Caburao, E. A. (2025). *What Is Compliance Management?* Sydney, Australia: SafetyCulture.

Fruhlinger, J. (2020). *The Sarbanes-Oxley Act Explained: Definition, Purpose, and Provisions*. San Francisco, CA: CSO.

Moosa, I. (2007). *Operational Risk Management*. New York: Macmillan.

Rogula, J. (2025). *Optimizing Your Enterprise Risk Management Strategy*. New York: Risk Management Magazine.

12 Compliance Staff

A compliance officer is an individual who ensures that a company complies with its outside regulatory and legal requirements as well as internal policies and bylaws. Compliance officers have a duty to their employer to work with management and staff to identify and manage regulatory risk.

Compliance officers have a duty to their employer to work with management and staff to identify and manage regulatory risk. Their objective is to ensure that an organization has internal controls that adequately measure and manage the risks it faces. Compliance officers provide an in-house service that effectively supports business areas in their duty to comply with relevant laws and regulations and internal procedures. The compliance officer is usually the company's general counsel, but not always.

- A compliance officer is an individual who ensures that a company complies with its outside regulatory and legal requirements as well as internal policies and bylaws.
- Compliance officers have a duty to their employer to work with management and staff to identify and manage regulatory risk.
- In the event of a regulatory breach, it is important for the compliance officer to have appropriate disciplinary measures in place to avoid a future recurrence.

A compliance officer is an employee of a company who helps that company maintain policies and procedures to remain within an industry's regulatory framework. The duties of a compliance officer may include reviewing and setting standards for outside communications by requiring disclaimers in emails or examining facilities to ensure they are accessible and safe. Compliance officers may also design or update internal policies to mitigate the risk of the company breaking laws and regulations and lead internal audits of procedures (Srivastav, 2021).

The compliance officer must have a thorough knowledge of the company, and an awareness of where possible regulatory breaches may occur. It is essential that the compliance officer effectively communicate the company's key ethical principles and compliance regulations. Compliance officers organize

DOI: 10.4324/9781042000258-13

regular training sessions for employees to communicate key regulatory changes and updates. This is particularly important in a heightened regulatory environment where change is constant. The compliance officer must work with business units and management to ensure appropriate contingency plans are in place that set guidelines on how to respond to a possible compliance breach.

The compliance staff is also responsible for ensuring that company operations comply with internal standards. Without this type of staff who actively monitors and drives compliance management, companies run the risk of violating applicable laws and regulations, thus exposing themselves to potential reputational damages and fines.

Compliance Guidelines

As compliance guidelines become more stringent, more and more companies, from medium-sized businesses to large corporations, are relying on compliance staff. Compliance personnel ensure that the company stays abreast of regulatory standards and fulfills the role of an in-house expert, keeping an eye on all developments and ensuring that compliance processes are fully implemented.

Compliance officers provide a link between specialist departments and the management. They regulate the flow of information between management and specialist areas, while respecting different responsibilities and confidentiality requirements.

To avoid conflicts of interest, the compliance officer position should not be situated within or report directly to the legal department. Compliance officers ensure that the company complies with the law while ensuring that the business runs smoothly. Ideally, the position is located directly under the board of directors, guaranteeing independence and also a direct reporting line to senior management. This ensures that unfiltered reports reach the management.

Compliance is a complex issue that affects all areas of a company and requires adherence to many laws and regulations. As was stated in the previous chapter compliance and regulatory, laws is a dynamic and ever-evolving field, driven by an intricate web of legislation. As a one-man band, a compliance officer can quickly become overwhelmed, depending on the size of the company. Establishing a compliance department ensures that a team is present to help take on tasks such as those related to the compliance management system, risk assessments and training.

Because compliance staff communicate directly with the management and is involved in business decisions, they also play an advisory role. Unlike external consultants, however, they actively help to shape these business decisions and seek solutions to achieve business objectives while complying with all laws and regulations.

In the event of a regulatory breach, it is important for the compliance officer to have appropriate disciplinary measures in place to avoid a future recurrence. It is the compliance officer's duty to ensure continual monitoring and review of compliance procedures to help identify possible areas where improvements could be made. Compliance officers are expected to provide an objective view of company policies. The influence by other employees, including management and executives, overlooking infractions may result in significant fines or sanctions that may lead to financial loss or even business closure. Larger companies typically have a chief compliance officer (CCO) to direct compliance-related activities.

Compliance Responsibilities

A compliance officer is a vital figure within an organization, responsible for ensuring that the company adheres to all relevant laws, regulations, and internal policies. They play a critical role in mitigating risks, conducting audits, and fostering a culture of ethical behavior and compliance.

Compliance officers develop and implement policies, educate employees on compliance matters, and act as liaisons between the organization and regulatory bodies. Their work ensures that the company operates within legal boundaries and maintains its integrity, protecting it from potential legal and financial repercussions.

The core responsibilities of the compliance officer are risk mitigation and maintaining ethical standards within the organization. It includes the following:

Regulatory adherence: Reviewing regulations and updating internal policies; conducting training sessions to educate employees on compliance standards; and monitoring operations to ensure compliance with established policies.

Audits and risk assessments: Planning and conducting regular internal audits; evaluating risk factors and developing mitigation strategies; and documenting findings and implementing corrective actions.

Reporting violations: Identifying and documenting compliance violations; communicating violations to regulatory bodies as required; coordinating with legal teams to ensure accurate reporting; maintaining detailed records of all reported violations and actions taken; and ensuring timely submission of reports to avoid regulatory penalties.

Risk mitigation is reducing, controlling, or eliminating risks that could hinder an organization from achieving its goals and objectives. Identifying risks, assessing their effect, and applying measures to mitigate their impact are the primary goals. After identifying potential risks, the compliance officer and/or a project team will perform a risk assessment to determine how significant those risks are. This assessment describes the types of risks, their impact on the project if they were to happen, and the probability that these risks would happen. These cost estimates, along with the mitigation costs, guide the choice of appropriate risk mitigation strategies. Risk mitigation is the process of minimizing the impact of potential risks by creating a plan for handling, minimizing, and eliminating setbacks whenever possible (Altomonte, 2025).

Risk management: Identifying potential legal and reputational risks and implementing strategies to mitigate identified risks; developing risk management plans in collaboration with other departments; and regularly updating risk management strategies to reflect new threats.

Compliance reporting: Collecting and analyzing compliance data and preparing comprehensive compliance reports; presenting findings to senior management and regulatory bodies; and ensuring transparency and accuracy in all compliance reports.

Several additional position titles for compliance risk managers are as follows:

- Compliance specialists and compliance analysts
- Regulatory affairs specialists
- Compliance coordinators
- Regulatory specialists
- Compliance associates
- Regulatory analysts
- Compliance consultants
- Regulatory affairs associates
- Environmental compliance specialists
- Risk and compliance analysts

A compliance business representative can also work closely with human/people resources and develop a general intake session, workshop, or questionnaire that may help facilitate future issues, disputes or conflicts. This individual ensures that an organization adheres to regulatory requirements and internal policies. They play a pivotal role in maintaining the integrity and reputation of a company by fostering a culture of compliance and ethics. Their scope of responsibility extends across various industries, including finance, healthcare, and manufacturing, as they interpret and apply complex regulatory frameworks set forth by governing bodies. They should possess a deep understanding of pertinent legal standards and be adept at implementing procedures to prevent, detect, and address any breaches of compliance. Some of the common compliance intake questions are:

- What specific issue, dispute, or conflict brings you here today?
- Describe, in detail, the problem or conflict you are experiencing.
- What result or outcome are you looking for?
- Have you received any feedback from others on your team or the company that would assist in reaching a resolution or settlement?
- Have you taken any steps already in an attempt to resolve this or these issues?
- How can we be of assistance?

Compliance Failure Cases

Compliance fails of 2024 show the real-world consequences of noncompliance for the companies that faltered and also for their customers and employees. The human costs that come from these narratives can't be ignored either.

US regulators fined **TD Bank** nearly $3.1 billion for allowing three separate money laundering schemes to funnel more than $670 million in dirty money through its network. Perhaps the worst part of all this was that the regulators hadn't been investigating TD Bank but rather stumbled onto the money laundering scheme while investigating a Mexican drug cartel (Nicodemus, 2024). Regulators concluded that the chronic underfunding of the bank's anti-money laundering (AML) program by corporate leadership caused the program to atrophy. Over several years, obvious red flags of money laundering activity were missed or ignored. Huge backlogs developed in transaction monitoring and the compiling of suspicious activity reports. Worst of all, the corporate culture de-emphasized the importance of rooting out and reporting potential criminal activity, leaving employees with no motivation to blow the whistle. They knew nothing would be done, so why bother?

A second compliance failure involved US airplane manufacturer **Boeing**. Up until ten years ago, Boring was the envy of corporations around the world. A big part of its success was its exact standards and safety measures. People felt safe flying on their planes. It seems that those days may be gone, and it's directly related to failures in compliance. Boeing's reputation is now in tatters following a seemingly unending series of disasters, including crashes, parts failures, and one airplane door that literally fell off mid-flight.

Much of the trouble started with two fatal plane crashes of 747 MAX airplanes in 2018 and 2019, caused by a malfunctioning flight control system. In the aftermath, the company entered into a deferred prosecution agreement (DPA) with the Department of Justice (DOJ) in 2021, as part of a $2.5 billion settlement. Several more bumps in the road followed, until the beginning of 2024 when a series of in-flight failures led to waves of Boeing plane groundings and inspections. Meanwhile, the DOJ notified Boeing that it had breached the DPA and charged it with making material misstatements to the Federal Aviation Administration regarding compliance and safety issues. The DOJ judged that the company had failed in its attempt to design and implement an effective compliance and ethics program, and The Federal Aviation Administration halted production expansion of the 737 MAX, and the DOJ fined the company another $243.6 million (Mintz and Miller, 2025).

A third compliance failure involved **Capital One**. In 2019, Capital One experienced one of the most significant data breaches in US financial sector history. Over 106 million individuals were affected, with personally identifiable information (PII) including names, addresses, dates of birth, self-reported income, credit scores, and, in some cases, Social Security, and bank account numbers exposed.

Capital One had migrated much of its infrastructure to AWS, relying heavily on cloud-based tools for data storage and application hosting. A misconfigured Web Application Firewall (WAF) was exploited to access AWS metadata services, which then provided temporary credentials. These credentials had permissions to list and download files from Amazon S3 buckets where sensitive data was stored. The breach resulted not from a traditional software vulnerability or outside attacker but from the misconfigured firewall in Capital One's **Amazon Web Services** (AWS) cloud infrastructure. This incident serves as a foundational case for attorneys advising on data governance, cloud risk, incident response, and regulatory compliance.

Three foremost questions about businesses that fail compliance rules are:

- What is the difference between non-compliance and misconduct?
  Non-compliance is a failure to follow laws and regulations, while misconduct implies intentional wrongdoing or improper behavior within the workplace.
- What is the most common non-compliance issue?
  The most common workplace non-compliance issues vary by industry. However, many businesses struggle to keep up with employment laws, including wage and hour laws, anti-discrimination laws and harassment prevention, workplace safety, recordkeeping, and employee benefits.
- Who is held accountable for non-compliance?
  Compliance accountability may impact multiple levels of the organization. Company leaders, such as executives and board members, are responsible for ensuring a compliant culture and adequate controls. Managers and supervisors are also accountable for implementing compliance policies and monitoring their teams. Individual employees can be held responsible if they knowingly violate regulations or company policies. Consequences for non-compliance may apply to the individuals responsible for the violation or to the organization.

References

Altomonte, L. (2025). *What Is Risk Mitigation?* Sydney, Australia: Safety Culture.

Mintz, S., and Miller, W. (2025). *The Story of Boeing's Failed Corporate Culture*. New York: The CPA Journal.

Srivastav, A. K. (2021). *What Is Compliance Officer?* Mumbai, India: Wall Street Mojo.

13 Conflict Management

As a trainer/facilitator for the American Management Association, I have been involved in teaching conflict management as one of the core training courses offered for managers and supervisors. This type of conflict management is a learned skill and one that improves over time and is focused on utilizing strategies to resolve an issue or problem between two or more people. What are the effects of poor conflict management? Disagreements in the workplace are inevitable, as employees have different personalities, goals, and opinions and being able to solve conflict a work in a healthy and effective manner has incredible benefits, including:

Stress reduction: Conflict can be stressful, and everyone handles it differently. Working while under any level of stress is going to impact employees and their well-being. Resolving conflict at work means all parties involved feel heard and accounted for and can work with ease. Stress occurs when people perceive that events are placing excessive demands on them. The relationship between the workplace and our psychological, cognitive, and physiological responses to stress is complex, impacted by a broad set of occupational and work demands as well as environmental stressors.

Retention improvement: As a manager, your job is to create a safe workplace for your employees. That includes dealing with conflict as it arises. A manager who has the best interest in mind for creating a positive work environment—one that includes accepting differences in a healthy manner—is one that an employee will more likely want to stay with.

Better relationships: While conflict is normal and is bound to occur, how it's handled is important for long-term success in the relationship. Dismissing conflict outright is grounds for one or both parties to feel ignored and even resentful. Having the right strategies in place for resolving conflict can lead to better relationships because both parties have the tools to come to a resolution in a productive manner.

DOI: 10.4324/9781042000258-14

Collaboration Strategies

Confronting an enterprise problem should employ problem-solving strategies. Collaboration involves an attempt to work with others to find win–win solutions to the problem at hand (the one that most satisfies the concerns of both parties). The win–win approach sees conflict resolution as an opportunity to come to a mutually beneficial result. It includes identifying your opponent's underlying concerns and finding an alternative that meets each party's concerns. Collaborating may be appropriate:

- When consensus and commitment of other parties are important.
- In a collaborative environment.
- When addressing the interests of multiple stakeholders is required.
- When a high level of trust is present.
- When a long-term relationship is important.
- When you need to work through hard feelings, animosity, etc.
- When you don't want to take full responsibility.

The potential advantages of collaborating are leading to solving the actual problem with win–win outcomes; reinforcing mutual trust and respect to building foundations for effective collaboration in the future; and shared responsibility of the outcome. Some qualifications of collaborating include a requirement to a commitment from all parties to look for a mutually acceptable solutions and may require more effort and more time than some other methods. A win–win solution may not be evident. For the same reason, collaborating may not be practical when timing is crucial, and a quick solution or fast response is required. Once one or more parties lose their trust in an opponent, the relationship falls back to other methods of conflict resolution. Therefore, all involved parties must continue collaborative efforts to maintain a collaborative relationship.

When collaboration is not available, convenient, or working, enterprise parties can look to compromise. Compromising looks for an expedient and mutually acceptable solution that partially satisfies both parties. It can be useful to reach temporary settlement on complex issues. Several possible advantages of compromising are achieving faster issue resolution. Compromising may be more practical when time is a factor and can provide a temporary solution while still looking for a win–win solution. Using compromise may result in a situation where both parties are not gratified with the outcome (a lose–lose situation). It may not contribute to building trust in the long run and may require close monitoring and control to ensure the agreements are satisfactorily met.

Collaboration Risk Management/CRM

Collaborative Risk Management (CRM) is a systematic approach that involves multiple stakeholders working together to identify, assess, and manage risks.

Table 13.1 Collaborative crisis response components

Component	*Description*
Management	Connecting efforts across all employees
Communication	Internal and external sharing of updates
Solution-shaping	Involving all stakeholders to maintain trust
Leveraging	Using all resources for effective responses

Unlike traditional risk management, which often occurs in silos, CRM fosters a culture of collaboration, transparency, and shared responsibility (Sada, 2024). This approach leverages the collective expertise and perspectives of diverse stakeholders to address risks more effectively and enhance organizational resilience. CRM is essential for several reasons:

- Enhanced risk identification: Collaboration among stakeholders helps identify a broader range of risks, including those that may be overlooked in a siloed approach.
- Improved risk assessment: Diverse perspectives contribute to a more comprehensive and accurate assessment of risks.
- Better risk mitigation: Joint efforts lead to more effective and innovative risk mitigation strategies.
- Increased resilience: Collaborative risk management enhances organizational resilience by fostering a proactive and adaptive risk culture.
- Regulatory compliance: Collaborative approaches ensure compliance with regulatory requirements by promoting transparency and accountability.

Collaborative crisis management is important because it protects reputation and credibility, preserves business continuity, and mitigates legal and regulatory risks. Preserving a positive reputation is paramount. Effective crisis management helps mitigate the impact of negative incidents on brand image and public perception. By handling crises transparently and responsibly, companies can minimize reputational damage and maintain trust among stakeholders.

Collaborative crisis response is included in Table 13.1.

Crisis Plan

Undoubtedly, any crises can disrupt normal business operations. Having a crisis management plan in place ensures a structured approach to navigate through challenges swiftly, minimizing operational disruptions and financial losses. Crises can often lead to legal implications or regulatory scrutiny. A well-prepared crisis management strategy, including legal counsel, aids in compliance, reducing potential legal repercussions and associated financial penalties.

Ten essential conflict management strategies include the following:

- Addressing the conflict: Don't overlook the problem.
- Clarifying the issue: Take time to comprehend the cause of the conflict.
- Bringing parties together: Talk with the people involved.
- Identifying a solution: Find a way to resolve the issue.
- Monitoring and follow-up: Check in on the situation after the conflict is resolved.
- Practicing active listening: Understand the other party's perspective and what you can do about it.
- Modeling empathy: Show empathy by acknowledging people's emotions and encouraging them to talk about them.
- Solving problems: Use problem-solving skills to find solutions that work for everyone.
- Negotiating: Exchange information to persuade the other party and reach a settlement.
- Communicating openly: Allow people to express themselves to build healthy relationships.

Identifying early detection of enterprise conflict before it escalates will make it very difficult to manage. Some elements of early intervention that can be undertaken include the following (Herbert, 2023):

Reduce escalation: When conflicts are addressed early, it is less likely for them to escalate into bigger problems. The longer a conflict goes on, the more likely it is for emotions to get involved and for the conflict to become more difficult to resolve.

Save time and energy: Resolving conflicts early can save leaders and their team members a lot of time and energy. The longer a conflict lingers, the more work must be done to resolve the conflict. This can consume a lot of time and resources, ultimately leading to less productivity.

Maintain a positive workplace culture: This type of culture is one in which people feel valued, respected, and supported. When workplaces allow conflicts to fester, it creates an environment that feels like you're walking on eggshells. This leads to decreased job satisfaction, decreased morale, and decreased retention of talent. By addressing conflicts early, leaders can help maintain a positive workplace culture where people feel heard and understood.

Strengthen relationships: When conflicts are resolved early, relationships between team members can be strengthened. By addressing an issue early on, directly, and constructively, team members may gain a better understanding of each other's perspectives and ultimately work more effectively together.

Improve decision-making: Conflicts can have a negative impact on decision-making processes. Sometimes, unconsciously, emotions can get in the way of making the best decision. Leaders can prevent emotions from interfering with the decision-making process.

The TEP Model (Tranquil, Evaluate, Permit)

- Tranquil: Reduce emotional intensity using verbal and non-verbal cues.
- Evaluate: Understand the root cause(s) and emotional triggers.
- Permit: Guide toward resolution with clear, achievable steps

Thomas–Kilmann Study

As introduced in Chapter 2, researchers Kenneth W. Thomas and Ralph H. Kilmann studied workers and their routine conflicts in the workplace in 1974. Over time, they were able to observe a pattern of ways in which people resolved conflict; most methods could be distilled down to five core methods. These five options formed the basis of the Thomas Kilmann Conflict Model Instrument and the Thomas Kilmann Conflict Resolution Model.

Five Thomas–Kilmann Conflict Management Model (1974)

COMPETING (Win–Lose)
COMPROMISING (Win–Win)
COLLABORATING (Win–Win)
AVOIDING (Lose–Lose)
ACCOMMODATING (Lose–Win)

- Collaboration is high assertiveness and high cooperativeness.
- Competition is high assertiveness and low cooperativeness.
- Accommodation is low assertiveness and high cooperation.
- Avoidance is low assertiveness and low cooperation.

Although there are many reasons there are disagreements in business, many conflicts revolve around:

- Personal values or beliefs (real or perceived)
- Perceptions of the issues, problems
- Conflicting goals or objectives
- Power aspects and dynamics
- Communication style

TKM Examples

AVOIDING: When a team member begins to question another member's methodology on a specific issue, the first person tries to change the topic or physically leaves the work space.

COMPETING: The project team leader becomes defensive about their ideas and becomes combative when others state objections.

COMPROMISING: Rival vendors for your organization want to cooperate with your marketing efforts in an attempt to engage more clients/customers.
ACCOMMODATING: When a valued business partner needs to take two days off for important personal reasons, a company leader agrees to pick up the slack and complete some of the task.
COLLABORATING: If the chief executive of IT has major issues with her team's new suggestions for innovation, then she would agree to work with them to arrive at solutions that would be mutually agreed upon.

Good managers/leaders will understand when to use each of these conflict styles. Life is too chaotic to just pick one and stick with it. We must give ourselves permission to move from style to style based on the circumstances. The key is to ensure that the team and organization's goals are at the forefront of these choices each time. It is also important that business leaders understand which style we tend to favor, and how that tendency affects others. For example, competitive leaders may tend to railroad over others and fail to take the time to understand other options. Avoiding leaders may inadvertently build an untrustworthy culture if they aren't willing to address elephants in the room at times. Accommodating leaders may allow others to push their agenda more than is healthy. Even collaborative leaders must remember that there are times when a decision must be made without taking the time to address and include everyone's input (Hedlund, 2019).

The workplace is an intricate maze of some tough circumstances, and this conflict model is simply a tool to help organize ideas and come up with solutions that can achieve consensus and success. The choice of the conflict resolution mode depends on: (1) the immediacy of the problem; (2) the comfort level with assertiveness and cooperation for the given conflict; (3) priority on resolving the problem or on a long-term relationship with the conflicting party; and (4) one's position in the enterprise power hierarchy.

Conflict Styles

The solution to successfully managing conflict is choosing the right style for each situation. For example, it might make sense to use avoidance or accommodation to deal with minor issues, while critical disputes may call for a more assertive approach, like a competitive conflict management style. Important questions to ask are as follows:

- How essential are your needs and wants?
- What will happen if these needs and wants aren't met?
- How much do you value the other person/people involved?
- How much value do you place on the issue(s) involved?
- Have you thought about the outcomes of using differing styles?
- Do you have the time and drive to address the situation right now?

The answers to these questions can help one decide which style to pick in a particular situation based on what you've learned about the various conflict management styles. Conflicts inevitably develop when one spends time with other people, whether at work or home. However, when conflicts aren't resolved, they can lead to various negative consequences. These include the following:

- Hurt feelings
- Resentment and frustration
- Isolation and feelings of depression
- Passive aggression and communication issues
- Increased stress
- Low morale
- Reduced productivity

Many of the most skilled negotiators can shift styles mid-negotiation. One can begin with *competing* to establish seriousness and then move to *collaborating* to explore mutual gains. One can then use *compromising* to close gaps and finally position *accommodating* to achieve goodwill.

American businesses lose $359 billion yearly due to unresolved conflict and low productivity (Kauth, 2020). The physical, emotional, psychological, and interpersonal tolls are incalculable. Can we seek a better understanding of conflict and transform its devastating effects? To reap the benefits of resolving conflict, certain helpful skills should be applied, and there are many conflict resolution skills that are effective for the business space.

- Self-awareness: Self-awareness is recognizing a feeling as it happens. Individuals with high self-awareness have moment-to-moment awareness and navigate life adeptly.
- Self-control: Self-control is the ability to manage unruly impulses and emotions effectively. Because emotions play a central role in conflict, the ability to stay composed despite heightened emotions is essential to constructive resolution.
- Assertive communication: This is a dynamic communication style in which the speaker maintains self-respect, expresses personal needs, and defends their own rights without abusing or dominating others. While an aggressive communication style may shut down a conversation, assertiveness encourages dialogue.
- Collaboration: The goal of collaboration is to consider all the important needs of the primary parties and develop a solution that meets these needs.
- Empathy: The ability to share and understand the emotions and feelings of others. Our understanding of another person's perspective can increase the likelihood of emotional connection and collaboration.
- Listening: Active listening is one of the most underrated and underutilized conflict resolution skills. Listening during conflict achieves key goals,

primarily putting an end to cyclical arguing and opening the door to empathy and understanding.

When dealing with conflict of any kind in the workplace (whether it is with customers, co-workers, or supervisors), it is important to remain calm. Losing one's patience and/or temper will only increase the tension of the situation. How will you remain calm the next time you encounter a situation that is stressful?

Several pointers for remaining calm when interacting with others in the workplace:

- Avoid emotional impulse reactions.
- Does it really matter or is it small stuff?
- Decide how to respond . . .
- How should I respond effectively?
- How much control do I have in the situation?
- Do not attack.
- Discover a way to overcome the initial reaction.
- Generate calmness and understanding.
- Maintain objectivity.
- Promote healthy communication.
- Resolve conflicts constructively and creatively.
- Turn frustration and anger into effective problem-solving (Wilson, 2022).

Conflict management personality types have different indicators of their decision-making interests and strategies. Those who are prone to *thinking* understand the opinions of all parties, create logical alternative solutions, are firm in their stance, and focus on analyzing and tolerating others in the situation. Those who are prone to empathize with the interests of all parties create solutions for growth, would rather change than make others change, and focus on accepting and appreciating others.

Personality types who are prone to *judging* make decisions based on agreed-upon standards, take the necessary time to efficiently solve problem-solve, have a clear idea of the outcome, decide when to review, and don't like to bring up conflict again once it's solved. Those who are prone to *perceiving* use facts and check assumptions, exercise negotiation, actively listen, take breaks, and seek mediators to ensure harmony.

Brainstorming

Adapting to various conflict styles and attempting to flush out varied resolution ideas can be accomplished through brainstorming sessions. Brainstorming can be a good first step in creatively attempting to resolve a problem. Brainstorming boosts creativity, encourages collaboration, and generates a wide range of ideas without fear of judgment. It's a powerful tool for problem-solving and innovation in both group and individual settings. Brainstorming allows individuals to think critically about ideas and solutions, form connections, and share ideas with peers. This allows the workforce to explore and expand their ability to think critically and laterally. Brainstorming for solutions is often hailed as the go-to method for generating a wide range of ideas, from solving complex business problems to coming up with new product concepts and marketing strategies. However, while brainstorming can be incredibly effective, it also comes with its share of limitations. Not all brainstorming sessions produce the desired outcomes, and sometimes, the very openness that makes brainstorming successful can also hinder progress. Groupthink, lack of structure, or the domination of conversation by a few individuals can stifle the creativity of others. Moreover, without proper facilitation and focus, brainstorming can drift into chaotic territory, yielding ideas that are impractical or irrelevant. In a well-facilitated brainstorming session, everyone has the opportunity to contribute ideas, and this democratic approach guarantees that all voices are heard, including those who may not typically speak up in more structured or hierarchical settings. By allowing everyone to contribute, brainstorming taps into the collective intelligence of the group, which often leads to more diverse and creative solutions (Roberts, 2024).

For example, New York City wants to improve its quality of life by changing the design of neighborhoods to be safe, stimulating, healthy, resilient, and clean. The elected leaders and community groups begin by asking for as many ideas as possible from city residents and urban design experts with no constraints such as budget. This technique is a group problem-solving method that involves the spontaneous contribution of creative ideas and solutions. It requires intensive, freewheeling discussion in which every member of the group is encouraged to think aloud and suggest as many ideas as possible based on their diverse knowledge.

This creative method focus principles of (1) quantity over quality; (2) withholding any criticism and immediate feedback; (3) welcoming ideas and thoughts that are "outside the box"; and (4) building on the creative suggestions and drawing connections to ascertain the best solutions.

> *If you wish to advance into the infinite, explore the finite in all directions.*
> ~ Johann Wolfgang von Goethe

Needs Assessment Elements

Offering effective and efficient conflict resolution and negotiation platforms that address individual and company needs is to identify and prioritize the party's needs, which is called a needs assessment. A needs assessment allows for the construction of a more objective picture of needs than merely depending on one person's perspective. To clarify the major substance of a problem, the needs assessment should attempt to develop and answer the following questions:

- What is the most constructive way to define the problem or issue?
- Does the problem/conflict focus on differing, interest, values, perception?
- What are the major central issues?
- Are there secondary or supplementary issues?
- Can these issues be addressed and negotiated?
- What are the significant interests of each party?
- What interests do the parties have in common?
- What are the core options to reach resolution or agreement?
- Are there any constraints that might impact the negotiation process?
- Do the parties have experience using alternative dispute resolution procedures?
- What will a winning agreement/negotiation look like?

Keeping in Mind

- Develop conflict awareness: Differentiate between a disagreement and a conflict.
- Modes of conflict management: Select the appropriate management approach for any situation; understand your own conflict approach.
- Responding to conflict: Communicate assertively without eliciting defensiveness from the other party.
- Handle difficult conversations: Select appropriate language to express ideas clearly; plan for difficult conversations in a way that focuses on achieving desired results: prepare for potential barriers during difficult conversations.

An example of handling a difficult conversation involving a team's underperformance could look like:

ISSUE: The Public Relations team is constantly missing deadlines.
TASK: Matching responsibility with empathy.
TACTIC: Use facts to secure the conversation, then explore any underlying reasons by focusing on individual team member activities and impact.
CONVERSATION STARTER:
"We've observed several missed deadlines recently, and we are concerned about how that's affecting the team and the company. We will need to meet and talk about what's been getting in the way?"

Personality Relationships

Individual psychological orientations in both interpersonal and business orientations can lead to issues with conflict resolution methods. Several dimensions of interpersonal relations can impact the resolution of conflict and crisis (Wish, Deutsch and Kaplan, 1976):

- Cooperation-competition: Such relations as co-workers are usually on the cooperative side, while business rivals are on the competitive side.
- Power distribution: Business partners are typically on the equal side, while boss and employee may be on the unequal side.
- Task-oriented versus social-emotional: Close friends are social-emotional, while business rivals are task-oriented.
- Formal versus informal: Relations within a business bureaucracy tend to be formal, while relationship norms between very close friends are informal.
- Intensity versus importance: Important relationships, as between child and parent are on the important side, while unimportant relationships, as between salesperson and customer are on the superficial side.

The conflict resolution individual in the organization that is tasked with resolving conflict issues will use a style that is consistent with their own orientation to conflict. Three styles of conflict management personalities (Filley, 1975) are as follows:

- The *tough battler*: conveys strategies that show determination to make small concessions to reach tough, but fair agreements.
- The *friendly helper*: a flexible approach to compel the disputants to express understanding for the other side's issues and concerns.
- The *problem solver*: the primary emphasis on satisfying each party's issues and concerns.

Breakdowns in Relationships

Conventional research states that good communication can improve relationships and increase intimacy, trust, and support. The converse is also true: poor conflict management can weaken bonds and create mistrust, and even contempt!

Some examples of negative and even destructive conflict management attitudes and patterns that can exacerbate conflict include the following:

Being self-protective: Rather than addressing complaints with an objective eye and willingness to understand the other person's point of view, defensive people steadfastly deny any wrongdoing and work hard to avoid looking at the possibility that they could be contributing to a problem.

Overgeneralizing: When events happen that negotiators are not be keen on, some blow it out of proportion by making sweeping generalizations.

Being right: It's destructive to decide that there's a "right" way to look at things and a "wrong" way to look at things. Don't mandate that the other side see things the same way, and don't take it as a personal attack if they have a different opinion. Look for a compromise.

Playing the fault game: Some individuals handle conflict by criticizing and blaming the other person for the situation. They see admitting any weakness on their own part as a weakening of their credibility and avoid it at all costs, and even try to shame them for being "at fault."

Avoiding/stonewalling: When one person wants to discuss troubling issues, sometimes people defensively stonewall or refuse to talk or listen. This displays disrespect and, in certain situations, even contempt, while at the same time letting the underlying conflict grow. Individuals often stop communicating and walk away, which escalates the conflict. They take breaks to avoid continuing discussions.

Insisting on resolutions at the wrong time: When there is a rush, team members and the other side to accept quick resolutions without proper time spent on examining the whole issue. Quick fixes may be implemented instead of real solutions.

Mishandling power dynamics: Conflicts that stem from issues related to tradition, hierarchy, and authority can cause problems in company structures and valid concerns are shut down when they are raised by team members who may not be in positions of authority.

Conflict and conflict management is a predictable part of professional enterprise life. When conflicts are not appropriately managed, they will remain unresolved and can escalate, leading to a range of negative consequences, including decreased productivity, high turnover rates, and damage to an organization's reputation. Identifying the causes of conflict is the first step to preventing and managing it. Effective conflict management is crucial for a thriving, harmonious, and productive working environment. The most frequent examples of mismanaged conflict failures, not mentioned above, include the following:

Personality clashes: According to a Charted Institute of Personnel and Development research project, the most common cause of workplace conflict is "differences in personality styles or working." Personality traits, such as introversion versus extroversion, assertiveness versus passivity, and risk-taking versus caution, can create friction. An extroverted, assertive employee might dominate meetings, leaving introverted colleagues feeling overlooked or undervalued.

Conflict can also arise due to how employees manage workplace pressures. Some might become more aggressive or demanding, while others might withdraw or become overly anxious. These differing responses can lead to conflicts in high-pressure situations.

Differences in values: Diverse personal values can lead to disagreements, especially when these influence work decisions and practices. Factors that can lead to conflicts are ethical standards, work ethics, and company policies. Conflicts may arise over company policies that align or misalign with employees' personal beliefs. For example, policies on remote work, gender equality, or corporate social responsibility may be contentious if they do not align with the values of all employees.

Change and uncertainty: Organizational changes often lead to uncertainty about job security, roles, and prospects, causing anxiety and stress among employees. This heightened stress can reduce their ability to cope with additional pressures, leading to conflict. In the absence of clear communication, rumors and misinformation can spread, exacerbating fears and misunderstandings. This can lead to further anxiety and conflicts among employees.

Employees may resist changes due to fear of the unknown or discomfort with new processes and expectations. This resistance can manifest as passive or active opposition, creating friction between employees and management.

Limited access to resources: Inadequate access to resources such as time, money, equipment, or human resources can lead to competition and conflict among employees and this can create high-pressure situations where employees feel stressed about meeting deadlines or achieving targets with insufficient support. This stress can exacerbate conflicts and reduce overall productivity and morale.

Resource scarcity can also lead to a competitive rather than collaborative environment, where employees or departments are less willing to share information, knowledge, or support, fearing that doing so might jeopardize their own resource needs.

Conflict Mishandling

There are three distinct patterns of what mishandling of conflict at the workplace look like. The first is *over assertion* when individuals use their authority to dominate or silence others. This leads to resistance and reputational impairment. The second is *underutilization*. This takes the form of a failure to use legitimate power when needed in the conflict. The consequences are indecision and chaos. The third pattern is *opacity* and is marked by a withholding of data or decision evidence and rationale. This will often breed mistrust in the organization.

Power imbalances occur when one party in a conflict has significantly more power than the other. This disparity can create an environment where the less powerful individual feels vulnerable, marginalized, or unable to voice their concerns effectively. As a result, conflicts involving power imbalances often lead to outcomes that favor the more powerful party, leaving the less powerful party dissatisfied or disempowered. Effectively addressing power imbalances in workplace conflicts requires a multifaceted approach that considers the needs and perspectives of all parties involved.

An example of a mishandled conflict involving a company supplier:

✓ *Situation*: A supplier ships an incorrect product, and you respond with annoyance and say, “This is intolerable, and we are reconsidering our partnership.”

✓ *Bearing*: The supplier becomes defensive and offers excuses, and the rapport deteriorates.
✓ *Tactical Reframe*: "We're under a heavy burden to distribute. We need better delivery scenarios. We're both under pressure, how can we solve this together?"
✓ *Outcome*: Opens dialogue, surfaces constraints, and creates a recovery plan.

Poor enterprise communication can exacerbate the successful handing of conflict. Consider Miguel, a team leader at a company where communication from management is inconsistent and policies are unclear and confusing. His team frequently receives vague instructions, leaving Miguel unsure about how to address common situations, such as handling client complaints or navigating internal team issues.

For instance, Miguel's team was recently instructed to prioritize vendor satisfaction but without detailed guidelines on escalation processes or conflict resolution methods. As a result, his team is confused, leading to mistakes, frustration, and a sense of being unsupported. Team morale plunges and productivity suffers as workplace conflicts arise from miscommunication and unclear expectations.

Part of a solid resolution to address this conflict is for senior management to recognize the necessity for clearer communication. Company management should begin by consulting with Miguel and other team leaders to identify the key areas of confusion to uncover recurring issues in communication patterns and policy interpretation that affect team performance. Then management can create an array of comprehensive written guidelines outlining clear expectations for common circumstances, from client handling to internal conflict resolution. These could be communicated through interactive seminars and workshops designed to engage employees and ensure understanding. A final point would be to institute monthly feedback sessions where personnel could discuss any new communication issues or suggest improvements.

An additional area of concern with the mishandling of conflict can often occur within an enterprise's leadership. Picture a circumstance where two senior executives, Lauren and Sven, are at odds over the direction of a major project. Lauren, known for her guarded, data-driven leadership style, believes in a precise approach. Sven, however, has an energetic communication style and favors bold, rapid execution to foster innovative ideas. Their ongoing disagreements spill into team meetings, creating confusion and strain among employees. Each employee believes they must follow a different direction, leading to delayed projects and declining productivity as the two teams receive opposing instructions.

Recognizing the need for intervention, the company's CEO suggests bringing in a neutral third-party mediator. This individual urges both leaders to become more self-aware about their approaches, guiding them to understand each other's perspectives so they may reach a compromise. The resolution begins with Lauren's data-driven approach, then pivots to Sven's swift execution strategy. This fusion of different styles allows both leaders to feel valued and respected. By addressing conflict in the workplace proactively, organizations can avoid conflict that could filter down to teams, preserving morale and ensuring alignment across the company.

An additional example of the mishandling of business conflict often occurs with an overbearing boss who micromanages everything, making it hard to function. The resolution to this issue is not as easy as it may appear. The employee can build trust by proactively providing status updates before asked and extend regular reports or set up weekly check-ins, so the boss feels informed, but not over-involved. During a private conversation, express that you value their input but work best with more autonomy. If they are challenging, demonstrate how autonomy will improve your efficiency.

Don't look where you fall, but where you slipped.

~ African Proverb

This example often occurs in many business conflicts: A magnificent idea gets presented by someone else on your team as their own and they take credit even if though their contributions are minimal. Part of the resolution could involve being non-confrontational by stating in a team meeting, "I'm glad my idea resonated with you! Let's collaborate on processing it further." To protect your work in the future, keep a written anecdotal record of the ideas through emails, shared documents, or meeting notes. If it happens repeatedly, address it directly with the individual or bring it to team leader.

References

Filley, A. (1975). *Interpersonal Conflict Resolution*. Glenview, IL: Scott, Foresman.

Hedlund, W. (2019). *The Five Styles of Conflict*. Rochester, NY: Transforming Leader.

Herbert, L. (2023). *The Power of Proactive Conflict Management*. Sunnyvale, CA: LinkedIn.

Kauth, K. (2020). *Cost of Workplace Conflict*. Mediate.com. www.mediate.com/articles/kauth-cost-workplace.cfm.

Roberts, J. (2024). *20 Pros and Cons of Brainstorming*. https://prospluscons.com.

Sada, J. (2024). *Comprehensive Guide to Collaborative Risk Management*. Sunnyvale, CA: LinkedIn.

Thomas, K. W., and Kilmann, R. H. (1974). *The Thomas-Kilmann Conflict Mode Instrument*. Mountain View, CA: CPP, Inc.

Wish, M., Deutsch, M., and Kaplan, S. J. (1976). Perceived dimensions of interpersonal relations. *Journal of Personality and Social Psychology*, *33*, 409–420.

14 Integrative Problem-Solving and Salience

Integrative negotiation involves problem-solving in which all parties work side by side to achieve outcomes that are mutually beneficial to all. This is an interest-based negotiation. Parties agree to find resolutions that are close to their planned target points developed in the planning stages. These resolutions depend upon open communication among cooperative, trusting individuals who explore opportunities for mutual gains while preserving, or improving upon, their relationship. The process of evaluating options in integrative negotiation must focus on those best options for mutual gain. Consider the following problem:

> *A technology manufacturing enterprise is concerned about remaining competitive in the market and particularly about the growing trend among its competitors to move their operators overseas where labor costs are lower. Their concern involves keeping prices for their products competitive. The union is concerned about a growing threat of the prospect of layoffs and the impact competition may have on depressing wages, reducing annual pay increase percentage rates, and placing more of a burden on union members to cover the cost of some benefits.*

Evaluating options for these issues will result in both the company and the union recognizing they have several shared interests. Their problem-solving sessions can result in several options they might consider (Griffith and Goodwin, 2016):

- Formulate management and labor teams to address how they can realign job duties and assignments to ensure the existing labor pool is fully used.
- Offer early retirement plans with appropriate incentives.
- Implement some partial hiring freezes for areas that can be covered adequately through realignment.
- Offered reduced work schedules for interested employees.
- Eliminate costly fringe benefits that aren't widely used.

DOI: 10.4324/9781042000258-15

Integrative Thinking

Integrative thinking (Riel and Martin, 2017), as defined in *Creating Great Choices*, involves taking different ideas and examining the problem they are trying to solve, with the end goal of opening to new thinking and innovation. People tend to think about difficult decision-making in the workplace as a matter of choosing from a pre-selected list of options, usually handed down to them from management. Integrated thinking reframes decision-making by moving it away from the process of settling on a compromise, toward actively breaking a challenge or opportunity down into its core elements and reassembling them into a new option that doesn't compromise. Integrated thinking allows two opposing solutions to be combined into a stronger option through a carefully designed and structured process.

> *The ability to constructively face the tensions of opposing models, and instead of choosing one at the expense of the other, generating a creative resolution of the tension in the form of a new model that contains elements of the individual models but is superior to each.*

The formal articulation of integrative thinking as a distinct mental model uses the underlying principles of synthesizing opposing ideas, which have been practiced intuitively throughout history by innovators and great thinkers; Martin's work provided a structured framework and brought this powerful approach into the forefront of business strategy and leadership.

As the former Dean of the Rotman School of Management at the University of Toronto, Roger Martin delved into understanding the cognitive processes behind integrative thinking, meticulously studying the thinking patterns of CEOs and business leaders renowned for their strategic prowess. His research culminated in his book, *The Opposable Mind: Winning through Integrative Thinking* (2007). In this work, Martin laid out the core tenets of integrative thinking, contrasting it with conventional "analytic" thinking. He argued that while analytic thinking excels at breaking down problems into smaller, manageable parts, it often falls short when dealing with inherently complex and ambiguous situations. Integrative thinking, on the other hand, thrives in these environments by embracing complexity and seeking to synthesize seemingly contradictory ideas.

Integrated thinking helps business teams to explore, remix, and test new methods of working that encourages people to have the confidence to take risks and think expansively to yield more interesting outcomes. In today's unpredictable, interconnected world, leaders face problems like discerning between profit versus purpose, and innovation versus stability. Integrative thinking can help to navigate these pressures by encouraging holistic decision-making while balancing short-term performance with long-term transformation (Crandell, 2022).

By adding tools and frameworks such as integrative thinking, one can close the gap between wanting to solve the problem and the practical action needed to make it happen. Four steps to assist in solving the disparity, problem, or issue are as follows:

Step 1: Define the problem and understand the options and identify potential answers.
Step 2: Examine the stakeholder issues and how potential outcomes will impact them.
Step 3: Explore the possibilities of various resolutions and how they can be applied to whole or specific parts of the problem
Step 4: Assess and test the prototype solutions to improve or discard them, which allows all parties to learn if other approaches will be more effective.

Decisions made through the integrative thinking process may later be explored as a poor or regrettable decision. One's thought process might point to the regret that stems from one of two causes:

- ✓ Unknown salient features—you didn't consider a factor that you should have.
- ✓ Undervalued salient features—you thought about a factor but did not give it the proper weight.

For integrative negotiation to succeed, the parties must be motivated to collaborate rather than to compete. Parties in negotiation maximize their outcomes when they assume a healthy, active self-interest in achieving their own goals while also recognizing that they are in a collaborative problem-solving relationship (Kelley and Schenitzki, 1972). Trained integrative tactic-oriented enterprise negotiators can set high goals and can persuade the other party of the validity of their views (Gentner, Lowenstein and Thompson, 2003).

> *Integrative thinking is fostered by a belief that better answers are possible, even if they are not immediately evident. A new, superior answer is out there lurking somewhere—waiting to be discovered.*

Barriers to Integrative Thinking

Integrative thinking offers many benefits. This type of thinking helps to generate creative and solutions that are not possible with traditional problem-solving techniques. It helps individuals to develop critical thinking skills and an ability to see multiple perspectives, while encouraging collaboration and teamwork. Yet, unlike traditional problem-solving techniques, integrative thinking does not seek to find the best solution, but to find a solution that incorporates the benefits of multiple perspectives. This approach does not prioritize one idea over the other but seeks to find a way to reconcile the opposing ideas. Integrative thinking does not rely on trial and error but rather on an organized and thoughtful process of combining different perspectives.

Several of the most common challenges that can mislead veteran leaders include the following:

- Unyielding mental models: Managers often default to familiar frameworks and that makes it hard to hold opposing ideas in tension long enough to synthesize something new.
- Uneasiness with ambiguity: Integrative thinking flourishes in the gray zone, but many leaders want clarity and certainty.
- Time pressure: This demands reflection and dialogue and in fast-paced environments, leaders often default to quick fixes or conventional solutions.
- Insufficient framing of the problem: Integrative thinking starts with how the problem is framed. If the initial framing is too narrow or biased, the synthesis will be limited or skewed.

An example of an enterprise that overcame the common challenges of integrative thinking is **Tesla**. Integrative thinking played a crucial role in Tesla's success by enabling the company to overcome the traditional trade-offs between environmental performance and luxury. While many people associate electric vehicles with being small and lacking luxury features, Tesla defied this stereotype by designing EVs that are not only environmentally friendly but also high performance and luxurious. This was made possible through the company's integrative thinking approach, which allowed them to combine different elements in a way that was previously unseen in the automotive industry.

Integrative thinking allowed Tesla to combine environmental sustainability, progressive technology, and luxury into electric vehicles. The company recognized that consumers wanted not only an environmentally friendly vehicle but also one that looked sleek and luxurious. Through integrative thinking, Tesla was able to combine the aesthetics of a luxury vehicle with the functionality of an electric vehicle, creating a product that appeals to a broader range of consumers. Second, integrative thinking played a vital role in improving battery technology for electric vehicles. Tesla understood that for EVs to be widely adopted, they needed to address the issue of limited range and long charging times. Through integrative thinking, Tesla developed advanced battery technology that not only increased the range of their vehicles but also reduced charging times, making electric vehicles more practical and convenient for consumers (Kispert, 2023).

Difference of opinion leads to inquiry, and inquiry to truth.

~ Thomas Jeffereson

Unfortunately, barriers to integrative thinking can hinder an individual's or company's ability to think critically. These are seven of the top obstacles that hinder and distort the ability to think critically:

- ✓ Using emotion instead of logic
- ✓ Past personal biases
- ✓ Cognitive rigidity with inability to entertain conflicting suggestions
- ✓ Small-picture and incomplete thinking
- ✓ Fear of change
- ✓ Prejudgment assumptions
- ✓ Group thinking
- ✓ Binary thinking that limits creativity
- ✓ Inability to discern between facts and opinions

Regular practice is essential for enhancing and maintaining integrative thinking skills, as it directly impacts an enterprise's problem-solving abilities. Engaging in systematic practice sessions that involve critical thinking exercises and problem-solving challenges is crucial to overcoming the barrier of not practicing enough. By actively seeking out opportunities to test and enhance critical thinking skills, one can strengthen the capacity to analyze situations, evaluate information, and make sound business decisions (Laymon, 2024).

Six questions to ask that may uncover barriers or roadblocks to integrative thinking are as follows:

- Are decisions often made without exploring opposing viewpoints?
- Do team members rely heavily on initial data or assumptions?
- Are short-term results prioritized over long-term strategy?
- Are complex problems oversimplified?
- Does management discourage dissent or alternative perspectives?
- Are individuals hesitate to challenge dominant ideas?

Opinion is the medium between knowledge and ignorance.

~ Plato

Salience

Salience refers to the degree to which a particular stimulus, information, or event stands out and captures an individual's attention within a given context. It is an essential concept that helps explain how individuals process and prioritize information, make decisions, and respond to their environments. A salient stimulus is one that is easily noticed, perceived, and remembered due to its distinctiveness, relevance, or emotional impact.

Salience can be influenced by various factors, such as the following:

- Novelty: New or unusual stimuli are more likely to capture attention and are considered salient.

- Intensity: Stimuli with greater intensity, such as bright colors, loud sounds, or extreme temperatures, are often more salient than less intense stimuli.
- Emotional impact: Stimuli that evoke strong emotions or are associated with significant personal experiences are more likely to be salient.
- Relevance: Stimuli that are relevant to an individual's goals, values, or interests are more likely to be perceived as salient.

Understanding salience helps in decision-making where knowing what stands out can shape choices. Salient information is easier to remember and with respect to conflict resolution, it can assist in identifying what's most emotionally or contextually prominent and can help address root issues.

In the context of decision-making and problem-solving, salience plays a crucial role in shaping individuals' choices and preferences. Salient options are more likely to be considered and incorporated into the decision-making process, while less salient information may be overlooked or undervalued. The role of salience in human behavior and decision-making is essential for a wide range of applications, including marketing, public policy, negotiation, and education. By recognizing the influence of salience on individuals' choices and preferences, researchers and policymakers can develop more effective interventions, strategies, and communication approaches to enhance decision-making quality, improve well-being, and promote more efficient resource allocation in various personal, educational, and professional contexts.

The popular concept of "finding common ground" suggests that recognizing similarities, as opposed to differences, can lead to positive interactions among group members. This adage is supported by research on intergroup contact theory, with findings indicating that a key pillar in mitigating intergroup bias is positive and meaningful intergroup contact. Similarity attraction theory suggests similar findings, primarily that individuals are attracted to those like themselves, which elicit positive affect in interpersonal interactions. These writings offer valuable insights for individuals who take part in interactions in which favorable outcomes are dependent on effective intergroup interaction, such as negotiation. While thorough research has been conducted on the benefits of similarity in interpersonal interactions, surprisingly little work has examined how perceptions of similarity affect one's evaluations of a negotiation counterpart or the negotiation process when the negotiating counterpart is an out-group member. Recent studies test the effect of focusing on similarities versus differences on attitudes toward a forthcoming negotiation and perceptions of the negotiation partner, and whether perceived similarity mediates the impact on attitudes toward the negotiation (Pollack, Park-Stamm, Shaw and Weiner, 2022).

The two most fundamental strategic choices are deciding where to play and how to win.

~ Roger Martin

What are several important norms and how can they support collaborative professional learning to enhance problem-solving skills in business negotiation? Norms are a social contract that supports a team's collaborative work. In collaborative situations, it's helpful to explicitly define and agree on a set of norms to guide how the group works. The word norm commonly refers to something that is usual, typical, standard, or expected. In the context of problem-solving and collaboration, norms are agreed-upon definitions of productive behaviors and mindsets that should be usual, or "the norm," whenever a group is working together.

Negotiation Norms

The collaborative problem-solving norms of negotiating parties can influence the possibility of win–win resolution and success. Several vital norms that are helpful in negotiation scenarios are as follows:

- Pausing before responding or asking a question allows time for thinking and enhances dialogue, discussion, and decision-making.
- Using a paraphrasing starter that is comfortable for you—"So . . ." or "As you are . . ." or "You're postulating . . ."—and following the starter with an efficient paraphrase assists members of the group in hearing and understanding one another as they converse and make decisions.
- Posing questions to explore and to specify thinking. Questions may be posed to explore perceptions, assumptions, and interpretations and to invite others to inquire into their thinking. For example, "What might be some conjectures you are exploring?"
- Putting ideas on the negotiating table is the heart of meaningful dialogue and discussion. Label the intention of your comments. For example, "Here is one idea . . ." or "One thought we have is . . ." or "Here is a possible approach . . ." or "Another fiscal responsible consideration might be . . . ."
- Providing data, both qualitative and quantitative, in a variety of forms supports team members in constructing shared understanding from their work. Data has no meaning beyond that which we make of them; shared meaning develops from collaboratively exploring, analyzing, and interpreting data.

(Garmston and Wellman, 2013)

Any negotiation team that is too busy to practice the skills of collaboration is also a group that is too busy to improve. Ironically, the parties that are most in need of the skills of collaboration are often those most resistant to them. Groups functioning most effectively are the same ones who recognize the need for regular collaboration and problem-solving training. Those in difficulty are very often the ones who are too busy to examine how they are working together or how they are failing to work together.

An elementary and straightforward way to adapt and remember some of the above-mentioned problem-solving norms are to:

A	Ask probing questions
E	Engage fully in all discussions
I	Integrate new information
O	Open up to new ideas
U	Utilize what is learned and agreed upon

Collaborative negotiation can help build trust, respect, and cooperation and can create a positive relationship that can lead to future business opportunities. Following are some guidelines for collaborative negotiation:

- Prepare: Consider the end goal and what a productive outcome would look like.
- Be open: Be honest and open with the other party.
- Listen: Take the time to listen to understand.
- Summarize: Summarize early and often.
- Take a break: Sometimes stepping back can help you see the whole picture.
- Share information: Ask questions to get people to think outside the box.
- Point out consequences: Remind both parties of the consequences of no deal.
- Agree on timelines: Set realistic, flexible, and consistent start and end dates, deadlines, and checkpoints.

Many individuals negotiations succeed or fail because of the numbers discussed. That is, people believe that the outcome is a function of what one is willing to pay and what the other person is willing to accept.

Category Norms

There are basically three negotiation-based categories—adversarial, collaborative, and consultative. Nearly all negotiations can be classified as one of these three types.

Adversarial negotiations: When business negotiations become adversarial, each side is attempting to force the other. In this scenario, negotiations become a zero-sum game. Simply, a competitive negotiation style means there is a winner and a loser. Few enter a negotiation with this approach. The problem, however, is that the negotiation process can quickly become adversarial if one side loses focus on the importance of building relationships, which create opportunities or future business.

Collaborative negotiations: These are superior to adversarial negotiations because the aim is to work together. This is a more effective negotiation style because it seeks common ground. With collaboration, both sides can reach a deal in a way that allows for future business opportunities. Some cast aside this approach believing that collaboration allows the other side to make any demands they want. In truth, collaboration leads to a successful close because it encourages negotiators to find a center that satisfies each side.

Consultative negotiations: The consultative approach to negotiating is the most effective of the three approaches. It is effective because it seeks to understand the other side's underlying perceptions. Moreover, it also equips the negotiator with the ability to overcome demands issued from the other party. A consultative style puts greater control in the hands of the negotiator by equipping them with the skills to shape the other side's perceptions of value.

There are numerous solutions offered in recent research that can assist in achieving mutually beneficial agreements. Parties can expand the pie before dividing it. Expanding the pie means increasing the total value of what's being negotiated. Instead of dividing the existing resources, one looks for ways to add more value. To implement this, negotiating parties should attempt to ask questions to uncover the needs and interests of the other party and think of creative solutions, like bundling services or offering additional products, to increase the value available.

Not every issue in negotiations carries equal weight. Some are serious, while others are less important. Leveraging trade-offs on low-priority issues means making concessions on things that matter less to you in exchange for something more valuable. Trade-offs help reduce conflict and speed up the negotiation process. In collaborative negotiations, creating contingency agreements is a clever way to manage uncertainty. A contingency agreement is a backup plan both parties agree on if things don't go as expected. Contingency agreements reduce risks for both parties. They help build trust and avoid conflicts down the road. If something changes, you already have a plan that everyone agrees on.

When two or more parties are negotiating, it's crucial to rely on objective criteria to make decisions. Objective criteria are facts, data, or standards that everyone agrees on. Using objective criteria keeps negotiations fair and prevents arguments. It removes emotions from the conversation and focuses on facts.

Competitive Model

The competitive model shares some similarities with several of the first two models, but it's tailored more toward getting the absolute best possible deal, often at the expense of the other side. It's a common approach in many high-stakes negotiations, like corporate buyouts or legal disputes, where each party is trying to amplify their own gain.

Competitive negotiation is a crucial aspect of business interactions, as it involves bargaining and reaching agreements with both competitors and suppliers. This process plays a significant role in shaping the success and profitability of organizations. From a competitive standpoint, negotiation allows businesses to secure favorable terms, such as lower prices, exclusive deals, or advantageous contracts, giving them a competitive edge in the market.

When examining competitive negotiation, it is essential to consider different perspectives. Suppliers, for instance, may regard negotiation as an opportunity to maximize their profits and ensure the sustainability of their business. On the other hand, competitors may engage in negotiation to shield their market share or form strategic alliances.

Competitive negotiation can encourage the parties to research the market, assess their alternatives, and prepare their arguments and evidence. This can help them identify their target price, reservation price, and use them as benchmarks to evaluate the offers and counter offers. By using competitive tactics, such as anchoring, framing, or conceding, the parties can influence the other side's perception of the value and the cost of the deal and persuade them to accept their terms or make concessions. For example, a buyer can use anchoring to set a low initial offer and then use framing to emphasize the benefits of the offer for the seller, such as saving time, reducing risk, or increasing reputation. A seller can use deception to pretend that they have an improved alternative and then use conceding to offer a small discount in exchange for a rapid decision.

This approach requires shrewd skills, an in-depth understanding of what is desired, and careful preparation. When using this model, it's fundamental to remain professional and strategic, focusing on facts, leverage, and timing. However, this style can easily ruin relationships if not managed carefully. It works well when the negotiation's outcome matters more than keeping things amicable and harmonious for the long term.

Ultimately, negotiation, using any of the above-mentioned models, becomes a balance between strategy and adaptability. By understanding the different models of negotiation, one can better adapt to any scenario. Successful negotiators are those who not only understand the strategies behind each model but also know when and how to apply them.

References

Crandell, S. (2022). *Integrative Thinking: Step Away from the Vantage Point*. Atlanta, Georgia: Korn Ferry.

Garmston, R. J., and Wellman, B. M. (2013). *The Adaptive School: A Sourcebook for Developing Collaborative Groups*. Lanham, MA: Rowman & Littlefield Inc.

Gentner, J., Lowenstein, J., and Thompson, L. (2003). Learning and transfer: A general role for analogical encoding. *Journal of Educational Psychology*, *95*(2).

Griffith, D. B., and Goodwin, C. (2016). *Conflict Survival Kit: Tools for Resolving Conflict at Work*. Boston, MA: Pearson.

Kelley, H. H., and Schenitzki, D. (1972). Bargaining. In C. G. McClintock (ed.), *Experimental Social Psychology*. New York: Holt, Rinehart & Wilson.

Laymon, R. (2024). *What Are Some Common Barriers to Effective Critical Thinking and Problem-Solving*? New York: Strategic Leaders Consulting.

Martin, R. (2007). *The Opposable Mind: How Successful Leaders Win Through Integrative Thinking*. Boston, MA: Harvard Business Press.
Pollack, J., Park-Stamm, E., Shaw, N., and Weiner, A. (2022). Negotiating with those like me: Similarity salience increases positive attitudes in imagined negotiation with an out-group member. *Peace and Conflict: Journal of Peace Psychology*, *28*(4), 521–527. Stanford, CA: Crown.
Riel, J., and Martin, R. (2017). *Creating Great Choices*. Boston, MA: Harvard Business Review Press.

15 Organizational Tension/Conflict

Tension is the primary link between conflict and creativity. Conflict signals dissatisfaction with something or someone. This dissatisfaction brings tension into the system, the enterprise, and the negotiation (Coleman and Deutsch, 2000). Managing and overcoming tension is what sets the world's best negotiators, athletes, and poker players apart from the rest. They're not only at ease in a state of tension, but they also thrive in it, using it to their advantage in a calm and collected fashion.

But tension is an inevitable part of any negotiation process. It's only natural: if both parties are looking to gain at the expense of the other, the moment those desires clash, there's bound to be a degree of conflict and discomfort. Many of the best business negotiators understand that it's not their job to dissipate tension as it arises. Rather, it is their job to manage that tension in such a way that enables both parties to meet their fundamental needs in a creative breakthrough.

Since tensions are inevitable, leaders of teams and business units must the first to acknowledge this reality. We must then devote time, resources, and strategies to navigate these tensions. The temptation might be to try to solve, fix, or overcome them. However, this might not possible, because tensions are a fundamental, ever-present part of organizations. What we can do is navigate these tensions and create an organizational context that accommodates them in a way that people can manage effectively. The result will be a higher level of serenity, calmness, and tranquility, rather than stress, anxiety, and discomfort.

Creating such contexts means striving for organizational harmony. Organizational harmony is an essential concept for improving the well-being of people in any tension-filled organization. It removes obstacles and, among other things, fosters a better organizational climate wherein everyone is committed to collaboration and mutual support.

This is only possible when one can identify positive, healthy tension as the opportunity that it is. Healthy tension is a positive force that motivates both parties to put in the legwork and uncover innovative solutions they wouldn't have otherwise considered. The tension between creating and claiming value is pivotal in business negotiation strategies (Mnookin, Peppet and Tulumello,

DOI: 10.4324/9781042000258-16

2000). Share too little information about your interests in a negotiation, and you will have difficulty identifying possible value-creating trade-offs. Share too much, and the other side may take advantage of you.

Tension Management

One of the primary common sense tension principles in enterprise is: *The main job of the leaders in any organization is to manage productivity by regulating the level of tension within the organization.* The term "tension" is not a synonym for "stress." Stress is a negative, nonproductive feeling of anxiety and strain, usually surfacing when people are put under pressure for extended periods of time. Unlike stress, tension can generate productive energy. For example, the tension that athletes experience while preparing to perform can actually provide an edge which heightens their performance.

Organizational Harmony

Several factors can contribute to organizational tension and conflict, often stemming from communication breakdowns, personal values, or competition for resources (Pollack, 2025).

- Unclear responsibilities: When roles are not clearly defined, team members may overlap in duties, leading to frustration and miscommunication.
- Personality clashes: Different personalities bring diverse viewpoints, which, while beneficial, can sometimes spark conflict. When personality clashes escalate, they can obstruct team cohesion and lead to resentment or misinterpretation.
- Resource shortage: Limited budgets, equipment, or workspace often creates a competitive environment where employees must vie for resources. This situation commonly triggers tension and increases the likelihood of workplace conflict.
- Differing interests: Conflicts often arise when personal goals overshadow organizational objectives. For instance, an employee may prioritize personal achievements or targets over team goals, leading to tension with colleagues who view tasks through a more collaborative lens.
- Ineffective communication styles: Miscommunication—whether due to tone, phrasing, or misinterpreted intentions—often sparks or amplifies organizational conflicts.
- Power differences: Employees with decision-making authority might unintentionally foster resentment if others feel excluded from essential discussions or undervalued. This imbalance can lead to dissatisfaction and decreased engagement.

Creative Tension

For many individuals common sense tells us that tension exists in any organization. In addition to the predictable road bumps, every organization faces unpredictable challenges that produce tension. Many internal forces produce tension. An accountant's goals may conflict with those of the quality control department. Likewise, quality control may pursue outcomes that clash with manufacturing. Whenever gaps exist between what people in the organization want and what they have, tension results.

Peter Senge (1990) introduced the concept of creative tension as a potential aid in facilitating creativity and change. According to Senge's theory, we create positive tension when we clearly articulate our vision and our current reality, thus making the gap between the two apparent. Learning organizations are those where people continually expand their capacity to create the results they truly desire, where new and expansive patterns of thinking are nurtured, where collective aspiration is set free, and where people are continually learning to see the whole together. Senge also postulates several "laws" that are pertinent to tension, stress, and organizational conflict:

- Today's problems come from yesterday's "solutions."
- The harder you push, the harder the system pushes back.
- The easy way out usually leads back in.
- Small changes can produce big results, but the areas of highest leverage are often the least obvious.
- You can have your cake and eat it too—but not all at once.
- Dividing an elephant in half does not produce two small elephants.

Creativity has always dealt with limited options and resources. Innovative and creative people experience a high output of creativity and innovative ideas when there is a maximum of restriction. If you lead a team, a business unit, an organization, or simply work within one, you've likely faced many challenges. Among those, one might have had to choose between two equally unappealing options of many varieties. Managing conflicting demands from various stakeholders, achieving goals without compromising a positive work environment, empower teams while maintaining control, or balance a long-term vision with short-term needs. These tasks, which feel at odds in their very nature, can feel daunting and nearly impossible to accomplish.

Tense negotiation scenarios will often provoke stress, anxiety, and discomfort. Research on goal conflict reports a negative association between goal conflict and well-being. It is natural to experience tense feelings when navigating such complexities. After enduring these situations, it is common also to question yourself: "What am I doing wrong to counter such tensions?" However, it is important to recognize that these tensions are not a result of personal shortcomings. Instead, they are inherent to the nature of organizations.

This shift in mindset changes our relationship with tensions. Since tensions are inevitable, our responsibility as leaders of teams, business units, organizations, or as organizational members is to first acknowledge this reality. One must then devote time, resources, and strategies to navigate these tensions. What we can do is navigate these tensions and create an organizational context that accommodates them in a way that people can manage effectively. The result will be a higher level of serenity, calmness, and tranquility, rather than stress, anxiety, and discomfort. Creating such contexts means striving for organizational harmony. Organizational harmony is an essential concept for improving the well-being of people in any tension-filled organization. It removes obstacles and, among other things, fosters a better organizational climate wherein everyone is committed to collaboration and mutual support.

The organizational harmony that is sought comes from building rapport that can demonstrate respect and reduce hostility, which will encourage co-operation. Successful negotiators should remain calm under tension, manage their own emotions, and avoid language that could escalate conflict. Following are the four key skills:

✓ Empathy and rapport-building: showing genuine concern for the subject.
✓ Patience and time management: allowing emotions to stabilize before decisions are made.
✓ Clear communication: speaking in plain, courteous terms.
✓ Problem-solving under pressure: reframing demands and creating alternatives.

Harmony and Tension

In Chinese philosophy, "he" (和) signifies harmony through the blending of diverse elements, such as musical notes or culinary ingredients, highlighting dynamic relationships and continuous interaction. Confucianism, Taoism, and Mohism present harmony as an adaptable process, emphasizing the integration and cooperation of different forces. Unlike the static Greek perspective, Chinese traditions view harmony as an ongoing cycle of balancing diversity. This dynamic understanding underscores that true harmony arises from the continuous adjustment and engagement with diverse elements, achieving balance through mutual interaction and synergy. Harmony in the Chinese tradition is not merely the absence of conflict but a perpetual dance of intertwined elements.

The term "harmony" originates from the Proto-Indo-European root meaning "to fit," evolving through Proto-Greek "harmos" to denote "joint." This term expanded to encompass structure, agreement, pleasing sounds, and stable governance. Greek philosophy emphasized the concept of balance and proportion, extending harmony beyond music to life and the cosmos. For figures like Pythagoras and Plato, harmony meant the fitting together of different elements to create a coherent and aesthetically pleasing whole, reflecting a static order akin to musical chords within a structured framework, but always considering the presence of heterogeneity.

The theory of organizational harmony is the theory of fitness, emphasizing interdependence and the mechanisms needed to manage heterogeneity with a focus on integration. Put differently, it is a seamless integration of Western and Eastern conceptions of harmony. As such, organizational harmony aims to reconcile tensions without eliminating differences between competing elements; it also aims to embrace and navigate heterogeneity rather than eradicating it. Integrating the semantic, etymological, philosophical, and organizational traditions, organizational harmony, then, is defined as the active integration of heterogeneity within an organization while preserving part of it (Correa, 2024).

A major challenge confronting enterprise today stems from grappling with the challenge of navigating day-to-day issues while striving to maintain focus on long-term goals. Whether it's adapting to a post-pandemic reality or undergoing a digital transformation, leaders are frequently faced with balancing the pressing demands of the present with a compelling vision for the future. This is where a creative tension model comes in—a powerful framework for bridging the gap between current reality and desired vision.

Tension can drive change and innovation in business, while harmony can sustain trust and collaboration. Tension will often ignite debate, and harmony can encourage a sense of aligned purpose with employees. Tension often arises from competing ideas and priorities, and business harmony can arise from shared mutual respect.

The creative tension model, rooted in systems thinking, highlights the natural tension that arises when individuals or organizations confront the difference between where they are and where they want to be. The creative process is driven by the gap between vision and reality. When one imagines what we want to create, one can visualize a future that highlights what's missing in the present. This is often referred to as structural tension and rather than viewing this tension as a source of stress or conflict, creative tension encourages leaders to use it as a motivating force to drive transformation. By acknowledging the gap between current reality and future aspirations, business leaders can harness the tension productively, creating an environment where innovation and growth thrive (Lim, 2024). How can environmentally creative tension be managed?

- By being aware of the potential problems of creativity
- By developing emotional intelligence
- By embracing diversity and inclusion
- By encouraging collaboration and collective creativity
- By rewarding making mistakes and welcoming failure

> *Happiness is when what you think, what you say, and what you do are in harmony.*
>
> ~ Mahatma Gandhi

Table 15.1 Healthy versus unhealthy tension

Healthy tension	*Unhealthy tension*
Solid goals delineated	Unclear and fractured goals
Clear perspectives defined	Ambiguous viewpoints hover
Mechanisms for accountability	Misaligned challenges in authority
Resource constraints are absent	Conflict in resources and conversations
Little fragmentation of respect	Friction, dissent, and stagnation

Business Harmony/Customer Service

Implementing effective customer service strategies sets a business apart from the competition, inspires word-of-mouth marketing, fuels company growth, and increases harmony throughout the entire organization. One approach is to establish consistent, high-quality communication with customers. Proactive conflict managers strive to create a culture where employees and customers and related stakeholders feel valued.

Rule 1	Strive to be helpful to all, even if there is no immediate profit
Rule 2	Provide what is promised: quality—products—services
Rule 3	Create inducements for desired behaviors
Rule 4	Identify and anticipate needs of all stakeholders
Rule 5	Empower individuals to resolve disputes at the lowest level possible
Rule 6	Devise, evaluate, and revise operating and procedural systems

Harmony and customer service skills are made up of the expertise, approaches, and understanding that are needed to make stakeholders as satisfied as possible. These skills are developed through several different avenues, including training, validation, and experience. There are generally two different types of these skills: hard and soft. Both types of skills are equally important, and successful managers are able to strike a good balance of hard and soft skills.

The hard skills are technical skills, ones that can generally be taught and measured. Knowledge and proficiency of hard skills are usually built through training and typically focus on the specific tasks that are needed to complete a job. The soft skills are more difficult to quantify since they tend to be personal attributes. Soft skills are aspects that are developed in someone's temperament so while there can be some training to teach them, these skills are largely learned by an individual over time.

Managing the Right Tension

Every leader and every company face the problem of how to make progress on seemingly conflicting objectives at the same time. And of all the competing objectives, three pairs stand out: profitability versus growth, short term versus long term, and the whole organization versus the parts. In each case, more progress on one front usually comes at the expense of progress on another: Going for more growth damages profitability and working toward higher profitability slows growth. Efforts to build for tomorrow distract everyone from producing results today, but when managers shift the focus to today's results, they compromise the future strength of the company. Attempts to create companywide benefits hold back individual business units, then attempts to unleash the individual potential of the business units bar the way to capture the benefits of being one company.

An American Psychological Association survey found that 31% of staff felt stressed out during their workday (Tetrick and Winslow, 2015). Several key insights for addressing workplace stress involve identifying stressors and developing coping strategies tailored to individual and organizational needs. Techniques such as time management, regular breaks, and mindfulness can significantly reduce stress and enhance productivity. It is prudent to encourage open communication and develop and cultivate support systems aimed at creating a healthier, more resilient work environment.

Often tension, problems, and conflicts occur during the many meetings convened by the company, project teams, executive and management consultations and the like. Mel Silberman (2006) has listed *12* ways to improve meetings and manage rising tensions:

- Send out agendas in advance.
- Be prepared with supporting facts and opinions.
- Select problems that can be managed and solved.
- Don't waste time. Stick to the issues at hand.
- Agree on a definition of the problem before moving on to solutions.
- Allow adequate time for each problem-solving step.
- Encourage positive confrontation.
- Focus on the issues, not the people.
- Take turns chairing long meetings.
- Vary the pace of the meeting between reporting and discussion.
- Classify and rank alternative solutions before deciding on the best ones.
- Determine a date on which to check on implementation of the decision.

The problem is not so much that managers don't recognize these tensions; they are all too familiar to anyone who has ever run a business. Rather it is that managers are often not focused on the tension that matters most to their company. Although companies have to manage all three tensions all of the time to some extent, at any point in time, only one of them is critical to unlocking better performance. More often than not, executives pick the wrong tension as their priority. This is hardly surprising because the tensions often masquerade as one another. A business's apparent problem reconciling short term with long term, for example, may actually reflect a growth versus profitability issue.

Finally, many companies often manage tensions in lockstep. When the priority is today's earnings, some managers tend to push for higher profitability rather than faster revenue growth because they are confident they can increase profitability more quickly and with less investment than they can influence revenue growth. Companies that give priority to revenue growth often seek it by freeing up the individual parts of the company to stimulate new ideas, more experimentation, and greater adaptation to local markets. This means that managers need to carefully think through their companies' problems to make a solid diagnosis.

Cognitive Dissonance

Cognitive dissonance is a psychological concept introduced by psychologist Leon Festinger (1957) that describes the mental discomfort we feel when we hold two or more conflicting beliefs, values, or attitudes, especially when our actions contradict those beliefs. This motivates people to seek harmony and consistency within their minds, prompting them to change their beliefs, modify their actions, or rationalize their choices.

In psychology, cognitive dissonance occurs when a person holds contradictory beliefs, ideas, or values and is typically experienced as psychological stress when they participate in an action that goes against one or more of them. According to this theory, when two actions or ideas are not psychologically consistent with each other, people do all in their power to change them until they become consistent. The discomfort is triggered by the person's belief clashing with new information perceived, wherein they try to find a way to resolve the contradiction to reduce their discomfort.

In *A Theory of Cognitive Dissonance* (Festinger, 1957), psychologist Festinger proposed that human beings strive for internal psychological consistency to function mentally in the real world. A person who experiences internal inconsistency tends to become psychologically uncomfortable and is motivated to reduce the cognitive dissonance. They tend to make changes to justify the stressful behavior, either by adding new parts to the cognition causing the psychological dissonance (rationalization) or by avoiding circumstances and contradictory information likely to increase the magnitude of the cognitive dissonance (confirmation bias).

How can an enterprise cope with and reduce this discomfort? Four steps are as follows:

- Change beliefs: "Perhaps including sugar in our product isn't that bad."
- Change behaviors: "Remove sugar and replace with monk fruit juice."
- Rationalize: "Vendors can select one or both products with these sweeteners."
- Avoid conflicting data: "Small amounts of sugar in the product is not so bad."

Enterprises can suffer from cognitive dissonance in several ways, as established by research:

✓ Strategic dissonance: When a company's strategies, goals, and actions are misaligned or contradictory, it leads to dissonance that hampers performance (Wilkins and Ouchi, 1983). For example, a company pursuing cost leadership but repeatedly spending heavily on marketing.

✓ Organizational dissonance: Disagreement between executives' functional departments or employees on key metrics or priorities creates tension (Schwenk, 1988). For example, the marketing and R&D teams having differing views on new product priorities.

✓ Behavioral dissonance: When company practices, policies, and leadership messaging are incongruous with the desired brand image or culture, it causes discomfort. For example, an eco-friendly brand that fails to implement sustainable practices internally.

Cognitive dissonance and creative tension both share a common etiology; tension created by the perceived gap between the ideal and real. What distinguishes creative tension from chronic cognitive dissonance is the way the tension is resolved. Creative tension is a powerful motivator that drives positive change within organizations. Three essential elements must be present for creative tension to produce positive change:

Vision: Our vision is what allows us to see a preferred future state of being. Having a compelling vision of a preferred future is essential on a personal level, but how we communicate this vision to our team is even more critical.

Desirability: Unless a negotiation team finds the vision compelling, they will lack the motivation necessary to make the vision reality. Trust in the leader and believing in an overarching organizational purpose are important when seeking team motivation. Presenting a clear vision that the team finds both compelling and desirable adds to their willingness to close the gap between their current reality and the preferred future.

Self-efficacy: There is perhaps no greater driving force for creative tension than one's belief in their ability to attain the desired future state. Those that suffer from chronic cognitive dissonance do so because they either place little value in achieving their preferred future, or even more commonly, they believe that they are incapable of closing the ideal/reality gap (Small and McDonald, 2024).

Teams that experience creative tension see the task ahead as a means to an extremely desirable future. Once they embrace a clear vision that they find desirable and compelling, and they are confident in their capabilities, there is little that will stop them from achieving the desired result. For them, the task becomes their mission. Enterprise leaders want to be sure they are offering teams these elements and helping them experience that creative tension. It will help build their confidence and abilities, and the company will see a difference because of it.

A healthy dose of creative tension can be an incredibly powerful stimulus for teams who are looking to advance creativity and striving to innovate collaboratively when approaching business negotiations. Healthy competition and adversarial moments in any team can help to create inspired solutions, if they are well intentioned. Setting clear rules and boundaries helps to set the conditions for innovation to happen, and conflict need not be derogatory. When harnessed for the greater good, it can be an excellent motivator.

Cognitive dissonance has a significant impact on the workplace. It influences employees' attitudes, behaviors, and overall dynamics. It can also lead to reduced job satisfaction, lower morale, and increased stress. Employees may struggle to reconcile their values with company policies or unethical practices. This potentially results in decreased engagement and motivation. Also, cognitive dissonance can hinder effective decision-making as rationalizing their professional choices to align with their existing beliefs makes it more difficult.

Understanding these effects of cognitive dissonance psychology can help one take proactive measures to minimize its negative impact. Addressing it also fosters a more transparent and ethical work environment and improves employee well-being.

Solid leadership addressing creative tension should help people reflect on their practice continuously and from there, help them build personal goals that help them grow. Important to let team members know that you may not have all the answers, but that more people working together is the answer. Additionally, it may be prudent to gather research and data to support the vision so that you know you are moving in the right direction. Communicating the vision clearly and often will help everyone see the realities of where you are and to build a shared vision one should emphasize why you are doing what you do and encourage individuals to support one another as part of the greater whole.

Tension in Work Teams

The origins of conflict in teams are often predictable, allowing proactive leaders to mitigate tensions before they escalate. These primary sources of conflict include (Kaplan, 2024) the following:

- Communication issues: Miscommunication or lack of clarity in conversations leads to misunderstandings. Research highlights that poor communication is one of the most common causes of conflict within teams.
- Resource scarcity: Competition for limited resources can create friction, especially in resource-constrained environments. When teams feel they're competing for budget, time, or manpower, tensions often rise.
- Role uncertainty: When team members are unclear about their roles and responsibilities, it breeds confusion and frustration. Clear expectations and role definitions are key to minimizing such conflicts.
- Personality clashes: In any group, personalities will differ, and sometimes those differences result in conflict. Personality clashes can be exacerbated in high-stakes environments where stress levels are high.
- Goal misalignment: When personal goals are not aligned with team or organizational goals, conflict is almost inevitable. This misalignment can cause confusion and reduce group cohesion.
- Cultural differences: Teams are increasingly diverse, and while diversity enriches ideas, it can also bring about misunderstanding if cultural differences are not recognized and respected.

Coping

Renowned Swiss psychoanalyst, Carl G. Jung, viewed tension between opposites as a fundamental dynamic in the human psyche. The "problem of the opposites," as he referred to it, became the centerpiece of his psychological theory, so much so that he came to identify opposing energies as the "ineradicable and indispensable preconditions of all psychic life." For Jung, the "problem" developed when one side of the opposites (positive/negative, superior/inferior, masculine/feminine, fixed/volatile etc.) is favored while the other is dismissed and buried within the unconscious where it accumulates energy. When this happens, conflict between the conscious ego and the unconscious invariably arises.

However, rather than accepting this as an inevitable and unchangeable outcome, Jung also championed the idea that this underlying conflict could be transformed into constructive, "creative" tension. Instead of burying or attempting to solve the unfavored opposite, he thought that if we hold each polarity, the process of individuation occurs, facilitating the birth of an entirely new, integrated attitude of self-awareness. The benefits of learning to hold the tension of opposites are immense. For one, it creates space for opposite ideas, feelings, and behaviors to peacefully coexist. One can become more flexible, tolerant, and loving. It can enable us to see the flaws not only in our own personality but also of others, turning us into more empathetic and emotionally intelligent beings (Jacquet, 2024).

In short, it is not the actual work one performs on the job that is stressful. What is usually most stressful is the bombardment of pressures that are unavoidable and beyond one's control, such as excessive workload, a difficult boss or colleague, repeated adaptation to restructuring, negotiation headaches, and so forth. Some people find it harder than ever to deal with the challenges at work, while others sail through with ease. The number one factor that determines how well one performs under stress is the ability to cope with the stress—not specific job conditions or the amount of pressure you face.

A glaring coping error in negotiation is to irrationally stick to an initial course of negotiating action, even once it becomes clear that this course is no longer the optimal position. Related to this error is the negotiator's tendency to seek out information and data that confirm any preexisting beliefs and to filter out information that runs contrary to those beliefs (Bazerman and Neale, 1992).

One experiences tension to the degree that the challenges one faces seem out of control and resilience refers to the ability to handle and rise above the multiple stresses in the workplace by controlling what one can control.

Being prepared for periods of tension and stress can make it easier to get through them. And knowing how to manage our well-being can help us recover after a stressful event. Some may refer to our ability to manage stress as resilience. There are things we can try to build our resilience against stress. But there are also factors that might make it harder to be resilient, such as experiencing discrimination or lacking support.

Answer the following eight questions along four parameters (1 = Strongly disagree; 4 = Strongly agree)

- I find myself turning my teammates' requests of me into obligations.
- Setbacks often cause me to feel inept.
- I often focus on the potential for failure rather than success.
- When projects go badly, I begin to think it's my fault.
- I often interpret guidelines as though they are obligations.
- I usually give myself credit for team successes.
- I have little trouble seeing the role of my abilities in progress.
- When something works well, I see how my skills have worked.

> *One of life's best coping mechanisms is to know the difference between an inconvenience and a problem.*
>
> ~ Robert Fulghum

Tension and stress occur when people perceive that events are placing extreme demands on them. The degree of tension experienced depends on one's perception. To analyze the eight-question survey, review other colleague's responses in a small group discussion and relate that to several of the group exercises in the appendix.

Michelangelo never wanted to paint the ceiling of the Sistine Chapel because he considered himself a sculptor. John Lennon and Paul McCartney wrote some of pop music's most iconic songs, but they could scarcely agree on anything. And Mario Puzo never really wanted to write *The Godfather* but did it because he needed money. All of these iconic works have one thing in common: they're products of creative tension, a situation where there is discord, or a gap between where something is and where you want it to be.

Creative tension isn't just limited to artists, musicians, and authors. We've all experienced some level of tension in our lives. In fact, the world is built on opposites: balancing family and work, spending and saving, giving and receiving. Though contradictory, we need these pairs, a concept known as "the unity of opposites." We can't have hot without cold, light without dark, or life without death.

The contemporary world usually struggles with tension. The dominant cultural narrative is to get rid of tensions because they're seen as bad (Zhang, 2022). Having tension between work and life, for example, makes us feel like we're not doing either thing right. Rather than aiming to get rid of tensions completely, we should find ways to balance them. Similar to how our physical world is literally built on tension, proper tension is also needed in the way we work. Often our best creative work comes when we draw energy from those tensions. We need idleness as much as busyness, a fulfilling career and a loving family, and the freedom of choice but also constraints to keep us on track.

Two crucial aspects of cognitive dissonance in the workplace involves employees feeling that the right course of action, as the organization dictates,

Table 15.2 How cognitive dissonance surfaces at work

Issues	*Examples*
Ethical conflicts	The values of integrity and honesty
Unfair treatment	Fairness in salaries and promotions
Toxic workplace	Miscommunication, workloads
Job satisfaction	Disengagement and burnout
Conflicting policies	Work–life balance dilemmas

goes against their values or ethics. Some might justify actions they wouldn't normally condone when forced into such a corner. This can include manipulating data, overlooking safety protocols, or even engaging in dishonest practices. A second aspect of cognitive dissonance in the workplace is resistance to change. Organizations evolve, and change is an integral part of growth. However, when changes planned by management contradict what employees have known or believed, it can magnify cognitive dissonance. Whether it's a shift in company values, a restructuring of teams, or the introduction of new procedures, employees may become resistant if they perceive these changes as clashing with their existing beliefs or past experiences.

This resistance is often not just a reluctance to embrace the new but a psychological defense mechanism against the uneasiness of dissonance. The result can be prolonged transition periods and decreased work proficiency.

Navigating the multilayered landscape of the modern workplace is challenging enough without the added strain of cognitive dissonance. Clearly, psychological tension from conflicting beliefs or values can significantly shape workplace dynamics, influencing everything from individual productivity to team cohesion. However, with awareness and proactive measures, enterprises and individuals can effectively manage and reduce the impacts of cognitive dissonance by fostering open communication, ensuring consistent messaging, and valuing employee well-being.

Tension Illustration

Recently, the COO of a company hired a conflict management consultant to conduct an assessment to determine the reasons that the employees often seem disgruntled and unhappy. The consultant's assessment revealed that many workers were dissatisfied because the merit bonuses were not distributed fairly.

Employees with seniority wanted their time with the company work and loyalty rewarded. Several workers who logged a lot of overtime wanted these efforts recognized. A cadre of newer employees informed the COO that they had obligations like expensive mortgages to deal with and felt that a fairer distribution of bonuses should be made. Additionally, employees near retirement have voiced hopes that bonuses given now would positively impact their pension payouts. The company COO has a clear understanding of all of these employee issues, so how should the COO proceed?

Key strategies (Stabell, 2022) for high-stakes negotiation to counteract pressure and create better outcomes are as follows: (1) slow down the conversation to control the narrative: controlling the tempo of the conversation is just as important as controlling its content; (2) leverage crisis framing to reshape perspectives: reframe crises as opportunities to shift control and create leverage; (3) master tactical empathy to gain influence: don't just listen to words—listen to fears, concerns, and underlying motivations; and (4) separate emotion from urgency: do not mistake emotional urgency for real urgency.

References

Bazerman, M. H., and Neale, M. A. (1992). *Negotiating Rationally*. Free Press.

Coleman, P., and Deutsch, M. (2000). *The Handbook of Conflict Resolution*. San Francisco, CA: Jossy-Bass.

Correa, M. (2024). Organizational harmony: A fresh framework to navigate tensions. In *The Leadership & Happiness Laboratory*. Cambridge, MA: Harvard Kennedy School.

Festinger, L. (1957). *A Theory of Cognitive Dissonance*. Stanford University Press.

Jacquet, P. (2024). *The Jungian Confrerie*. London: Jungian Analysis & Psychotherapy.

Kaplan, S. (2024). *How to Manage Team Conflict in Your Workplace*. New York: Psychology Today.

Lim, T. (2024). *Harnessing Creative Tension to Lead Organizational Change*. Jersey City, NJ: Forbes Coaches Council.

Mnookin, R., Peppet, S., and Tulumello, A. (2000). *Beyond Winning: Negotiating to Create Value in Deals and Disputes*. Boston. MA: Harvard University Press.

Pollack, J. (2025). *What Is Organizational Conflict and 5 Strategies for Managing It*. Los Angeles, CA: Peacebuilding Systems.

Schwenk, C. R. (1988). *The Essence of Strategic Decision Making*. MA: Lexington Books.

Senge, P. (1990). *The Fifth Discipline: The Art and Practice of the Learning Organization*. New York: Currency/Doubleday.

Small, J., and McDonald, M. (2024). *7 Surprising Steps to Grow Your Practice Through Leadership*. Dallas, TX: Line of Sight Coaching.

Stabell, K. P. (2022). *Negotiating Under Pressure—Conflict Resolution in Crisis Situations*. Ann Arbor, MI: Center for Conversational Conflict Resolution.

Wilkins, A. L., and Ouchi, W. G. (1983). Efficient cultures: Exploring the relationship between culture and organizational performance. *Organizational Culture*, *28*, 468–481.

Zhang, S. (2022). *How to Embrace Creative Tension and Do Your Best Work*. San Franciso, CA: Dropbox.

16 Relational Identity Concepts

A broad-based approach to understanding conflicts and negotiations within and across communities, nation-states as well as communities defined by common ethnic, economic, or political interests is termed *relational identity theory* (Shapiro, 2010). This complex theory examines how relationships interact during negotiation dynamics. Relational identity theory (RIT) is a framework for understanding and managing conflict by addressing the emotional aspects of relationships. RIT Relational is based on the idea that identity is relational, and that it develops through interactions with others. It can be applied to a variety of contexts, including work relationships and collaborative supply relationships. It can help people understand how unaddressed relational identity concerns can lead to rigidification. RIT, sometimes referred to as social identity theory, is the exploration of how relations between individuals and groups work. This theory is used to best understand how people work and learn together. This theory plays an important part in forming teams and making strategic groups that work together.

Emotions are a vital dimension in conflicts among nation-states and communities affiliated by common ethnic, economic, or political interests. Yet the individuals most responsible for managing such conflicts like heads of state, CEOs, intellectual or religious leaders are often blind to the psychological forces affecting their interests. During 20 years of international research, consulting, and teaching, the relational identity theory (RIT), a theoretical and intellectual framework, was originated to help individuals understand and deal with key emotional dimensions of conflict management. Shapiro argued that national and communal bonds are essentially tribal in nature and how a tribe's unaddressed relational identity concerns make it susceptible to the tribes effect, a rigidification of its relational identity.

Some of the ways in which existing relationships change in this dynamic are as follows:

- Negotiating within internal and external relationships takes place over time.
- Beyond discussion of key issues, negotiation is one way to learn more about the other party and increase interdependence.

DOI: 10.4324/9781042000258-17

- Resolution of simple distributive issues has implications for the future.
- Negotiating within relationships may not reach closure.
- Parties may defer negotiations over tough issues.
- Issues on which parties really disagree may not go away.
- In some negotiations, relationship preservation is the overarching goal.

(Lewicki, Saunders and Barry, 2021)

Breakdown in communication is one of the major forces that pulls business relationships apart. Workmate relationships often come apart for a variety of reasons, including (1) dissatisfaction with the work connection; (2) disillusionment with the power or hierarchical enterprise structure; (3) difficulties with individual characteristics (psychological or behavioral tendencies that interfere with task accomplishment; and (4) inability to cope with stresses imposed by work conditions and settings (Knapp, Vangelisti and Caughlin, 2014).

Identity Defined

Identity is a complex and multifaceted concept that has been the subject of study in various disciplines, including psychology. Traditionally, identity has been understood as something internal and individual, a kind of essential core that defines who we are. However, it is increasingly recognized that identity is not something static or isolated but is built in interaction with other people and contexts. The idea that identity is relational implies that it does not exist in a vacuum, but rather develops through our relationships with others. This identity is not static or fixed but rather develops and evolves throughout life in response to the experiences, relationships, and contexts in which we find ourselves. Our values, beliefs, goals, and aspirations can change over time, which impacts our identity and how we define ourselves and react in many situations.

A relational identity in enterprise often refers to how a company positions itself based on the relationships it fosters with its customers, often emphasizing community, belonging, and shared values, with examples including Airbnb promoting a sense of "home away from home" through unique travel experiences and Coca-Cola building a brand around happiness and shared moments with others. These two companies strive to create a feeling of connection and belonging with their customers beyond just selling a product. Their focus is on connection and community building. The company Patagonia actively promotes environmental activism, connecting with customers passionate about sustainability. Warby Parker emphasizes social responsibility by providing affordable eyewear and supporting eye care initiatives.

The term brand personality refers to a set of characteristics that is attributed to a brand name. An effective brand increases its brand equity by having consistent traits that resonate with one or more consumer segments and provides a company with qualitative value in addition to those benefits derived from the functional desirability of its products and/or services.

The process of identity negotiation has several components, one of which includes those self-presentation processes people perform in the service of establishing who they are. Identity negotiation cannot be equated with self-presentation, however. Self-presentational activity represents a collection of behavioral tactics designed to achieve various interaction goals. In contrast, the process of identity negotiation refers to a much broader set of processes through which people strike a balance between achieving their interaction goals and satisfying their identity-related goals, such as the needs for agency, communion, and psychological coherence. To this end, individuals generally conform to various principles of identity negotiation that not only facilitate smooth interpersonal interactions but also promote intrapersonal harmony. Furthermore, the motivational forces that regulate identity negotiation processes remain operative well beyond the cessation of self-presentational activity (Swann and Bosson, 2008).

Renegotiation Enterprise Examples

With the challenges present in the current economy, it's possible that one will need to rework contracts with suppliers, sellers, licensees, and so on. Renegotiation permits businesses to adapt to changing circumstances while maintaining long-term relationships. Without a clear renegotiation clause, disputes can arise if one party wants to change the terms, but the other does not. Navigating the renegotiation process successfully is key to preserving valuable business relationships and creating lasting benefits for all parties. Often one may need to renegotiate when a contract ends and needs have changed. Perhaps a negotiation was finalized that didn't meet the organization's needs, or a problem has arisen and the terms of the original agreement can't be met as planned. In those cases, one might not have a choice but to go back to the table.

At other times, there may not be any pressing reason to go back to the table, and we might tend to leave things as they are for the time being. This can be a huge mistake. As things evolve in the marketplace, we can miss out on big opportunities if we aren't paying constant attention to what a new contract might offer us.

We should treat renegotiation as an ongoing part of an active and engaged relationship with all buyers, suppliers, and partners. When we do this, we build the strength of our relationships as well as the terms of each contract and build ourselves a stronger position for future renegotiations.

One of the least common situations for renegotiation is when things seem to be going along just fine, but a good negotiator sees a way to improve the terms of a contract and wants to find a way to bring parties back to the table. The key is to make sure that you are always watching the big picture of the marketplace and your long-term relationship with the vendor, provider, or buyer. This means looking not only at what you have to offer but also at what's happening with competitors. Are they offering new incentives or advantages that are weakening your negotiating position? If so, over the course of a stable contract you are likely losing ground if you aren't paying attention.

When conducted properly, renegotiation functions as a way to continuously improve business relationships, ultimately creating greater value for everyone. All business relationships are human relationships and maintaining that relationship over time is part of building your strength in renegotiation. If you are consistently in touch with a partner, you are in a position to ask exploratory questions at any time. This reduces the tension that might come up if you decide it's time to renegotiate an existing contract (Karrass, 2020).

Below are three examples of enterprise conflict that required renegotiating their brands personality: **British Petroleum, Chipotle,** and **Samsung**. When this conflict or crisis occurs that targets and affects the company's brand personality, managers and supervisors will need to negotiate terms and solutions that "right" the brand.

The British Petroleum oil spill in 2010, also known as the Deepwater Horizon oil spill, was the largest marine oil spill in US history. On April 20, 2010, the Deepwater Horizon oil rig exploded and sank in the Gulf of Mexico. An estimated 134 million gallons of oil spilled over 87 days. The spill had a devastating impact on the environment. The spill killed or injured many species, including sea turtles, sperm whales, Bryde's whales, and marine invertebrates. It also damaged habitats and recreational areas and injured natural resources like fish and birds. In addition to resurrecting its brand name, they paid a record-setting $5.5 billion Clean Water Act penalty and up to $8.8 billion in natural resource damages.

In another example, in 2015 Chipotle suffered a brand crisis across Washington, Oregon, California, Minnesota, Ohio, New York, and Massachusetts when hundreds of people fell ill due to *E. coli* and salmonella after eating there. Dozens of victims experienced symptoms severe enough to require hospitalization and to make matters worse, the company's stock prices plummeted. Victims, customers, and stakeholders alike weren't happy with the situation. However, the company rallied by strengthening its food safety requirements, replacing contaminated ingredients, and deep cleaning its locations. Founder Steve Ells issued an open letter defending Chipotle and outlining all the measures the company was taking to fix the problem. The trouble didn't end there. In 2018, 646 people contracted food poisoning caused by Clostridium perfringens bacteria after eating at an Ohio Chipotle. Facing pressure from investors, company executives negotiated a deal where Steve Ells stepped down from his role in 2018. Industry pro Brian Niccol took his place and worked with the Chipotle team to turn the company around, and it worked, against all odds.

In 2016, Samsung experienced a crisis to its confidence and market value. Shortly after its release, multiple Samsung Galaxy Note 7s caught fire. Several of them actually exploded. The company had to stop making the Note 7 and it sent replacement phones to customers and lost stock value to the tune of $26 billion. The US government even recalled the Note 7 phone and the replacements. On top of it all, both were banned from air travel. It was estimated that Samsung lost $17 billion in sales. The company spent four months working as intensely as if the company were a startup. Over 500 engineers tested over 200,000 devices and 30,000 batteries. Three separate third-party safety auditors investigated the problem, too. In the end, the company discovered that some of its factories had been jamming batteries into ill-fitting cases, resulting in faulty (and sometimes exploding) devices.

After the crisis, Samsung put together a battery advisory board, set up new tests to identify potential points of failure, and created software that made any Note 7 still out in the world entirely unusable. Sales have rebounded since then, and Samsung's willingness to investigate itself and fix its mistakes helped maintain its reputation.

In times of this type of turmoil, uncertainty will reign. The status quo is upended and maintaining brand awareness and trust is critical. Companies that remain connected and committed to their employees, customers, and partners will thrive. Beyond meeting customer expectations, being proactive during difficult times will be good for a business's bottom line. Three key takeaways throughout a renegotiation of a brand during a crisis are as follows:

- Be seen: Stay the course with company advertisements. Retreating during a crisis risks undermining customer expectations and long-term profitability.
- Act: Consumers aren't looking for excuses; they want action. They want to be reassured that the brand they're backing is doing the right thing.
- Prepare for what's next: What new marketing, customer service, or product innovation opportunities await? Tune in and listen to your customers. Growing your brand in step with them will further strengthen their trust in the enterprise.

Social Identity Theory

Identity theory should not be confused with social identity theory, which emphasizes group process and intergroup relations rather than role behavior. Identity theory focuses on the self as comprised the various roles an individual occupies (e.g., mother, friend, employee), while social identity theory posits that the groups to which people belong (e.g., political affiliation, ACLU member, nationality) can provide their members with a definition of who they are.

Social identity theory, developed by Henri Tajfel, explains how individuals define themselves based on their group memberships, such as nationality, religion, or social class and it suggests that people seek to enhance their self-esteem by identifying with in-groups and differentiating from out-groups. This can lead to group favoritism, prejudice, and stereotyping as people favor those who belong to their own group (McLeod, 2023). Social identity theory was developed as an integrative theory, as it aimed to connect cognitive processes and behavioral motivation. Initially, its main focus was on intergroup conflict and intergroup relations more broadly. For that reason, the theory was originally referred to as the social identity theory of intergroup relations. Henri Tajfel, who became one of the most famous and influential social psychologists of the twentieth century, began his life in Poland. Born into a Jewish family, he later pursued third-level studies in chemistry at Toulouse University and at the Sorbonne in Paris.

Tajfel explains that the three core processes encompass social categorization, social identification, and social comparison. This illustrates that people sort themselves and others into groups to simplify the social world and that helps predict behavior. Individuals adopt the identity of the group they belong to and internalize group norms and people compare their in-group to out-groups to maintain or enhance self-esteem.

A variety of studies have measured only the salience of identities. Some have measured the content, or self-meanings of identities (the set of beliefs that define an identity). But these approaches do not address the reflexivity of identities. Identities have been defined as reflexively applied cognitions about the self-in-role, meaning that our perceptions of our identities are influenced by what we think others think of us as we enact our various roles in our personal lives and work. This psychological process leads individuals to categorize themselves and others into social groups (or work team groups) and they may identify with certain groups that positively contribute to their self-concept while comparing their in-groups favorably against out-groups

Relationships can substantially influence the outcome of most negotiations. Five important aspects that help negotiations to be successful include the following:

- Trust: Strong relationships can build trust, which is a key factor in negotiation.
- Cooperation: A strong relationship can help negotiators work together effectively.
- Alignment of interests: A strong relationship can help align interests, which can lead to win–win outcomes.
- Conflict management: A strong relationship can help negotiators manage conflict.
- Economic outcomes: Negotiators who build positive relationships with their counterparts can attain better economic outcomes.

The process of negotiating includes all the verbal and nonverbal actions of and interactions between the involved parties while they search for a mutually agreeable solution. Like other social issues in organizational life, the process of negotiation is not objectively determined and experienced. It rests on the co-construction that takes place during the interaction (McGinn and Keros, 2003). Relationships affect this co-construction in several ways: through the choice of interaction partner; through attributions and emotions;

through shared knowledge structures; through procedural rules and norms; and through coordinated action and information sharing.

An initial step in any negotiation is choosing the party or parties with whom to try to shape a deal. Deciding whom to bring to or allow at the bargaining table can be thought of as a matter of search. A bounded rational argument would assert that parties attempt to reduce search costs, just as they attempt to reduce other information-processing costs. Turning to someone with whom ties are already established reduces the cost of searching. In situations in which trust is critical to successful negotiations, selecting known others as partners can not only reduce costs but also bring additional benefits.

Building Trust

Parties in close, positive relationships develop and share their own, unique way of interacting with one another and interpreting the social world around them (Berger, 2002). These shared systems of meanings or understandings facilitate agreement on how to make sense of the issues in and surrounding a negotiation between close parties.

Crucially, trust building is an ongoing, proactive process that involves direct and empathetic interaction as well as a continuous commitment to actions that reinforce a company's dependability and concern for its stakeholders. As business leaders, how one communicates has an impact on a team's level of commitment and the quality of work they deliver, which, in turn, has real and significant implications for the business. To become a more effective communicator and a trustworthy leader, several fundamental principles of leadership communication include the following:

- Genuineness. Always be authentic. That's where others' trust in you begins. Leaders should be genuine and emotionally honest, using realistic, everyday language.
- Acclimated. Be attuned to others. Know what's going on in the organization and the industry and be aware of how what's happening in the outside world affects them. Remain sensitive to the needs of employees and to individual's cultural differences.
- Flexibility. Be adaptable when circumstances change. At times, one may need to be more results focused. In other instances, one may want to be more assertive.
- Confirming. Be affirmative. Loyalty will be present if one is always supportive and appreciative of others.
- Success-oriented. Place a priority on achievement. Take initiative and push for excellence in others.

Leadership trust is a must-have for managers and other leaders. Working in a high trust work environment improves employee engagement, well-being, and psychological safety. And all these areas impact employee turnover. So, if one is to look to increase employee retention, developing employee trust is an excellent place to start.

Constructing trust can be broken down into two distinct types. These types of trust are developed in different ways. Both are important and work together synergistically. So, it's critical that business leaders simultaneously develop both types of trust. The two types are practical trust and emotional trust (Wooll, 2022).

Practical trust is the more traditional type of trust and the one that usually first comes to mind when thinking about how to trust someone. Earning this kind of trust will get one the reputation of being someone who's reliable and competent. Without this kind of trust, people may tend to micromanage you. Communication can break down, and productivity will decrease.

Emotional trust is developed by going above and beyond what's expected and creating meaningful bonds with work teams. It requires a level of emotional intelligence. Successful leaders tend to have higher levels of emotional intelligence, so this is a splendid skill to start developing. Emotional trust can surely be created at an organizational level. Take Netflix, for example. 70% of their employees on Glassdoor would recommend working at Netflix to a friend. This is because Netflix hires with inclusivity and integrity in mind. Their employees work in a high-trust environment. They are also given more decision-making and information-sharing freedom.

> *Trust is the highest form of human motivation. It brings out the very best in people. But it takes time and patience.*
>
> ~ Stephen Covey

Fundamental principles of leadership communication to keep in mind are: (1) *authenticity*—using clear language and being emotionally honest; (2) *connection*—awareness of the workforce and being sensitive to their needs; and (3) *affirmation*—being supportive and appreciative of the workforce.

Unfortunately, building trust is sometimes easier said than done, particularly if you operate in an industry not known for trust. We've all heard stories about dishonest used car salesmen, but many other industries, such as technology, also face their fair share of skepticism. All too often, this distrust is deserved. Some actionable steps one can take to build trust are to focus on foundational elements, adapt to client goals, and ensure that communications align with actions,

Trust Building Strategies

Seven strategies to build trust in an organization are for leaders, supervisors, and administrators to (Reddington, 2023):

- Communicate openly and honestly.
- Explain the environment behind changes.
- Involve more individuals in the decision-making process.

- Connect people to the larger picture.
- Listen actively and ask probing questions.
- Be transparent about enterprise goals and priorities.
- Provide occasions for growth and development.

Additionally, other key strategies include transparency and openness; consistency and reliability, empathy and human connection; and authenticity and integrity. Integrity is the backbone of trust and involves (1) holding the line on ethical boundaries; (2) calling out any misalignment early; (3) protecting confidentiality; and (4) making decisions that match stated values, even when costly. This works because integrity can create moral predictability.

Zak (2017), author of *Trust Factor: The Science of Creating High-Performance Companies*, reported that individuals employed by high-trust companies saw that following:

- A 60% increase in career satisfaction
- A 50% increase in productivity
- A 66% increase in team unity

When trust is questionable or missing, however, many areas suffer. Job performance slows down, employee engagement is low, and turnover is high. Therefore, trust in leadership is crucial to a healthy workplace, a conflict free environment, and sustainable shared success.

Inside high-trust organization, one finds employees who feel safe to take risks, express themselves freely, and innovate. When trust is instilled in this organization, tasks get accomplished with less difficulty because people are more likely to collaborate and communicate with each other in productive ways. As a result, outcomes tend to be more successful.

According to a study by Paul Zak (2017), he found that individuals at high-trust companies reported 74% less stress, 106% more energy at work, 50% higher productivity, 13% fewer sick days, 76% more engagement, 29% more satisfaction with their lives, and 40% less burnout than people at low-trust companies.

In contrast, employees at low-trust organizations are often bogged down by office politics and infighting. They are more likely to withhold information and hoard resources because they don't feel safe sharing them. As a result, decision-making is slower and less effective.

Leadership skills and actions that help build trust in the workplace include the ability to master self-awareness and empathy. Excellent leaders understand themselves and their employees as people. This humanistic approach to leadership leaves the ego at the door, making space for transparency and this enhanced self-awareness also lets trusted leaders assess their decisions and reduce biases. Additionally, these leaders embrace learning opportunities that develop these soft skills. They understand how fundamental they are to building employee trust.

The implication for managing conflict often relies on the existence of trust between individuals. Trust is often the first casualty in conflict (Coleman and Deutsch, 2000).

As relationships develop and change over time, so does the nature of trust in those relationships. Our trust in another person also varies in different situations and contexts, and so different types of trust, and even trust and distrust, may coexist in the same relationship.

Coleman and Deutsch draw on their account of trust to characterize relationships based on four variables: calculus-based trust, calculus-based distrust, identification-based trust, and identification-based distrust.

Research shows that calculus-based trust can be built by engaging in predicable, constant, reliable ways. The authors offer several strategies for managing calculus-based distrust. First, have explicit agreements on goals, deadlines and penalties, and on monitoring procedures. Develop alternatives to relying on another and use those alternatives as a threat. Show the other how their performance may be (unintentionally) provoking distrust and attempt to understand the logic of another's seemingly inconsistent behavior.

Identification-based trust can be fostered if the parties take time to develop their common interests, values, perceptions, motives, and goals. Identification-based trust has a strong emotional component and so is sensitive to a few non-logical factors. This makes managing identification-based distrust difficult. One strategy is to increase the parties' calculus-based trust. Another is to openly acknowledge areas of distrust and jointly develop ways to work around those areas.

Frequent or severe violations of trust (or conversely of distrust) are likely to change the trusting relationship. Violations of calculus-based trust are likely to encourage calculus-based distrust (and vice versa). Such violations of trust can be managed in a relatively straightforward manner, by determining the cause of the lapse and the likelihood of further such lapses.

Violations of identification-based trust have a greater effect on the parties' emotional well-being. Violations of identification-based trust are likely to end the relationship itself, if they are not properly addressed. To repair such a violation parties must first communicate to identify and understand the breach, and then explicitly recommit themselves to their trusting relationship.

This account of trust has several implications for conflict management. First, trust facilitates effective conflict resolution. Second, conflicts diminish trust and build distrust. Third, the authors argue that "creating trust in a relationship is initially a matter of building calculus-based trust" (p. 101). Identification-based trust can further strengthen a relationship, as the parties come to have a shared interest in maintaining their relationship. Distrusting relationships are more prone to conflict, and those conflicts are more prone to increase distrust. Most relationships are a mixture of both types of trust and distrust and so are marked by varying degrees of ambivalence. Finally, trust can be rebuilt. However, since the rebuilding process is often lengthy, conflict management may be more effective if it emphasizes managing distrust.

Trust Repair

Outsourcing, mergers, downsizing, shifting business models, the rise of AI, return to office mandates and more are creating turbulence for companies. Add in the broader economic uncertainties, and we have the natural breeding grounds for distrust. Changes like these result in confidential discussions about restructuring, budget cuts, and other hard decisions that directly impact employees. These discussions demand secrecy at precisely the moment when transparency could support morale and engagement. The result is a trust paradox.

While trust is critical for staff engagement and morale, only 21% of employees currently trust their leadership according to one Gallup survey (and a more recent survey shows it has declined since then). Even fewer, at 18%, trust that their leaders will explain the effect of any changes made on their organizations (Randel, 2025).

Theories of trust repair theory in business refers to a set of strategies and principles focused on rebuilding broken trust within a professional relationship, typically between a leader and their team, colleagues, or clients, after a breach of confidence or a significant mistake has occurred. It involves acknowledging transgression, taking responsibility, demonstrating genuine remorse, and actively working to regain trust through consistent positive actions. Repairing trust after a transgression is a complex, multi-stage process that depends on the nature of the violation, the relationship between the parties, and the willingness of both sides to engage in reconciliation.

Trust means having confidence that an organization is (1) competent enough to reliably deliver on its promises and obligations, (2) has goodwill toward stakeholders and cares about their interests, and (3) adheres to ethical principles and acceptable conduct, especially in business negotiations. A failure that makes stakeholders doubt any of those key elements will damage trust for trust repair involves the actions an organization takes to restore those positive perceptions and regain the confidence of stakeholders after it has been lost.

> *Trust is the key that unlocks the door of every successful partnership, whether in business or personal life.*
>
> ~ Mark Zuckerberg

After acknowledging a trust transgression, the company workforce needs some transparent context about resulting findings. Executive decisions should be translated into human terms, helping teams understand and begin to adjust to new realities.

Trust repair at the enterprise level means sharing what you can about market conditions, strategic changes, and the reasoning behind difficult choices. Confidentiality might prevent full disclosure, so it is important to be honest about those constraints: “I can’t share details about specific decisions, but

I can tell you about the specific market pressures and budget realities that drove the overall restructuring."

Great leaders, according to Gallup research (McLain and Pendell, 2023) "explain where the company is coming from and where it's going" while also establishing "what the company will always do and what it needs to do now." Especially during turbulent times, employees are looking to you for assurance about what they can rely on.

A helpful practice is to meet with fellow leaders, share the questions your teams are asking, and support one another in providing meaningful answers.

Key aspects of trust repair theory are to acknowledge the breach or transgression and to take responsibility and express remorse. Companies often blame trust violations on rogue employees, but these violations are predictable in organizations that allow dysfunctional, conflicting, or incongruent activities to take root.

In the aftermath of the well-publicized corporate scandals of Enron, WorldCom, and Tyco circa 2001 and 2002, there were major efforts in the United States to restore trust and enforce corporate compliance. Among other things, the US Congress passed the Sarbanes–Oxley Act of 2002, featuring enhanced whistleblower protections, holding CEOs and CFOs personally responsible for financial statements, and establishing the creation of the Public Company Accounting Oversight Board, harsher sentencing rules, and even new organizational guidelines to encourage boards to adopt changes to organization structures and processes to target more systemic approaches to prevent wrongdoing. Corporate spending on compliance increased an estimated $6 billion annually (Schaller, 2010) and leading business schools created ethics centers and made ethics training mandatory.

Yet despite these reform efforts, corporate trust violations have gone unabated and public trust in business has plummeted. A full recitation of the significant trust violations of recent years would go on for pages, covering Olympus Corporation's accounting fraud, Barclays' LIBOR rigging scandal, News Corporation's phone-hacking scandal, and the BP Deepwater Horizon oil spill.

In fact, some of the most insidious practices from the Enron era (notably, disguising financial weakness with off-balance-sheet debt) were front and center again during the global financial crisis of 2008. In the wake of that financial crisis, the US Congress passed the Dodd–Frank Wall Street Reform and Consumer Protection Act, which extended and tightened the financial regulatory system and strengthened consumer protections.

Team Dysfunction

Patrick Lencioni levels of team dysfunction focus on the following:

Absence of trust: This occurs when team members are reluctant to be vulnerable to one another and are unwilling to admit their mistakes, weaknesses, or need help. Some fear of conflict: being incapable of engaging in unfiltered, passionate debate about key issues. It creates situations where team conflict can easily turn into veiled discussions and back-channel comments. In a work setting where team members do not openly air their opinions, inferior decisions result.

Absence of commitment: Without commitment, it is difficult for team members to commit to decisions, fostering an environment where ambiguity prevails.

Avoidance of accountability: When teams do not commit to a clear plan of action, even the most focused and driven individuals are hesitant to call their peers out on actions and behaviors that may seem counterproductive to the overall good of the team.

Inattention to results: Work team members naturally tend to put their own needs (e.g., ego, career development, recognition) ahead of the collective goals of the team when individuals are not held accountable. If a team has lost sight of the need for achievement, the business ultimately suffers.

When teams are working in harmony, these dysfunctions cease to cause problems. Lencioni's model highlights the results when the team lacks trust, and this should be the area one concentrates on the most. Understandably, when trust is breached, the damage can be extensive. The repercussions may extend beyond cooperation on a professional level, leading to a fundamental distrust of one's values and business intentions. The range of reactions may be best understood through the nature of the violation.

Before moving on to the strategies to rebuild trust, it should be noted that not all trust can be repaired and repaired trust may never be the same as pristine trust. Whether or not one achieves forgiveness in the business world, the important thing is that the company moves forward with authenticity and sincerity.

Researchers (Sharma, Schoorman and Ballinger, 2023) have identified three philosophical mechanisms for trust repair.

Defensiveness after trust transgressions is a common and damaging situation. Several guidelines (Block, 2023) to facilitate constructive trust repair discussions are as follows: (1) stay focused and clearly define the issue(s); (2) be an active listener; (3) understand that total agreement is not essential; and (4) do not personalize, but rather stick with the issue(s)

Table 16.1 Philosophical trust repair mechanisms

Mechanism	*Description*
Attributional	Focuses on how the trustor interprets the cause of the violation.
Social equilibrium	Seeks to restore balance in the relationship through reciprocity
Structural	Involves formal systems or third-party interventions to rebuild trust

How Not to Handle a Crisis

Few corporate scandals in recent memory offer as stark a lesson in how not to handle a crisis as the demise of **Agrokor**, once the largest food manufacturer in Southeast Europe. At its peak, in 2017, Agrokor was more than just a company. It was an economic pillar, employing over 60,000 people across the Balkans (including 40,000 in Croatia, making the country's largest employer) and accounting for 15% of Croatia's GDP. The first cracks appeared in early 2017 when Moody's and S&P downgraded Agrokor's credit rating. What followed was a rapid unraveling that exposed deep-seated issues within the company and Croatia's broader economic landscape.

Agrokor's handling of the crisis was plagued by a series of critical missteps that exacerbated the company's problems and eroded stakeholder trust. At the heart of these failures was a stark lack of transparency. As reports surfaced of financial misreporting and massive debt, mainly to Russian bank Sberbank, Agrokor's leadership failed to provide clear, honest communication about the company's financial state. This opacity was compounded by delayed action; the company's slow response to the unfolding crisis allowed speculation and fear to spread, further eroding trust among employees, suppliers, and the general public. Leadership inadequacies further hampered Agrokor's crisis response. The company's reaction to the crisis was to claim innocence and file a lawsuit against the Croatian government rather than taking responsibility and spearheading efforts to address the company's issues. This defensive posture did little to inspire confidence or demonstrate a commitment to resolving the underlying problems.

This case serves as an illustration of how major state-owned banks, which act as pillars of a nation's financial sector, can fall victim to the dangers of blindly trusting external private advisers. It also highlights how financial mismanagement can be further compounded by geopolitical risks and the complexities of navigating legal proceedings in European countries, particularly for sanctioned entities (Dimitrov, 2025).

Effective crisis management is critical for maintaining an organization's reputation, financial health, and stakeholder trust. A single slipup, particularly crisis management mistakes in leadership or missteps in corporate crisis response, can lead to long-lasting damage. Therefore, it is vital to understand and address these potential pitfalls before they escalate. Common crisis management mistakes to avoid include a lack of preparedness, poor communication, overlooking stakeholder needs, slow response timing, and weak leadership.

> *Management is doing things right; leadership is doing the right things.*
>
> ~ Peter Drucker

Business managers should steer clear of making the following six errors when addressing a business crisis:

- Do not *minimize* the problem by stating that it's under control.
- Do not *postpone* or delay a response since it fuels misinformation and speculation.

- Do not *overlook* internal stakeholders, which can lead to leaks and fear.
- Do not *mislead* and make statements that cannot be backed up or proven untrue.
- Do not *neglect* empathy without displaying human concern.
- Do not *communicate* mixed leadership messages that can confuse employees and the public.

In 2014, **Theranos**, a blood-testing startup pitching a supposedly revolutionary technology, was flying high. While existing technology required one vial of blood for each diagnostic test conducted, Theranos claimed to be able to perform hundreds of tests (supposedly over 240) ranging from cholesterol levels to complex genetic analysis, with just a single pinprick of blood. Automated, fast, and inexpensive, Theranos seemed to be offering technology that could revolutionize medicine and save lives.

Elizabeth Holmes, founder and CEO of Theranos, had famously dropped out of Stanford to found the company using her tuition money, and was just 30 when Theranos was at its peak. Having raised over $700 m in investment from the likes of Larry Ellison and Tim Draper, the company had become the rising star of Silicon Valley and was valued at over $9 billion, while Holmes, with a share of more than half that, was heralded as the female Steve Jobs.

The only problem was that the technology did not work. Theranos employees revealed lies that were made to board members that fostered a culture of intimidation and secrecy. The technology had repeatedly failed quality assurance and, crucially, results sent to real patients that were fundamentally incorrect, upon which life-changing medical decisions were being made. It would seem that the company had been built on nothing more than audacious lies.

The reaction from Theranos was astonishing. At first, Holmes vehemently denied the claims made against her and the company. Nonetheless, in 2018, Holmes stepped down as CEO and was charged with criminal fraud, having allegedly misled investors and deliberately made false claims made about the efficiency of the company's blood testing technology.

Three months later, the company officially shut down following investigation by the FBI, leaving thousands of former employees uncertain about their future and in January 2022, Holmes was found guilty on four charges of defrauding investors, and ten months later, she was sentenced to over 11 years in prison. More information around the downfall of Theranos was revealed in the trial, with prosecutors accusing Holmes of destroying evidence in Theranos' final days in business (Roff, 2024).

References

Block, J. (2023). *After a Breach of Trust Don't Make It Worse*. New York: Psychology Today.

Coleman, P., and Deutsch, M. (2000). *The Handbook of Conflict Resolution*. San Francisco, CA: Jossy-Bass.

Dimitrov, P. (2025). *Agrokor's Legacy: How Ivica Todorić Became Croatia's Most Controversial Businessman*. Research Initiative. support@researchinitiative.org.

Karrass, C. L. (2020). *Effective Negotiating*. Los Angeles, CA: Karrass.com.
Knapp, M., Vangelisti, A., and Caughlin, J. (2014). *Interpersonal al Communication and Human Relationships*. Boston, MA: Pearson.
Lewicki, R., Saunders, D., and Barry, B. (2021). *Essentials of Negotiation*. New York: McGraw-Hill.
McLain, D., and Pendell, R. (2023). *Why Trust in Leaders Is Faltering and How to Gain It Back*. Gallup. www.gallup.com/workplace
McLeod, S. (2023). *Social Identity Theory in Psychology*. London: SimplyPsychology.org.
Randel, M. (2025). *Rebuilding Trust After Difficult Decisions: A Relationship-Based Approach*. San Francisco, CA: Simpler Media Group.
Reddington, R. (2023). *How Leadership Trust Guides High-Performing Teams*. San Francisco, CA: Better Up.
Roff, C. (2024). *Everything You Need to Know About the Theranos Scandal*. Hampshire: Pan Macmillan.
Schaller, J. (2010). Almost ten years after the Enron meltdown. In *The Hidden Challenge of Cross-Border Negotiations*. Boston, MA: The Magazine HBR.
Shapiro, D. L. (2010). Relational identity theory. *American Psychologist*, *65*(7).
Sharma, K., Schoorman, F. D., and Ballinger, G. A. (2023). How can it be made right again? A review of trust repair research. *Journal of Management*, *49*(1), 363–399.
Swann, W. B., and Bosson, J. K. (2008). Identity negotiation: A theory of self and social interaction. In *Handbook of Personality: Theory and Research*. New York: The Guilford Press.
Wooll, M. (2022). *How to Build Trust in the Workplace: 10 Effective Solutions*. San Francisco, CA: Better Up.
Zak, P. (2017). *Trust Factor: The Science of Creating High-Performance Companies*. Grand Haven, MI: Brilliance Audio.

17 Power and Conflict Issues

Power and conflict issues are central to how enterprises operate; they influence decision-making, employee relations, leadership effectiveness, and overall organizational performance. Power and conflict are related concepts that can be studied in many disciplines, including business, economics, social sciences, and the humanities. Power is the ability to meet one's needs, and conflict can exist when each party involved has some degree of power. Things to consider when thinking about power and conflict are power imbalances, and different overarching goals.

Manifestations of Power

Power and conflict in business settings are critical aspects that can significantly influence organizational dynamics, culture, and overall success. Following are some key areas where power and conflict manifest in business:

Organizational structure

- Hierarchical power: In traditional organizational structures, power often flows top-down, which can lead to conflicts between different levels of the hierarchy. For instance, conflicts may arise between managers and employees over decision-making authority.
- Decentralized power: In more modern, flat organizations, power is distributed more evenly, which can reduce but not eliminate conflicts. These structures often rely on collaboration, which can sometimes lead to disagreements over responsibilities and roles.

Leadership styles

- Authoritative leadership: Leaders who exert a high level of control may face resistance from employees who feel their autonomy is being undermined, leading to conflict.
- Democratic leadership: While more inclusive, this style can lead to conflicts as differing opinions and ideas clash.

DOI: 10.4324/9781042000258-18

Workplace dynamics

- Competition: In highly competitive environments, conflicts can arise as employees vie for promotions, recognition, and resources.
- Collaboration: While teamwork is encouraged, differing working styles and personalities can lead to interpersonal conflicts.

Strategic decisions

- Resource allocation: Decisions about how resources (like budget, personnel, or time) are allocated can lead to power struggles and conflicts.
- Change management: Implementing new strategies or changes within an organization often causes resistance and conflict among those who are affected.

External relations

- Negotiations: Power dynamics play a crucial role in negotiations with clients, suppliers, and partners. Conflicts can arise when there is a perceived imbalance of power.
- Regulatory compliance: Navigating laws and regulations can lead to conflicts, especially when business practices are challenged by external authorities.

As important as hierarchies often are in business, they can also breed resentment, competition, and tension. Creativity can get dampened, as can the willingness of employees to voice their opinions. As some employees get promoted and others do not, competition can turn to jealousy, rivalry, and perhaps petty gossip. Those who advance within a large organization might not always be the ones who deserve it.

Rudiments of good and positive relationships are built upon (1) trust—this becomes the vital foundation for successful employees in bonding with others and building a healthy relationships; (2) mutual respect—when employees value each other's opinions and ideas; and (3) mindfulness—a workforce that is careful with their words and practice active listening.

Building positive relationships with one's subordinates, peers, and supervisors is crucial to building and maintaining power as a leader/manager. These positive relationships mean that others are likely to give you the benefit of the doubt when difficult decisions need to be made (Raines, 2024).

A typical hierarchy in business looks like a pyramid:

Top level (executive management)—for example, CEO, COO, CFO

Makes strategic decisions and sets goals.

Middle level (managers, directors)

Converts strategy into operational plans; oversees teams.

Lower level (supervisors, employees)

Fulfills daily tasks and reports progress upward.

Social Science Experiences

While ensuring everyone is treated with optimal fairness and can share their opinions and ideas is not always possible, there are many ways to create a positive hierarchy. One way is to make expertise the focal point. As obvious as expertise is in terms of workplace promotion, it does not always occur. Some people might get promoted because of how well they know certain individuals within the organization, because of how they look, or simply because they are the most vocal. When such people advance despite not having the expertise and other necessary qualifications, resentment among their former co-workers is inevitable. Those at the top of the organization should know the most about the company and how to move forward for maximum brand awareness and revenue. By making expertise and related experience the sole reasons for promotion, one will not only avoid workplace tension but also save the company from issues such as low-performance levels and shadow hierarchies.

Four common themes or perspectives are found in the social science literature:

✓ "Power over"
✓ "Power with"
✓ "Powerless and dependence"
✓ "Empowered and independent"

The power over approach tends to involve people who acquire power and will usually endeavor to consolidate it and extend it (Michels, 1911). The power with approach is the type that is jointly developed, coactive and non-coercive. Powerless and dependence are distinct though often highly correlated experiences where one has a lack of power coupled with a tendency to have some type of dependence on others (Kanter, 1977). The opposite side of powerlessness is having power with a concomitant sense of independence. Several businesses have explored empowerment in terms of employee participation, delegation of authority and structural decentralization.

Your most unhappy customers are your greatest source of learning.
~ Bill Gates

Power Struggles

Power is an elusive concept because it has so many manifestations. Everyone has many possible sources of power, most of which he or she is often unaware. Some are independent of conflict while others can be enhanced or diminished by the process of conflict. Structural power is derived from the situation. Power struggles often create conflict, especially when individuals are competing for authority or resources. This can escalate tensions. Conflict in enterprise also reveals the power structures. The singular question of who resolves conflicts and how they're handled often indicates where real power lies.

One form of structural power is formal authority. Changes in structural power usually require systemic fixes. Personal power is inherent in the individual, their personal characteristics, and traits. Personal power may come from communication skills, training, or experience.

Research over the past two decades has established the all-encompassing effect of power on people. Put simply: Power changes people. People who rise to the tops of companies and other organizations tend to prioritize their own goals and desires above those of others, fail to take other people's perspectives into account, tend to disregard other people's feelings, and are, well, less polite. They act to preserve their power, sometimes aggressively, when they feel that it is threatened.

When high-powered people work with teammates who are a potential threat, the high-powered people lash out. Conflict ensues. Because power is so valued, people within reach of the top tier of an organization will fight to retain their position at the top. Power conflicts in management teams are so common that teams one would expect to be the best, such as management teams, can actually be less effective than those lower down on the organizational chart. This is an enormous loss of potential for an organization relying on its most skilled and experienced employees (Greer, 2014). At worst, conflicts result in firings and outright failures. Business leaders and board members who ignore power struggles within their management teams do so at the organization's risk.

Power struggles are like unseen currents that can swamp an organization. They manifest in various forms, from subtle manipulations to explicit conflicts. To navigate this dangerous territory, it's crucial to recognize the signs and identify the different types of power struggles that may lie in wait beneath the surface.

Table 17.1 Four types of power struggles

Type of power struggles	*Description*
Interpersonal	Conflicts between individuals or colleagues competing for recognition, funds, or leadership roles
Departmental	Tensions between different departments or teams seeking autonomy, control over resources, or dominance
Hierarchical	Battles for influence or control within organizational hierarchies, often involving managers or supervisors

Nine key types of power are as follows:

- Formal: The authority given by an institution, by set policies or by virtue of one's position, such as CEO, board president or city council member.
- Legal: Rights and choices defined by law or policy. Related are the resources a person must pursue legal action.
- Information (data and knowledge): if one party to a conflict has information that the other doesn't then they may have power in a conflict. Expert power is intriguing because one doesn't actually need information to have expert power but instead must merely be *perceived* to have expertise. Simply having qualifications or certifications, or creating or gaining a reputation for wisdom, can be enough to give someone expert power.
- Association: This kind of power comes from the connection with other people or groups, such as political entities, trade associations, or any other organization.
- Resources: The ability to control resources whether tangible in the form of money, labor or time, or intangible, such as reputation, is a significant source of power
- Sanctions: The ability to confer benefits or rewards and impose sanctions or penalties. This reward power means having the capacity to offer benefits in exchange for carrying out a task or achieving a result. It may come in the form of raises, benefits, promotions, or public praise. However, this type of power is not always as effective as some think.
- Coercive: Having the capability to discipline or punish and penalize others. Although it may work in the short-term, coercive power creates unhappy, disengaged employees. It can also negatively affect employee retention efforts.
- Morals: Power can flow from an appeal to values, beliefs, and ethics or from an attack on the values of those with whom you are in conflict.
- Personal charisma: This kind of power derives from an individual's inherent make up, such as their perseverance, endurance, intelligence, communication skills, determination, and emotional strength. It often means they're well-regarded, respected and admired, and thus influence others as a result.

Common sources of conflict in enterprise considerations are as follows:

- Lack of solid communication: Communication is essential for ensuring clarity, alignment, and collaboration among stakeholders. However, communication can also be a source of conflict if it is unclear, inconsistent, incomplete, or inaccurate. To prevent or resolve communication-related conflicts, the business leaders should use effective communication techniques, such as active listening, paraphrasing, summarizing, asking open-ended questions, and providing constructive feedback.
- Competing interests: Stakeholders may have different or conflicting interests, goals, priorities, or values that influence their expectations and

preferences for the solution. To manage or resolve interest-based conflicts, the business leaders should identify and understand the underlying interests of each stakeholder group and try to find common ground, mutual benefits, or trade-offs that can satisfy their needs and expectations.

- Incompatible perspectives: Stakeholders may have different or conflicting perspectives, opinions, beliefs, or assumptions that affect their understanding and interpretation of the problem, the solution, or the situation. To address or resolve perspective-based conflicts, business leaders should acknowledge and respect the diversity and validity of different perspectives and try to foster a culture of openness, curiosity, and learning among stakeholders.

Leadership is not about having all the answers; it is about knowing how to get to the best answer.

~ Sherre DeMao

Misconceptions of Power

Power in business is often misunderstood, leading to ineffective leadership, missed opportunities, and toxic cultures. Power is often mistaken as dominance, control, or hierarchy, but in reality, it's about influence, trust, and adaptability. Misconceptions about power can lead to poor leadership, toxic cultures, and missed opportunities for collaboration and innovation.

Power plays a role in most conflicts. Popular misconceptions about power include the belief that it has some physical location, that there is only a fixed amount of it, that it operates in only one direction, and that the use of power is basically adversarial or competitive. Within the social sciences, there are four perspectives on power. Some theorists emphasize "power over"—the ability to compel someone to do something. This view suggests a view of power as coercive and competitive. Other theorists have developed the concept of "power with," which emphasizes the effectiveness of joint or cooperative action. A third set of theories focus on issues of powerlessness and dependence, while others explore the obverse: empowerment and independence. Empowerment theorists employ the notion of "power to," as in the power to act effectively without constraint or disability (Coleman and Deutsch, 2000).

Two misconceptions of power are that power only comes from position and only top executives or managers have real power. The reality is that power also comes from expertise, relationships, and influence. Employees without formal authority can still shape decisions through credibility, collaboration, or innovation. The second major misconception is that power equates to having control over others to force compliance. In reality, true power in modern organizations comes from inspiring, persuading, and enabling others, not domination. Effective leaders employ influence, not coercion.

In general, power is a fixed resource. Individuals often treat power like a pie. If someone achieves a gain, someone else stands to lose. However, in high-performing organizations, power is expandable where sharing information can increase collective capability, while empowering others increases your own influence. Zero-sum thinking often leads to territory wars and political dysfunction.

Power can be usefully conceptualized as a mutual interaction between the characteristics of a person and the characteristics of a situation where the person has access to valued resources and uses them to achieve personal, relational, or environmental goals, often through using various strategies of influence. Power is understood in relational terms, and power itself is distinguished from sources of power, the effective use of available power, and strategies for deploying power.

Power is not only what you have, but what the enemy thinks you have.
~ Saul Alinsky

By harnessing the power of leverage to make business easier and more profitable, any business owner can propel their business to greater heights. Leverage is the key to scalability. It means using various resources to achieve business goals more effectively and efficiently.

Not all power is bad, and optimistically it is well earned. Ideally, those in positions of power and influence got there due to their experience and authority. One can't ignore that sometimes it is connections that help. It's important not to ignore power imbalance in business. Instead of fearing an imbalance, identify what one brings to the table. Even the most junior employee has something valuable to contribute. Perhaps it is a fresh insight, digital expertise, or a unique perspective others might be blind to. Power dynamics exists in every workplace, but they don't have to be intimidating or negative. By fostering foster mutual respect, setting clear expectations, and maintaining autonomy one can create relationships that fuel both personal and professional growth. The key is to use power dynamics as a tool for learning and collaboration, instead of a source of conflict or insecurity. The most successful people don't just learn to navigate power—they learn how to harness it for mutual success (Gotian, 2025).

In business, harnessing power and leverage means getting more done with the same number of resources or achieving more with less. It's about amplifying output while keeping input at a manageable level. It's not tied to any specific resource; rather, it's a mindset, a strategy, an approach to doing business that prizes efficiency and impact over mere effort, making it possible to grow more without working more. To comprehend the power of leverage, one needs to know that it works by maximizing the effectiveness of resources in a way that proportionally exceeds the amount that's invested. It's about optimizing inputs to achieve outsized outputs. In other words, it's not a one-to-one equation, where one puts in one unit of effort and gets one unit of results. Instead, it's about putting in one unit of effort and getting multiple units of results and the essence of leverage is understanding that small things can compound into big results. Whether applied in finance, time management, or knowledge acquisition, leverage is about achieving greater results without necessarily increasing the number of resources used (Kaufmann, 2024).

Three rudimentary misconceptions about power are as follows:

- Power is a personality trait: Power is interpersonal, not intrinsic. One does not possess power in isolation; it is granted by others based on trust, necessity, or respect.
- Feeling powerful means you are powerful: One's actual influence depends on how others perceive and respond to you.
- Power is always visible: Some of the most potent forms of power are invisible, like social capital and emotional intelligence.

Enterprise power issues have enveloped Boeing ever since the Boeing 737 MAX was first announced in 2011. The jetliner that was supposed to represent the future of the aerospace giant has been plagued by problems. Despite being Boeing's best-selling model ever, the 737 Max's troubled history included a pair of fatal crashes, a number of forced landings, and ongoing safety and production issues that have resulted in significant financial losses and a severe blow to Boeing's reputation as one of America's most trusted companies.

Some of the results of this crisis involved Boeing borrowing $14 billion from US banks to navigate the financial strain caused by the grounding of the plane and the emerging COVID-19 pandemic. This loan was later supplemented by another $25 billion in debt, underscoring the financial challenges Boeing faces. In March 2020, the company shares hit $89, the lowest since early 2013, reflecting investor concerns about the company's future amid the 737 Max crisis and the impact of the COVID-19 pandemic on global air travel. Boeing also announced the first wave of job cuts, planning to reduce its workforce by 10% in response to the pandemic-induced drop in air travel. This move is part of broader efforts to cut costs and stabilize the company's finances.

One of the most significant factors contributing to the failure of the 737 Max was the flawed design of the MCAS system. Boeing engineers decided to rely on a single AOA sensor to provide input to the MCAS, despite the known risks of sensor failure. Instead of addressing many issues through structural changes to the aircraft, Boeing chose to implement the MCAS as a software solution. This decision, while expedient, introduced new risks that were not fully appreciated at the time. The definitive finding of this crisis had Boeing replace its chief executive and other senior managers and make changes to improve quality and accountability in its production (Johnson, 2020).

Power misconceptions in business often persist because of (1) cultural narratives where media often praise dominance and control; (2) hierarchical constructs that operate with rigid top-down models, reinforcing outdated views; and (3) leader's fear and insecurity who feel vulnerable and may hold on to control as a defense mechanism.

Squandering Power

Squandering power is something anyone can do. While it often happens when people first enter an organization, it can also happen to people who've spent many years, or even their entire careers, at an organization. Some of the most common mistakes that one can make to squander power are as follows (Barkacs, 2021):

- Not knowing what the goals are
- Inaccurately assessing the situation
- Failing to keep one's ego in check
- Underestimating dependence and interdependence
- Mistreating or disrespecting others
- Overestimating one's power and control

In 2019, **WeWork**, the office-sharing startup once hailed as the future of work, was poised for one of the most anticipated initial public offerings in recent years. With a peak private valuation of $47 billion, a charismatic co-founder in Adam Neumann, and the backing of SoftBank's Vision Fund, WeWork seemed unstoppable.

Then came the Initial Public Offering prospectus and within weeks, the company went from being Silicon Valley's hottest unicorn to a corporate cautionary tale. Investors flinched at the company's ballooning losses, questionable governance, and unusual corporate culture. The IPO was postponed, then canceled, and Neumann was ousted as CEO. What unfolded was not just the collapse of an offering but the public unmasking of a business model and leadership style that couldn't withstand market scrutiny.

After the IPO collapse, WeWork faced a money crunch and **SoftBank** entered with a $9.5 billion bailout, gaining majority control. Neumann walked away with a lucrative exit package reportedly worth hundreds of millions. Restructuring began under new leadership. The company scaled back expansion, cut thousands of jobs, and aimed for profitability. However, the damage to WeWork's brand and investor trust was severe.

The spectacle encompassing WeWork's collapse, complete with governance scandals, valuation freefalls, and an ousted founder, reinforced WeWork's place in business history as a symbol of squandered power and excess (Palmer, 2019).

Leveraging Resources

Karie Kaufmann (2024) also indicates that a robust business plan is another form of leverage that can significantly impact a company's trajectory. Serving as a roadmap, it outlines a clear path from where the business is currently to where you want it to be, detailing the strategies and actions needed to get there. A well-articulated business plan can help secure funding from investors who are persuaded by the clarity of vision and the thoroughness of the plan.

It also provides a framework to measure progress, set milestones, and realign actions when necessary.

Moreover, with a clear plan, companies can leverage their resources more effectively, provide direction for team members, and set benchmarks for assessing performance and making necessary adjustments. In essence, a solid business plan leverages foresight, strategic thinking, and tactical planning to guide a business toward its objectives in the most efficient way possible.

Understanding the magnitude of leveraging resources can help organizations optimize their resources to achieve their desired goals efficiently. Leveraging resources also enables organizations to take advantage of external resources that they may not have within their workforce. By utilizing these external resources, organizations can increase their effectiveness and efficiency, leading to improved performance and productivity.

One of the key benefits of leveraging resources is increased efficiency. When organizations leverage their resources effectively, they can streamline their processes, reducing the time, effort, and cost required to achieve their goals. This can free up resources that can then be allocated to other areas, allowing the organization to achieve even greater levels of efficiency.

Leveraging resources is also critical in enabling organizations to stay competitive in today's rapidly changing market. By leveraging their resources, organizations can adapt to changes and respond quickly to emerging trends. This allows organizations to stay ahead of the curve and remain relevant in their industry, ensuring long-term success and growth.

An added noteworthy benefit of leveraging resources is the ability to reduce risk. By utilizing external resources, organizations can mitigate potential risks associated with relying solely on their internal resources. This can include reducing the risk of employee burnout, project delays, or unexpected costs, allowing the organization to maintain a stable and predictable flow of operations.

A control of resources is about having one's hands on the perks, bonuses, and rewards. This isn't just about money; it's also about access to people, technology, information, or anything else people might need to get their jobs done. The enterprise gatekeeper for any of these resources wields a significant amount of power. This authority can make that gatekeeper a central figure in the workplace, as they enable projects and initiatives to move forward or stall.

Additionally, access to information is the modern-day equivalent of being the visionary. In today's knowledge-driven workplaces, information is gold. The individual with the latest data and insights has power. This could mean being knowledgeable to executive team decisions, understanding the market better than anyone else, or just being good at finding out what's going on around the workplace. Information power means one can influence decisions and opinions simply because they know something others don't.

In conclusion, leveraging one's resources is a critical aspect of achieving success in any field, especially in business. By understanding the importance of leveraging resources, organizations can improve their effectiveness, efficiency, and adaptability, reduce risk, and ultimately achieve their desired goals (Cheng, 2023). Through effective resource management, organizations can optimize their performance and maintain a competitive edge, ensuring long-term success and growth.

Effective Resource Management

Leveraging resources effectively is key to achieving business success. Effective resource management is all about maximizing the value of what one has. By strategically leveraging resources, businesses can improve efficiency, reduce costs, and drive growth. Some ways enterprise can make the most out of their available resources:

Human resources: talent development—invest in training and development programs to enhance employee skills and productivity.

Diverse teams—leverage the diverse backgrounds and perspectives of employees to drive innovation and problem-solving.

Financial resources: budgeting and forecasting—implement rigorous budgeting and financial forecasting to allocate resources efficiently; Technology Investment—use financial resources to invest in technology that can streamline operations and boost productivity.

Information resources: data analytics—utilize data analytics to gain insights into customer behavior, market trends, and operational efficiency.

Knowledge management—create systems to capture and share organizational knowledge to foster continuous learning and improvement.

Time management: project management—project time management is the process of analyzing work, developing a timeline, and establishing schedule control procedures to ensure projects are completed within a particular schedule. This is an ongoing process that spans across the initiation, planning, scheduling, execution, and monitoring phases of a project and project management software can help manage time throughout the project life cycle.

Projects can be intimidating and there is often a lot to do, with usually little time or money to do it. There is no room for mistakes, which can be costly and time-consuming. Stakeholders like certainty and while one cannot promise that everything will run like clockwork, one can certainly do the best to manage time. Project time management allows one to break a project down into more manageable parts, such as specific tasks.

By assigning time to each task in a project, one can control the project timeline and deliver as scheduled. Whether that's with a to-do list or more robust project management software, one can prioritize tasks based upon on their impact and urgency to ensure resources are focused on high-value activities (Tristancho, 2024).

Conflict is the blight of organizational productivity and engagement. When done with respect and curiosity, conflict can be healthy often leading creative resolutions. Too often, however, disputes are unresolved and escalate into aggressive or passive–aggressive behavior.

In the contemporary business landscape, marked by accelerated globalization and technological advancement, companies face unprecedented challenges and opportunities. Rapid digital transformation has reshaped industries, creating a dynamic and competitive environment where businesses must constantly innovate to maintain their market positions. This era of disruption has not only introduced new competitors but also shifted consumer preferences and raised expectations for personalized, efficient, and innovative products and services.

As a result, companies are obliged to rethink traditional strategies and adopt more integrated and adaptive approaches to remain relevant. The concepts of competitiveness, competitive intelligence, and strategic positioning have emerged as critical pillars in the formulation of such approaches. Competitiveness, at its core, refers to a company's ability to sustain a superior market position by leveraging its strengths and optimizing resource allocation to meet market demands effectively. Competitive intelligence, on the other hand, involves the systematic collection and analysis of data regarding competitors, market trends, and consumer behavior. It enables firms to make informed strategic decisions, anticipating potential disruptions and identifying emerging opportunities. Lastly, strategic positioning allows companies to carve out a unique place in the market, differentiating themselves from competitors and maximizing value for consumers (Dantas, Silva, Gomes, Vieira and Amaral, 2024).

The survival-orientation of competitiveness is its most potent characteristic. It is clear in its focus on winning and not losing. If a situation is one of eat or be eaten, live or die, win or go out of business, being a strong competitor is the way to go. Darwin's Origin of Species documents well this approach to survival. His phrase "survival of the fittest" describes pointedly the survival orientation of the win/lose perspective of power.

Clearly, the organizations most fit to compete will be the ones to survive in a highly competitive environment. Competition, for all its value as the friend of the consumer, improving quality and protecting price levels and spurring productivity, is, nonetheless, a power perspective with decidedly diminishing returns. When competition becomes unfriendly and predatory—unnecessary because survival is not at stake, win/lose ultimately becomes lose/lose, a very limiting, limited, and finite proposition.

Most organizations waste much time, energy, creativity, and productivity. Or they never develop because of power struggles. Turf battles, empire-building, dueling departments, back-stabbing, self-promoting decisions, ego trips, favoritism, passive aggression, duplication of effort, poor judgment, poor communication, personality conflicts, contentious employees, gossip, complaining, blaming, grievances, and lawsuits are just some of the things that happen in organizations that waste time and energy. They are activities that do not allow organizations to reach their fullest potential. All are forms of power struggles or attempts at avoiding them. All come from the finite, win/lose perspective of power.

Unproductive routines, corporate bureaucracy, and "administrivia" kill ambition and sap energy for far too many employees. That's demoralizing for employees and a waste for companies, which badly need the full energy and commitment of all their workers. Companies wind up in distress and squander the time, talent, and energy of their workforce when they lose focus, spend money on things that don't make a difference to employees or the future of the business, and use operating models that are out of whack.

By attacking the root causes of organizational drag, companies can eliminate unnecessary work, reenergize the workforce, and, at the same time, put the business on a better course. They can do this by following the three R's

- Refocus on strategic priorities.
- Reset the budgets.
- Redesign the operating model.

Having refocused the strategic priorities and reset budgets, it is important to redesign the operating model, that is, the way the company is organized to deliver on its strategy to eliminate any unnecessary work or dysfunctional processes that bog things down. Thinking "customer-back" or "frontline-back" provides a powerful lens through which to eliminate work. Companies can also look for complexity and inefficiencies that are hidden in the seams of the organization—in cross-functional, cross-geographical, or cross-business unit activities, where no executive or team has a single point of accountability. Every organization has seams, and these are fruitful areas for optimization and redesign. Where inefficiencies are found in ongoing operations, companies should consider "leaning out," centralization, or outsourcing.

Following these three steps can elevate a company's performance potential by creating an environment in which individual energy and creativity are converted to productivity. That can initiate a virtuous cycle in which improved performance liberates cash and capital to fund new growth opportunities and reward talent, unlocking new levels of organizational performance. Employees working in this winning environment will find that the new employee spirit can be sustained and that their work feeds their individual energy rather than destroying it (Garton, 2025).

Power and Accountability

Some organizations seem peaceful on the surface. Many of these are the organizations that are riddled with undue conformity, groupthink, sycophancy, buck-passing, responsibility avoidance, problem concealment, and apathy. In these organizations, the power struggles are still there, but in passive aggressive form (Broom, 2023).

An infinite perspective of power understands power to be abundant and offers no necessity for struggle. Winning and losing are not at issue when playing infinitely. In fact, the purpose of infinite play is to sustain play rather than determine who wins and who loses. Only at the end of a game is it known who the winners are and who the losers are. If play continues, there are no winners or losers in the finite sense. To assure that play continues, that the life of the organization continues, it befits players to cooperate with and be supportive of each other. Infinite play works toward a positive experience for all players. Dissatisfied players threaten an end to the game or, at least, decrease its productivity. The term win–win applies only in the sense that everyone must experience satisfaction if the game is to continue.

In the end, either the stress and resentment decrease the work quality of these employees or they leave believing that management has forced them to sacrifice themselves and their sense of well-being for the good of the organization.

Authority without accountability is inherently problematic. Unchecked power, when placed in human hands, is prone to abuse or mismanagement. History offers countless examples of absolute authority becoming corrupted, underscoring that responsible governance requires clear accountability measures at every level. In business organizations, authority is deliberately entrusted to directors by the owners of the company. These directors express their authority primarily through creating and enforcing policies. These policies guide company operations and directly shape its future outcomes and when a company's policies lead to failures or undesirable outcomes, responsibility primarily falls upon the directors who established or approved these policies. Directors/managers must be held accountable for the effects of their decisions, as authority is inevitably bound to the outcomes it creates.

There are, however, situations where failure is directly attributable to employees failing to comply with clear policies. In these instances, the employees bear direct accountability. Yet, even here, the managers are not completely absolved. Directors remain responsible for reviewing why the failure occurred, improving oversight, and adjusting policies to prevent similar future issues (Bourque, 2025).

Directors have a clear and continuous responsibility for comprehensive risk management. Proper oversight includes auditing, systematic code reviews, and explicitly accepting and managing residual risks. To place blame solely on an individual coder ignores the larger, systemic responsibility directors have in anticipating, preparing for, and mitigating these risks.

An employee who is not performing at the level needed by the organization is creating a loss for the organization. The employee must improve or leave to find some place where they are better suited. Employees will experience themselves as losing at the time of their dismissal for poor performance, and often they find their way to jobs for which they are better suited—an infinite play that doesn't seem so at the time. Accountability is crucial to infinite play.

> *A body of men holding themselves accountable to nobody ought not to be trusted by anybody.*
>
> ~ Thomas Paine

Do power and accountability have a direct relationship and what is the relationship between power and responsibility? There is essentially no difference between power and responsibility; they are the same thing, whether we recognize it or not. This is because power is the ability to influence the world, and responsibility is the quality of having causally influenced an event to occur.

Observations on the misuse of power are constant and reflect an underlying assumption about leadership. Business leaders exercise a variety of postures toward power. Some fear power and shirk responsibility; some desire power and lose sight of what it's for and who are comfortable with power and use it to serve the best interests of the corporation and their employees. Even the best leaders find that the act of serving the collective interests is complex and a minefield of competing interests.

There is abundant evidence to show that those leaders who fail to pursue the collective interest have disastrous impact on organizations including such things as: public embarrassment, decreased employee participation, decreased leader effectiveness, decreased employee motivation, and decreased employee performance (Rus, Knippenburg and Wisse, 2013).

If an organization or company is struggling or experiencing something less than thriving momentum, one should consider the accountability structures of the top leaders. High-powered leaders are the ones setting the tone of the organization's culture. Will it be moving in the right direction? Does the overall approach to leadership and organizational culture offer a platform to sustain performance?

Sustainable business performance is a company's ability to meet the needs of its customers and stakeholders while reducing its negative environmental and social impacts. It involves:

- Meeting customer needs: Providing quality products and services.
- Reducing negative impacts: Reducing adverse environmental and social impacts from business operations.
- Responsible resource management: Reducing wasteful spending and streamlining processes.
- Developing honest communications in negotiations that target integrity and reliability.

The balance between authority, responsibility, and power is fundamental to effective leadership and organizational success. These fundamentals form the backbone of any structured institution, yet their interplay can lead to efficiency or dysfunction depending on how they are managed. Authority is the right to make decisions, power is the ability to execute those decisions, and responsibility is the accountability for the outcomes of those decisions and their implementation. An imbalance among these elements, particularly in an administrative office, often results in abuse, inefficiency, and a breakdown of trust within the organization. In an ideal setting, authority, power, and responsibility are balanced. Individuals granted the authority to make decisions should also have the power to implement them and bear responsibility for the outcomes.

Environment Social Governance (ESG)

An enterprise's sustainability practices are typically analyzed against environmental, social, and governance (ESG) metrics. ESG is important because investors use it to assess long-term sustainability and risk and companies adopt it to strengthen reputation, attract talent, and ensure compliance. Additionally, governments and regulators are increasingly requiring ESG reporting.

The term ESG first came to prominence in a 2004 report titled "Who Cares Wins," which was a joint initiative of financial institutions at the invitation of the United Nations. By 2023, the ESG movement had grown from a UN corporate social responsibility initiative into a global phenomenon representing more than US$30 trillion in assets under management.

Environmental, social, and governance (ESG) metrics are often used to determine how ethical and sustainable an organization is. According to Chladek (2019), companies with high ESG ratings consistently outperform the market in both the medium and long term. While sustainability strategies might be an investment in the short term, they can lead to long-term benefits.

An ESG sustainability audit can help a company evaluate how well it's adhering to its sustainability goals and identify areas for improvement. Sustainability can be beneficial for a business in several ways: by attracting customers, clients, vendors, or buyers; attracting investors; and reducing costs. In addition to driving social and environmental change, sustainability initiatives can contribute to an organization's overall success. It may seem counterintuitive that spending more money on sustainable business practices can boost a company's profitability, but many studies show that the most sustainable companies are also the most profitable.

ESG matters in an enterprise because it impacts identifying long-term risks. ESG-aligned companies often attract more investment and a solid ESG performance can enhance brand loyalty and employee retention.

The United States does not have a federal mandate for environmental, social, and governance reporting. However, some regulations require an enterprise to disclose specific ESG information, and more rules will likely come.

For instance, in March 2024, the Securities and Exchange Commission (SEC) enhanced and standardized public companies' climate-related disclosures.

This new rule aims to improve transparency by requiring SEC-registered companies to include climate details in their official registration statements and reports.

Similarly, the US Federal Supplier Climate Risks and Resilience Rule came into effect in 2022. Its goal is to enhance the climate change resilience of federal supply chains. Suppliers must disclose climate-related risks to their operations, products, and services. However, this rule only affects major federal contractors with multi-million-dollar annual contracts.

The impact a company can have on its surrounding ecosystem has become vividly clear, whether it's on a global scale or within its local community. At the same time, people have become increasingly concerned about ESG issues such as human rights and executive compensation. And so, embedding sustainability in business is top-of-mind for executives and investors alike in today's eco-conscious business landscape.

Given that stock markets traditionally mirror public sentiment, investors have recalibrated their asset management strategy to focus on not only financial performance but also various ESG factors. Now more than ever, businesses are being scrutinized by institutional investors looking to align their investment strategies with their values, namely their ESG considerations. Since many investment decisions are influenced by ESG criteria, investors have taken a new approach to asset management. And while they may seem similar, there are a few key distinctions between ESG investing and other strategies such as socially responsible investing (SRI) and impact investing. ESG investing looks at various ESG factors alongside traditional financial metrics. However, there is an added opportunity and risk management component that factor environmental externalities into a company's valuation. Ultimately, financial returns remain the biggest priority when it comes to ESG investing (Krantz, 2024). SRI, or sustainable investing, focuses less on financial returns and more on ethical considerations.

References

Barkacs, C. B. (2021). *The Top 7 Mistakes You Might Make That Squander Your Power*. Psychology Today.

Bourque, S. (2025). *Power Must Be Balanced By Responsibility and Accountability*. Sambourque.com.

Broom, M. (2023). *Two Perspectives of Power & Conflict in Teams and Organizations*. Baltimore, MD: Cenor Human Systems.

Cheng, H. (2023). *Best Secrets for Leveraging Resources to Grow Your Business*. https://www.freedomtoascend.com.

Coleman, P., and Deutsch, M. (2000). *The Handbook of Conflict Resolution*. San Francisco, CA: Jossy-Bass.

Dantas, R. G., Silva, V., Gomes, J., Vieira, M., and Amaral, J. C. (2024). Competitiveness, competitive intelligence, and strategic positioning: An integrated approach for organizational success. *IOSR Journal of Business and Management*. www.iosjournals.org.

Garton, E. (2025). *Your Organization Wastes Time. Here's How to Fix It*. Boston, MA: Bain and Company.

Gotian, R. (2025). *4 Steps to Successfully Navigate Power Dynamics at Work*. Psychology Today.
Greer, L. (2014). *How Power Struggles Escalate*. CA: Standford Business.
Johnson, E. (2020). *Boeing's 737 MAX Crisis*. Vancouver, BC: Wall Street Star.
Kanter, R. M. (1977). *Men and Women of the Corporation*. New York: Basic Books.
Kaufmann, K. (2024). *Maximizing Impact: The Power of Leverage in Business*. San Diego, CA: Action Coach.
Michels, R. (1911). *Political Parties: A Sociological Study of Oligarchical Tendencies in Modern Democracy*. New York: Dover.
Palmer, A. (2019). *The Strangest and Most Alarming Things in WeWork's IPO Filing*. Englewood Cliffs, NJ: CNBC.
Raines, S. (2024). *Conflict Management and Leadership for Managers*. Lanham, MD: Rowman and Littlefield Publishing.
Rus, D., Knippenburg, D., and Wisse, B. (2013). Leader power and self-serving behavior: The moderating role of Accountability. *The Leadership Quarterly* 2(13–26).
Tristancho, C. (2024). *Project Time Management: Strategies, Tips & Tools*. Austin, TX: Project Manager.

18 Leverage in Negotiations

Power is a critical part of any negotiation, and understanding the power dynamic between all parties can lead the discussion toward more successful outcomes. Many people tend to think they're entering a negotiation from a position of weakness. Moreover, they might give the other side an enormous benefit of the doubt, imagining them with all the information they need to succeed. Because of this, beginner negotiators tend to hand over everything easily. Skilled negotiators usually enter discussions with the right principles on their side. They consistently evaluate their influence in comparison to the other party's strength. However, power does not derive from a single source. Some sources of power in a business negotiation are as follows:

- Circumstance power: Leveraging the immediate situation to gain an advantage.
- Comprehension of the other side: Understanding the individual's motivations and drivers to shape your approach.
- Informational power: Using research and data to strengthen your position.
- Organizational power: Drawing authority from your position or your company's reputation.
- Individual power: Channeling individual traits like confidence and drive to influence outcomes.

Interests, Rights, and Power

Enterprise negotiation is an essential part of most business life. It is critical to understand the concepts of interests, rights, and power in negotiation. Interests are the underlying motivations and needs that drive a person's behavior in a negotiation. They are the reasons why a person wants something and are often related to their goals and objectives. In a negotiation, it's crucial to identify one's own interests as well as the interests of the other party. By understanding the other party's interests, one can find ways to create value and reach a mutually beneficial agreement.

Rights refer to the legal or moral entitlements that a person has in a negotiation. They are based on laws, rules, and regulations, and are often

DOI: 10.4324/9781042000258-19

non-negotiable. In a negotiation, it's important to know one's rights and the other party's rights. By understanding the legal and moral frameworks, one can find common ground and avoid conflicts that may arise due to misunderstandings.

Power refers to the ability to influence or control the outcome of a negotiation. It can be based on a variety of factors, such as expertise, reputation, and resources. In a negotiation, it's important to identify one's own sources of power as well as the other party's sources of power. By understanding the power dynamics, one can find ways to level the playing field and create a win–win outcome (Howe, 2023).

The deliberate impression of interests, rights, and power in leadership starts with interests, which builds psychological safety and reveals hidden leverage. Successful leaders will use rights for clarification when some interests clash. Rights can anchor fairness and legitimacy. Finally, solid business leaders will reserve power as a last resort to be used carefully with transparency and clear accountability.

Types of Leverage

To navigate the complexities of negotiation, it is important to understand and utilize various forms of leverage. Several types of leverage one needs to master for effective negotiation include the following:

- Time: A critical factor in negotiations. It's not just about deadlines; it's about understanding and syncing your timing with that of all counterparts. Mismanaging time can turn it into a liability, especially under pressure to close deals quickly, leading to unnecessary concessions.
- Need: The degree of need that counterparts feel directly impacts leverage. The more crucial your solution is to address their problem, the stronger your negotiation position. Understanding and articulating the cost of inaction for your buyer amplifies your leverage.
- Relationship: Robust relationships built on trust and mutual understanding can simplify negotiations. People are more likely to make fair deals and less likely to drive hard bargains with someone they know and respect.
- Understanding: Understanding the counterpart's business, challenges, and objectives can significantly enhance one's leverage.
- Skill: Solid negotiation skills themselves can be a form of leverage. Practicing and refining negotiation techniques can level the playing field against more experienced negotiators.

Power and leverage are the fulcrum on which successful negotiations pivot (Rifenburgh, 2024). It represents the power, influence, and advantages that one party has over another in a negotiation. This negotiation strategy can take various forms, including:

- Information leverage: This means having access to valuable information that the other party does not possess.
- Resource leverage: Controlling essential resources, such as capital, technology, or physical assets, that are important and relevant to negotiation.
- Time leverage: Having power over the timeline or deadlines of the negotiation, which can put pressure on the other party.
- Alternative options leverage: This includes possessing any viable alternative options just in case the current negotiation fails, thus reducing your desperation to reach an agreement. Without desperation, there is less pressure on you as you negotiate.
- Relationship leverage: Having a strong and valuable relationship with the other party that can be leveraged for mutual gain. Whether the other parties are coworkers, family members, friends, or even previous customers, this type of leverage can help you succeed in your negotiations.

An enterprise is said to be overleveraged when it is carrying too much debt when compared to its operating cash flows and equity. An overleveraged business may have difficulty in paying its interest and principal payments and is often unable to pay its operating expenses because of excessive costs due to its debt burden, which often leads to a downward financial spiral. This results in the company having to borrow more to stay in operation, and the problem gets worse. This spiral usually ends when a company restructures its debt or files for bankruptcy protection. Companies typically restructure their debt or file for bankruptcy to resolve their overleveraged situation.

One of the biggest challenges for negotiators is when we believe the other side has more power and leverage. This makes us feel badly off. Successful negotiators know how to shift power from the other party back to them. Performing a power analysis before each negotiation is critical to developing

Table 18.1 Leverage

Type	*Description*	*Example*
Positive leverage	You possess something the other side wants.	You offer a limited pricing schedule.
Negative leverage	You can impose various consequences on the other side.	You threaten to only work with the competitors.
Normative leverage	You appeal to shared ideas and values.	You petition to industry norms.

an effective strategy. Three sources of power that have the most impact on leverage for either party include the following:

- Having a strong alternative: Possessing a strong alternative going into a negotiation will provide significant power and leverage. In negotiation terms, the best alternative is called the BATNA (Best Alternative to a Negotiated Agreement). There is probably no bigger source of power and leverage than having a great alternative—opportunity to go after, if the current deal falls apart.
- Uniqueness: If what one side provides is unique and different from everyone else in the industry, then this gives one tremendous leverage allowing that party to call the shots on the terms of the agreement. However, whatever the uniqueness is, it must be in demand.
- Expertise: There is extreme value in being an expert in something. Companies are sought out for the knowledge that they possess, and that knowledge is power.

Leverage and Liability

Liability is helpful when managed correctly, and many companies take on debt to grow their business, purchase necessary items, upgrade their facilities, or for many other reasons. Taking on debt is sometimes preferable to other means of raising capital, for example, issuing stock. Taking on debt doesn't give up pieces of ownership of the company and outside participants aren't able to direct how the debt is used. If a company can manage its debt burden appropriately, debt can often help a business become successful. It is only when a company stops being able to manage its debt that it causes severe problems.

Limitation of liability is a structural concept in much contract law designed to cap the amount of damages one party can recover from another. The limitations of liability outlined in a negotiated contract ensure that neither party will be held responsible for indirect or consequential damages exceeding the total amount paid under the agreement. This clause is vital for managing risk and protecting parties from significant financial losses due to unforeseen events or breaches of contract.

By defining the maximum compensation claimable and often excluding certain damages like indirect, consequential, or punitive damages, it provides a framework for fair risk distribution. Commonly found in service agreements, software licenses, and purchase contracts, these clauses are heavily negotiated to ensure balanced responsibility. For enforceability, they must be clear, reasonable, and mutually agreed upon, with courts scrutinizing their fairness. Understanding the limitations of liability is crucial for delineating financial exposure and making informed business decisions.

The limitation of liability is a legal concept used in contracts to set a cap on the amount of damages one party can recover from another. The primary goal is to manage risk and protect parties from extensive financial losses that could arise from unforeseen circumstances or breaches of contract that may have been fairly negotiated. It typically defines the maximum amount of compensation that can be claimed and can exclude certain types of damages, like indirect, consequential, or punitive damages. Understanding the limitation of liability is crucial for both parties in a contract, as it delineates the extent of potential financial exposure and can significantly impact the decision-making process in business dealings.

Negotiators should be aware of the exclusions from liability limitations. These can involve the following:

- Gross negligence or willful transgression: Actions that show a severe disregard for duty or intentional wrongdoing are typically excluded from the limitation.
- Breach of confidentiality: Violations involving the misuse or disclosure of confidential information might be excluded.
- Intellectual property infringement: Damages related to the infringement of intellectual property rights are often excluded.
- Breach of fundamental obligations: Core obligations that are essential to the contract may also be excluded from the limitation.

The enforceability of much of the above is strengthened if both parties had a fair opportunity to review, negotiate, and modify the terms of these clauses before agreeing to the contract.

As a small businessperson, you have no greater leverage than the truth.
~ John Greenleaf Whittier

Domains of Leverage

It can be helpful to map out a framework around leverage to accurately assess how this would function in an enterprise. In simple terms, leverage is the ability to use resources, like time, money, technology, or people to amplify the results. Five aspects, or questions, to be posed and discussed are as follows:

- What is the strategic objective? What outcomes are achievable?
- What stakeholders have power? Is the power formal or informal?
- What are the leverage amplifiers? Is it business capital, information, operational, alliance-based?
- What are the vulnerabilities? Are there limitations on time, regulations, resources?
- How can the leverage be used? Is framing or reframing important?

True business leverage isn't just about adding more resources; it's about multiplying the impact. The most successful companies understand that intelligent partnerships are the ultimate form of business leverage, allowing them to achieve exponential growth without a proportional increase in spending or manpower. A strategic alliance is more than a simple collaboration; it's a calculated move to combine complementary strengths, access new markets, and share risks, creating a value proposition far greater than the sum of its parts.

Take for example the Netflix and Amazon Web Services (AWS) Cloud partnership. Netflix's reliance on Amazon Web Services (AWS) is a captivating case study in leveraging a competitor's strength for one's own strategic advantage. Faced with the challenge of scaling a global streaming service, Netflix chose to outsource its entire infrastructure to AWS. This allowed Netflix to achieve massive scale and reliability while avoiding the colossal capital expenditure of building its own data centers. The business leverage here is converting a huge capital expense into a variable operational expense, freeing up resources to focus on its core competency: content.

This alliance thrives despite Amazon's Prime Video being a direct competitor to Netflix. The partnership works because the value exchange is clear and immense. Netflix leverages AWS's world-class infrastructure to power its global operations, and AWS leverages Netflix as a high-profile client that pushes its services to the limit, providing a powerful marketing case study and a massive revenue stream (Allen, 2025).

The core of this strategy was for Netflix to leverage AWS to handle a critical but non-differentiating function, infrastructure management. Netflix's true value lies in its content library and recommendation algorithm, not in managing servers. By offloading infrastructure to AWS, Netflix could focus 100% of its engineering talent and capital on the things that actually attract and retain subscribers. Allen states that the key strategic insight is that leveraging a competitor's service can be a powerful strategy if it allows you to outsource a critical but non-core function. This frees up capital and focus to invest in what truly differentiates your business, accelerating growth.

Boosting Your Leverage

Four key methods to strengthen one's leverage are as follows:

- Get data about the other side's true needs, wants, and fears. For example, if one is negotiating to purchase some customized IT software for the company and find out the seller really wants a foothold in the industry, you've strengthened your leverage.
- Improve the value of your alternative. Take practical steps to make the best alternative a viable option. The better a Plan B, the stronger is one's leverage.
- Consider how you might limit the attractiveness of the other side's alternatives.
- After evaluating the leverage and improving alternatives, determine how to effectively use it.

Leverage is a key aspect in any negotiation. If you can fortify it and use it wisely, you will substantially increase the likelihood that you can get what you want. Used unwisely, you may inadvertently destroy a potentially great deal.

Power and Control

Power has a direct link to control; in actual sense, power refers to the capacity to influence or control. Individuals often associate the use of power with the capacity to coerce or use force to make others respond as desired. Power in itself is not bad, but the way power is used can be just or unjust, coercive or benign. In an organization, all individuals have certain given powers; they have spheres of influence or control.

Each person in a relationship exercises power. It is only through individuals exercising some power that things happen. Power is a necessary ingredient in all organizational processes. There are two different types of power exercised in an organization, that is, personal and position power. Personal power exists in the form of personal charisma or capabilities (Roger, 2006). Position power is derived from the rank or positions one holds in an organization. In an organization, the base of power that individuals exercise is position, expertise, personality, or persuasive capacity. In whichever case, individuals exercise powers either through the use of force or through persuasion. Although personal power is different from position power, the exercise of personal power at different levels is what makes possible the achievement of position power. One's influence depends on the kind of decisions an individual can make and the effect.

Finally, there are different ways negotiators can exert control over the negotiation power process. **IBM** researchers Cynthia F. Kurtz and David J. Snowden (2003) have developed a process for building internal consensus in situations where high uncertainty exists. Facilitators lead managers in making sense of novel challenges and opportunities. A key goal is distinguishing complex cases from pure chaos. In the former, cause-and-effect relationships may be nonlinear and obvious only in retrospect. In truly chaotic environments, there is never a pattern to discern.

Thus defined, complexity calls for experimentation by "probing, sensing, and responding," write Kurtz and Snowden. Once patterns become more apparent, managers can reinforce positive dynamics and attempt to destabilize undesirable interactions.

Negotiators who function in volatile markets should first target deals that not only are attractive but also reveal the most information about how prices are moving. By contrast, chaotic situations are so turbulent that there are no trends to monitor. Instead, they call for crisis management. The boundary separating complex and chaotic situations is blurry. Indeed, one of the goals of IBM's decision-making process is to encourage managers to recognize what is potentially knowable "and thus worth testing" and what is likely beyond anyone's ken. Internal consensus on strategy is reached more easily when negotiators and managers overtly address how they make sense of the complicated worlds they confront. When those complicated issues are dissected and addressed, it might be the time to strengthen one's leverage. Four techniques to undertake this would include the following:

- Get information about the other party's true needs, wants, and fears.
- Improve the value of an alternative/Plan B
- Consider how you might limit the attractiveness of the other party's alternatives.
- After you've evaluated the leverage and improved your own Plan B, determine how to effectively use it

Leverage is a crucial aspect in any negotiation. If you can strengthen it and use it wisely, you will substantially increase the likelihood that you can get what you want. Used unwisely, you may inadvertently destroy a potentially great deal. Of course, leverage in business is the secret ingredient to multiplying success. It's like using a lever to lift a much heavier object than you could manage with brute strength alone. By channeling the power of leverage to make business easier and more profitable, any business can be boosted to greater heights.

References

Allen, P. (2025). 7 *Strategic Alliance Examples That Master Business Leverage.* ThinkinLeverage.com.

Howe, D. (2023). *Understanding Interests, Rights, and Power in Negotiation.* Canyon, TX: ProfSpeak.com.

Kurtz, C., and Snowden, D. (2003). The new dynamics of strategy: Sense-making in a complex and complicated world. *Armonk. NY: Systems Journal*, 42.

Roger, G. (2006). *Theory and Practice of Leadership*. New York: Sage.

19 Dispute/Conflict Reporting Forms

Incidents of all sorts and sizes occur, from conflicts in the workplace to accidents, injuries, or illnesses. It's critical that in all workplaces staff are empowered to report incidents that happen using an incident report form. When individuals report incidents, they are directly contributing to potentially preventing a future incident from happening again. It allows the enterprise to properly investigate and establish checks and procedures and implement risk controls in response to what has happened. Setting up an incident reporting process enables organizations to ensure their workforce can report when things go wrong and are encouraged to do so.

The significant benefits of incident reporting can address issues before they become more significant problems. It can save time and resources that could otherwise be spent dealing with more critical problems and can boost the overall well-being of every worker in the organization.

Reporting incidents helps the organization to keep track of the trends and patterns and discover anomalies and it helps management know the significant problems in the workplace and develop improved processes and safe procedures for workers (Nunn, 2026).

Flexible Template

This is a flexible template that can be used to report various types of events including workplace incidents, employee or team issues, injuries, client, or customer issues. It allows one to record information about all parties involved, details of the incident itself.

Describe the Specific Conflict:

What do you think the problem/issue is?

What is it that you need or want?

DOI: 10.4324/9781042000258-20

What are your perceptions?

Individuals Involved:

Plan of Action:

Is this a "win–win" solution?

Do we need to address other concerns?

Incident Reporting

Conflict, dispute, or incident reporting is capturing and documenting information about a specific incident or event. It can include data such as who was involved, what happened, when it happened, where it happened, what caused it to happen, and any other relevant details. This documentation helps organizations identify risks that need to be addressed to prevent similar incidents from occurring in the future.

By recording incident data, organizations can use key risk indicators to gain insights that allow for predictive analytics and proactive measures to prevent similar events from happening again. It can also help streamline the process of incident reporting with accuracy and efficiency. Incident reporting helps companies identify trends, analyze the root cause of an incident, and make necessary adjustments to prevent similar incidents from occurring.

- Track progress: Incident reports help companies measure their performance and track improvements over time. This allows them to take proactive steps toward creating a safer workplace environment for all employees.
- Track trends: Incident reports can help companies identify patterns of recurring issues or trends that may be indicative of a larger problem. This allows companies to take corrective measures and prevent costly incidents from happening in the future (Khonko, 2025).
- Improve risk management: Incident reports provide companies with data about their performance to make informed decisions and take proactive measures to improve their risk management strategies.
- Take actionable steps: Incident reporting helps companies determine what type of follow-up actions need to be taken and when they need to be taken to prevent future incidents.

Steps in Incident Report Creation

If an enterprise adopts and/or develops an incident reporting form, it would be prudent to establish a methodology for managing these reports. The following are some steps to consider when setting up an incident reporting form management system:

- Create a database or spreadsheet to store incident reports: This will allow the business to store and manage incident reports in a secure, organized manner. Management can establish a process for collecting incident reports and develop a clear process for how to document and report incidents.
- Train staff on incident reporting: Educate staff on incident reporting procedures, as well as how to use the database or spreadsheet.
- Monitor and analyze incident reports: Regularly review incident reports and look for patterns that could indicate underlying issues or potential risks and take action to address any issues. The data can be utilized to inform decisions and take appropriate action to address any identified issues. This process will help to ensure that all incidents are managed in a consistent and timely manner. Incident management typically involves the coordination of an organization's staff, resources, and operations to ensure that any incident is quickly identified, investigated, and resolved.

Conflict Reporting Form

Name:
Date:
Position:
Immediate Supervisor:

Please outline the concern(s), which resulted in your decision to initiate this process. Specific examples/dates detailing your concern(s) are encouraged. Ensure to include the impact it has on the work environment. Feel free to attach additional pages if more space is necessary.

What specific remedies would help resolve this issue?

Employee's Signature:
Date:

Upon completion, submit it to Human Resources or a Peer Review Committee.

The form will then be forwarded through your chain of command. Within 7 business days, the supervisor/administrator will respond to you in writing and will ask you to indicate if the issue has been resolved to your satisfaction (simply circle "Yes" or "No" below).

Date received in Human Resources
Received by ___________
Date submitted to Immediate Supervisor Received by Resolved: Yes No
Date submitted to Area Administrator Received by Resolved: Yes No
Date submitted to Division Supervisor

How Mass Media File Reports

When the media report about conflict, especially when working in a conflict zone, they are faced with many complexities. Often the facts are not revealed in a way that offers the level of understanding the situation demands. Journalists need to be sensitive, understand history, be aware of cultural issues, and put people before the story. Some of the things they should avoid can be relegated to enterprise conflict reporting (Katwala, 2024).

- Don't write the report in clichés.
- Don't believe everything other people tells you.
- Don't pursue the "definitive truth."
- Don't get things out of context.
- Don't accept information without question.
- Don't be led by another's agenda.

When writing a conflict report, keep in mind the following basics: (1) identify the conflict; (2) analyze and explain the basics of the conflict; (3) propose personal experience solutions; and (4) invite feedback to reflect and learn.

Conflict management and conflict reporting is an important skill for any professional who works with others, especially in situations where there are competing interests, values, or goals. Whether one is a mediator, a manager, a supervisor, a consultant, or a team member, one may need to write a conflict management report or presentation to document, analyze, and resolve a conflict situation

A closing reporting basic is to communicate effectively to the report reader(s). One needs to tailor the report to address the needs and expectations of the reader(s), such as their level of knowledge, their interests and concerns, and their company position. Using clear, concise language, which avoids jargon and technical terms, will provide examples and evidence to support the major points.

Societies have often been shaped more by the nature of media by which men communicate than by the content of the communication.
~ Marshall McLuhan

References

Katwala, J. (2024). *What to Avoid When Reporting Conflict.* Mountain View, CA: Creative Commons.
Khonko, A. (2025). *How to Write a Report on Conflict Resolution: Win Trust, Share Leadership, Document Right.* San Francisco, CA: DART.
Nunn, J. (2026). *What Is Incident Reporting?* Perth, Australia: Work Metrics.

20 Crisis Preparedness

Organizations that lack a crisis program can fall behind when a disruption hits. Rather than calmly moving ahead with a strategic response, unprepared organizations are constantly reacting to the next emergency, and there can be many, depending on the nature of the crisis. The crisis preparedness assessment gives the enterprise the information needed to formulate and prepare an appropriate response. If an assessment reveals a lacking and meaningful governance structure, the company can design one before a crisis develops.

Every business, no matter the size or type, is susceptible to unforeseen circumstances. Proactive crisis management planning is infinitely more effective and less costly than reactive problem-solving. Over 75% of businesses that have a crisis management plan in place experience a crisis within five years. Despite this, approximately three out of every four businesses don't have a formal, documented crisis management plan. Anticipating potential problems before they happen means getting ahead of the panic by staying focused and able to handle the situation.

Crisis and Issue Differences

It's essential to understand the difference between a crisis and an issue. Poorly managed issues can become crises, and poorly managed crises lead to long-term damage to a business' bottom line. Three of the key differences include the following:

Impact: A situation or event is usually a crisis if it threatens lives, the environment, or the organization's reputation. While an issue can have an impact, it is usually not critical.

Urgency: If one is under immediate pressure to make decisions and resolve a problem, that is a sign of crisis. Issues management usually involves time to assess all avenues and make considered decisions; however, in a crisis, the best decision can be the one you should have made minutes ago.

Time: While an issue can span weeks, months, and even years, crises generally have a clear start and end. Issues management involves a sustained

DOI: 10.4324/9781042000258-21

effort of activity and monitoring over time, whereas crisis management is an immediate response.

There are several common misconceptions about the development of crisis management plans. These misconceptions often lead to underestimation of their importance and effectiveness. Here are a few fundamental misunderstandings:

- Only for large organizations: There's a belief that crisis management plans are only necessary for large corporations. Businesses of all sizes can face crises, and having a plan is crucial regardless of the organization's size.
- Only for specific industries: Some assume that only certain high-risk industries need these plans. However, crises can occur in any sector, from IT failures to PR scandals, and all industries can benefit from being prepared.
- Just a PR strategy: While communicating with the public is foremost, crisis management is not just about public relations. It encompasses many actions, including ensuring employee safety, maintaining operations, and legal compliance.
- One-time effort: Another misconception is that once a plan is created, it's set for good. Crisis management plans require regular updates and reviews to remain effective, adapting to new risks and lessons learned from past incidents.
- Too costly and time-consuming: Some businesses avoid creating a crisis management plan, thinking it's too expensive or time-consuming. However, the cost of not being prepared can be much higher in terms of financial loss, reputation damage, and recovery efforts.
- It's all about immediate response: While immediate response is vital, effective crisis management also involves long-term recovery strategies and learning from the incident to improve future responses.

Understanding and addressing these misconceptions are essential for organizations to appreciate the full value of a comprehensive crisis management plan. Reviewing crisis management plan examples can help organizations create tailored plans for various scenarios, such as financial loss and technological failures.

Workplace Disruptions

Each of the below listed 12 enterprise disruptions brings with it its own unique set of circumstances and impacts on operations and personnel. Crisis plans can and should address these. Other business disruptions can include acts of nature and infrastructure issues.

- Biological hazards
- Business relocation

- Community unrest
- Computer failure, hacking
- Delivery malfunctions
- Labor disputes
- Mergers and acquisitions
- Negative publicity
- Power Outages
- Reduction in workforce
- Staffing issues
- Workplace violence

Business Crisis Plans

Organizations that lack a crisis program can fall behind when a disruption hits. Rather than calmly moving ahead with a strategic response, unprepared organizations are constantly reacting to the next emergency and there can be many, depending on the nature of the crisis.

The crisis preparedness assessment gives you the information you need to formulate and prepare an appropriate response. If an assessment reveals the enterprise lacking a meaningful governance structure, for instance, a design can be created before a crisis situation develops.

Every business should be able to identify potential vulnerabilities and devise ways to address them. Through careful evaluation of internal and external factors, targeted strategies to mitigate potential crises can be developed. Identified risks should also be categorized depending on their impact, namely, risks impacting cost, risks impacting performance, and risks impacting schedule. Proper monitoring of risks and their effects should also be done so changes that affect the impact of risk can be identified.

A business crisis plan is the core of an effective crisis management program, providing critical structure and guidance when an unplanned event strikes. Effective crisis plan development includes the following:

✓ Articulating scenarios that rise to crisis level and how to assess the impact.
✓ Defining how incidents are escalated: from where, to whom, through what channels.
✓ Providing clear delineation of who's involved in the response, expectations for those roles, and guidance for working together; defining a crystal-clear chain of command.
✓ Identifying key actions to consider and who's responsible for those actions and developing resource allocation plans.

Every predicament brings its own complexities, affecting different parts of the organization in varying ways. By designing, communicating, and practicing an integrated, enterprise-wide crisis management program, business leaders will be able to navigate those nuances with confidence when a disruption hits. Leading programs generally include the following:

- Guiding principles, purpose, and scale
- Program governance composition that defines executive sponsorship, oversight, and accountability
- Training, awareness, and response plan
- Stakeholder mapping
- Crisis management tools and technology
- A defined approach to engaging external vendors and third-party support services, as needed
- Significant response plans

In the process of developing a business crisis plan, the company will gain:

- A dynamic, agile, and crisis-agnostic tactical guide to mitigate negative effects.
- Clarity regarding consistent processes, responsibilities, and tools.
- An important component of continuous improvement and building resilience.

Every crisis brings its own complexities, affecting different parts of the organization in varying ways. By designing, communicating, and practicing an integrated, enterprise-wide crisis management program, the company will be able to navigate those nuances with confidence when a disruption hits.

Workplace crisis exercise example:

Your pharmaceutical facility, ADVENT Center, is a 3,000-acre pharmaceutical manufacturing center located in a busy urban area. The center provides a wide range of services and employs over 400 staff members.

Recently, ADVENT has been undergoing renovations to upgrade its infrastructure and improve sterile and hygienic processing areas. This has led to some interim disorganization and an increased risk of accidents due to many construction activities. The facility has strict safety protocols in place. However, the ongoing renovations have put additional pressure on maintaining these standards.

Incident: During a busy afternoon shift, the assistant chief pharmacist slips on a wet floor in the hallway and sustains a serious injury, including a fractured arm and a concussion. The individual is immediately incapacitated and unable to continue his duties. A colleague witnesses the incident and promptly calls for medical assistance.

Immediate actions: The injured pharmacist is taken to the emergency department for treatment, and the wet floor area is cordoned off to prevent further accidents.

Escalation: An internal probe has revealed that the floor was wet due to a leak from a nearby sink that had not been properly addressed. Further, the incident has caused significant concern among staff about workplace safety.

Crisis preparedness questions

- Who will take over the chief's duties during his absence? Is there a plan that delineates the chain of responsibility in the event of this type of incident?
- How can the organization ensure that all potential hazards are promptly reported and addressed in the future? Does a plan exist that describes the reporting of hazards, obstacles, or other problems?
- How will the organization inform the rest of the staff about the incident and any interim safety measures? Does the plan contain information about communications during an incident?
- Are there legal reporting requirements for this type of workplace injury?
- How will the company document the incident and the subsequent investigation for regulatory compliance?
- If pertinent, do regulatory agencies need to be involved in the report of the incident?

An integrated company crisis response delivers:

- Clarity and organization from day one of a crisis event.
- Rapid action that saves critical time.
- Facts and data a business needs to make important decisions.
- The ability to adapt to a response as the crisis evolves.
- Meaningful insights to apply the next time a crisis strikes the organization.

Vendor crisis exercise example:

The company, ROBUST Manufacturing, relies heavily on a key supplier for a critical component used in their best-selling product, a rug and carpet high-powered steamer. This component is sourced from a manufacturer located overseas. The lead time for this component is typically three weeks, and ROBUST maintains two weeks' worth of inventory.

Incident: ROBUST receives a critical email from the supplier stating that their factory has been severely damaged by a hurricane, and they expect a minimum eight-week delay in production.

Initial impact: The current inventory will last only two weeks, after which production will halt.

Escalation: The supplier informs the company that the delay might extend to ten weeks due to logistical challenges in their region.

Crisis preparedness questions

- What are the first steps the lead team will take upon receiving the notification?
- How will ROBUST communicate this disruption to its stakeholders, including customers and internal teams?
- What are the company's options for finding an alternative supplier?

- How will the company manage customer expectations and communicate potential delays?
- What steps will be taken to prevent similar disruptions in the future?

Ransomware crisis exercise example (Meers, 2024):

Backstory: You're a midsize professional services firm with 100 employees, including a three-person IT team.

Day 1, 7:05 am

After a long holiday weekend, a couple of early birds arrive at work and report to IT that they can't access files on their workstations or the network drive.

Day 1, 7:35 am

IT team members rush to the office and find that numerous files on the server and workstations appear to be encrypted.

Day 1, 7:55 am

The only file anyone can open is one that has appeared in every directory. It's called RECOVER-FILES.txt. Upon review, the team discovers that this is a ransom message and decides to notify the IT leader.

Day 1, 8:05 am

The team realizes that the IT leader is on a cruise and unreachable.

Day 1, 3:50 pm

Upon further investigation, 80% of your workstations and 50% of your servers and applications were encrypted. Forensic analysis found evidence of data exfiltration and indicated that the threat actors were active in your network for months before the attack. Recovery will probably take several days or weeks. Not all data is recoverable.

Crisis preparedness questions

- Does this qualify as an incident?
- What's the initial step after realizing that something odd is happening?
- What information/evidence do you need to collect?
- How do you know what data was compromised/exfiltrated?
- Who else in the organization needs to be notified and what should be shared internally?
- What are the reporting requirements after the incident is over?

Crisis Response Teams (CRT)

Engaging crisis response team members in safety plans for preparedness will produce lasting consequences. No matter what kind of emergency companies are preparing for, having a team of leaders and employees who feel ready to respond in a safe manner will ensure that the business isn't leveled by a critical event. Training in a safe environment around a response plan is a remarkable way to create a successful safety culture.

It doesn't take a lot of time or assets for an enterprise to plan and be prepared. Consider how emergencies may affect the company's ability to do business. Planning before a disaster will help to return to operations more quickly. The following steps are important:

- Identify operations that are critical to business functions and recovery. Determine which staff, materials, procedures, contacts, and equipment are necessary to keep your organization operating.
- Make a list of the most important contacts/clients and plan ways to communicate with them during and after a disaster.
- Coordinate with vendors, suppliers, and others the company depends on to do business.
- Keep copies of important records you may need to rebuild the business in a waterproof, fireproof, portable container. Keep a second set at an off-site location.
- Review the plans annually.

An organization's employees are the business's most important asset. It's important to talk to staff and employees often about what to do before, during, and after an emergency. Set up a call tree, an email alert, or a call-in voice recording to communicate with employees. When creating a plan, consider all employees' special needs. One should also encourage employees to prepare for emergencies at home. Remember: one of the best methods to ensure a company's recovery is to provide for your staff's well-being.

In addition to protecting staff and employees, it is important to protect the company's physical and virtual assets. It is critical to review any insurance coverage and understand what the policy covers. Consider expanding the insurance to include coverage for direct and indirect costs associated with a disaster. Think about what equipment is necessary for the survival of the business and where one will obtain replacement parts if it is damaged. Every organization depends on electricity, gas, telecommunications, sewers, and other utilities. Have a plan in place in case these services are disrupted. Additionally, protect data and information technology systems. Create back-up copies of all information and send them somewhere safe.

Rarely does a crisis happen in isolation. A mechanical failure can lead to an emergency medical crisis, which then causes a PR crisis, which may escalate into a financial crisis, and so on. The opposite is also true: A fast response through a crisis management plan can prevent the effects of even the most serious incidents from spreading.

> *Great leaders are almost always great simplifiers who can cut through argument, debate, and doubt to offer a solution everybody can understand.*
>
> ~ Colin Powell

Crisis Threats

In 2018, **Southwest Airlines** learned this lesson in an unfortunate way. Shortly after takeoff, Flight 1380 suffered a partial engine failure that set off a series of events leading to the rapid depressurization of the cabin and fatal injuries to a passenger. The plane was in one of the worst possible situations, with hundreds of passengers' lives at risk. How the crew and airline executives responded prevented a much more significant crisis. With her calm and decisive actions, Captain Tammie Jo Shults managed to land the plane safely despite the dire circumstances, preventing further loss of life. Meanwhile, the executive team quickly mobilized, providing clear and empathetic communication to both the passengers and the public. Their response showcased the importance of rigorous training and a well-prepared crisis management plan. However, the incident also served as a stark reminder of the need for continuous improvement in crisis planning (Agnes, 2024).

A crisis management plan helps guide an organization in worst-case scenarios, whether it's a mechanical failure that puts lives at risk, a data breach that threatens the company's reputation, or a natural disaster that disrupts operations. By having a well-prepared plan in place, the organization can respond swiftly and effectively, containing the damage and preventing the crisis from spiraling into a larger catastrophe.

Companies ought to begin preparing for the next unexpected event as the prior crisis resolves. Establishing a post-crisis review process, which evaluates the company's handling of the crisis, and its lessons learned, will assist a company with appropriately updating their response plan and identifying root causes of the crisis (Park, Mukhi and Doyno, 2023).

A post-crisis review plan should lay out the procedures that the company should take to evaluate the crisis response after the events have stabilized. A post-crisis plan should describe how the team involved will be evaluated, how investigations will be assessed, and how lessons learned will be incorporated. The post-crisis review should also focus on updating the crisis response plan. As a part of the post-crisis review, and subject to privilege and litigation considerations, the response team involved in the crisis should generate a written record of what happened, the causes of the crisis, the impact, how the concerns were resolved, and any preventative measures that can be taken.

Finally, a root cause analysis will allow the company to decide whether an independent investigation of the issues is warranted. Following a crisis, companies should also consider including internal and external auditors, legal counsel, and consultants in post-crisis review processes to discuss whether further risk assessments should be conducted.

Internal threats, conflicts, or crises stem from the nature of a business or from specific situations that originate inside of the organization. Examining the organization through this lens can show how working in a high-stress work environment or working with valuable or sensitive information can leave an organization vulnerable to new threats. A particularly stressful "active season" or an organization restructuring involving layoffs can increase the risk for workplace violence.

External threats are triggered by circumstances beyond the company's control. An aggressive group may be protesting a nearby business or government building, causing a significant disruption to the business. Nearby construction or special events (like large sporting events or concerts) can open your locations up to threats including from business disruption, industrial accidents, and terrorism.

Once it is clear what types of threats the organization should be prepared for, it is important to develop a plan to safeguard the safety and security of employees and the business. This ensures that when a conflict or crisis strikes, the company is not forced to wing it and hopes for the best. It is crucial to have plans to ensure employee safety, keep the organization in business, and communicate with clients and the public. Several apparent elements should be included in a crisis management safeguard plan.

- Risk analysis: A study of all potential crises a company may face. This includes both internal and external threats.
- Activation protocol: A crucial aspect of a crisis management plan is clearly defining what events will trigger it.
- Chain of command: An organizational chart identifying key decision-makers.
- Command center plan: A strategy identifying where those in charge of handling the crisis will work.
- Response action plan: A plan laying out who is responsible for which tasks as part of the response.
- Internal communication plan: A system (including a backup system) for communicating internally with employees.
- External communication plan: A system of communicating with the public and external stakeholders about the crisis and how it's being handled. Typically, a company spokesperson oversees informing the media and deciding what will be posted on social media channels.
- Required resources: A list of necessary resources in the event of a crisis. This can include food, water, blankets, and backup generators. Depending on the nature of the crisis, external resources may also be required, such as public relations specialists and legal teams.
- Crisis management training: Companies should regularly perform drills that put their crisis management strategies to the test to look for weak spots and inefficiencies.
- Plan review: After running drills, those in charge of the crisis management plan need to find ways to optimize it.

Economic downturns often result in companies making tough decisions, especially when it comes to their workforce. While laying off staff is to be expected during challenging times, delivery is critical. In December 2021, the CEO of **Better.com**, Vishal Garg, received harsh backlash for his approach to laying off about 900 employees. The layoff meeting, which took place over Zoom, was poorly delivered and viewed as overly callous and the real trouble started when Garg proceeded to host a follow-up call with the remaining employees. In an audio leaked to the public, the CEO can be heard explaining that the employees that were laid off were "stealing from customers" by slacking off.

The company itself didn't issue a response. However, Garg did apologize in an internal email that he "failed to show the appropriate amount of respect" to employees and was "committed to learning from the situation." This attempt was seen as superficial when Garg was later identified as the author of an anonymous post on a professional networking site that continued to slam Better.com's employees. Throughout 2022, the company continued to lay off employees on three separate occasions bringing the total number of layoffs to approximately 3,000 (Leighton, 2023). The key takeaway of this enterprise crisis is that even if a company is performing routine activities, delivery is important, especially when people are involved. PR professionals can learn the valuable lesson of not exacerbating the issue by continuing to double down on negative messaging after trying to apologize.

The outcomes of poor crisis management response plans on an enterprise are many. The potential damage from poorly handled crises illustrates how important a proper crisis management plan is. Three negative results are as follows:

- Damage to status. Constant negative press can destroy a brand's image. Damaging stories can flood traditional media, and digital content from websites and social media adds to the problem. A company's mistakes, actions, and inactions will be criticized and broadcast around the globe.
- Jobs to handle a crisis. This response can cause vital functions, such as customer service or production, to be short-staffed. If a crisis continues for a long time, elevated work stress and a poor reputation may increase employee turnover and hiring costs. If primary executives leave the company on short notice, the entire organization can be affected in unpredictable ways.
- Profits loss. Constant negative media attention can drive away potential customers, which in turn leads to lost revenue.

Crisis Plan Vulnerabilities

Crisis management is where leadership is truly stress-tested, and the most common pitfalls often stem from intellectual blind spots, structural gaps, or emotional missteps. Some of these pitfalls include the following:

- Lack of preparedness
- Poor and inconsistent internal and external communication
- Failure to involve stakeholders
- Misjudging the crisis event

- Decision-making bottlenecks
- Missing updates and debriefings post crisis

In the preparation of a vulnerabilities assessment for developing a crisis communications plan, it is important to consider the effects on key stakeholders in the organization, possible reactions and their need for effective communication. Key stakeholders include business groups, community leaders, competitors, customers, employees, investors, media organizations, the legal department, and regulatory agencies/officials.

Poor Crisis Plan Examples

What can occur when a crisis plan is not followed or implemented incorrectly? A crisis that shook **United Airlines** began on April 9, 2017, when a video capturing a violent altercation between a passenger and United Airlines staff went viral on social media platforms.

The incident occurred on a United Airlines flight where a 69-year-old passenger, David Dao, was forcibly removed from the aircraft by security personnel. The video showed a distressing scene, with the passenger being dragged down the aisle, sustaining injuries in the process. The airline's initial response had strengths and weaknesses. On the positive side, they promptly acknowledged the incident, expressed remorse, and apologized to those affected. Their recognition of a failure in customer service demonstrated accountability and a willingness to take responsibility for the situation. Furthermore, their commitment to conducting a review of policies and procedures indicated a proactive approach to addressing the underlying issues.

The weaknesses in United Airlines' initial response was seen by some as lacking in empathy and sincerity, failing to effectively address the distress caused to the passenger and the public. Additionally, the communication did not provide detailed explanations or immediate corrective actions, leaving room for doubt and skepticism. This lack of transparency and clarity could have contributed to further eroding public trust and confidence.

On top of this insensitive response, an internal email from CEO Oscar Munoz to United Airlines staff, which was leaked, described the passenger as "disruptive and belligerent" and said that "employees followed established procedures for dealing with situations like this."

This lack of empathy in United Airlines' response added fuel to the fire and caused another wave of backlash toward the company on social media. It wasn't until the following Tuesday that Munoz apologized for the forcible removal of Dr Dao, calling the incident "truly horrific" and offered his "deepest apologies for what happened." Munoz also said in the statement, "I want you to know that we take full responsibility, and we will work to make it right, I promise you we will do better." By the time the second official response from the CEO was released, United were continuing to struggle to contain the fallout from the incident (Creswell and Mahenswari, 2017).

This debacle demonstrates the importance of a company's crisis plan and the first response and how it is delivered and due to the high visibility of this incident, issues concerning corporate culture, stakeholder empowerment, and timely and accurate communications were brought to the forefront of public discourse. This is an important case because it is an example of an organization's worst-case scenario with stakeholder empowerment through highly visible communications. Social media gives stakeholders a new level of empowerment that they have not had before, making organizational issues very public. This enables the public to hold organizations captive when something doesn't go their way by gathering and posting videos and pictures to start a digital mob of enraged social media users.

A second example of terrible outcomes when a company's crisis preparedness plan is not followed is the **British Petroleum** Deepwater Horizon oil spill, which stands as one of the most catastrophic environmental disasters in recent history. On April 20, 2010, the oil drilling rig *Deepwater Horizon*, operating in the Macondo Prospect in the Gulf of Mexico, exploded and sank resulting in the death of 11 workers on the Deepwater Horizon and the largest spill of oil in the history of marine oil drilling operations. Four million barrels of oil flowed from the damaged Macondo well over an 87-day period, before it was finally capped on July 15, 2010. On December 15, 2010, the United States filed a complaint in District Court against BP Exploration & Production and several other defendants alleged to be responsible for the spill.

BP's response to the spill was marred by shortcomings and a lack of effective communication. The environmental and economic consequences were significant, with widespread damage to marine and coastal ecosystems and billions of dollars in cleanup and compensation costs. This example highlights the need for preparedness, transparency, and accountability in crisis management.

Another business failure involved **Ticketmaster**. In today's digital world, a brand's reputation can easily be affected by how it handles social media crises. In November 2022, following a chaotic presale ticket rollout that left fans waiting for hours on the ticketing website and many leaving upset and empty-handed, Ticketmaster canceled public ticket sales for Taylor Swift's "Eras" tour. Some Republicans and Democrats conveyed outrage on both sides of the aisle over the debacle, questioning whether Ticketmaster handled the Swift ticket rollout properly. It also brought up the criticism that Ticketmaster has excessive power in the live events and ticketing industries. Better planning and a robust communication strategy could have probably steered Ticketmaster clear of the storm. The high demand for Taylor Swift's concert tickets was foreseeable, and a well-prepared ticketing system alongside clear guidelines for customers could have mitigated the ensuing chaos. The essence of averting such crises lies in anticipating potential hurdles and having solid contingency plans in place (Chen, 2023).

Social Media Toolkit

It is key for any enterprise to understand how human error can be catastrophic in most crisis circumstances. Human error during crises can take many forms, including miscommunication, incorrect prioritization, delayed responses, and poor decision-making. These errors can lead to increased risk where poorly managed crises can escalate, causing more harm to people, property, and reputation; inefficiencies with time wasted on incorrect actions or decisions delays effective crisis resolution; and reputational damage that can harm public perception and trust.

In the above cases, a social media toolkit could and would have helped to mitigate, to some extent, the crisis' impact. A social media toolkit provides a step-by-step guide to company teams during a crisis to ensure they are utilizing social media channels in the right way. It sets out the strategies and tactics that the teams need to use to ensure that they harness social media channels effectively during a crisis or emergency and are engaging with online audiences in the right way. The toolkit contains information and resources to push out and amplify a social media campaign/cause. It is similar to a press kit for promoting a news item, but the audience is the business supporters and partners, rather than journalists or media contacts.

The toolkit at heart is a messaging exercise: when creating content for a social media toolkit, think about the values and interests of the audiences and how to strategically use text, visuals, and interacting elements to capture their attention. The key components of a social media toolkit include (1) guidance on effective social media strategy; (2) roles and responsibilities for social media response; (3) guidance on social media monitoring; and (4) key principles for publishing social media content.

Social media toolkits will make it easy for the organization's supporters and members to create relevant posts that promote a cause or event or a response to a crisis. They are related to a press kit, with one major difference: the audience. The information, hashtags, and graphics that one includes in the social media toolkit should resonate with a broader audience than any PR.

Each social media toolkit one creates should be specific enough to promote the message the enterprise wants but be extensive enough to allow the members to add their own creativity and ideas into the post they create.

References

Agnes, M. (2024). *How to Create a Crisis Management Plan: A Step-By-Step Guide.* Austin, TX: Alert Media.

Chen, F. (2023). *An Evaluation of Ticketmaster's Crisis Management During the Taylor Swift Ticket Fiasco.* San Francisco, CA: Medium.

Creswell, J., and Mahenswari, S. (2017). United grapples with PR crisis over videos of man being dragged off plane. *The New York Times*, April 11.

Meers, T. (2024). *Incident Response Tabletop Exercise and Scenarios.* Little Chute, WI: Heartland Business Systems.

Park, J., Mukhi, R., and Doyno, A. (2023). *Best Practices for Crisis Management Preparation.* Reuters.

21 Business Ethical Considerations

We are all encouraged to make ethical choices and apply ethics in all areas of our lives. But what does ethics mean, and why does ethics matter for business? We can think of ethics as the principles that guide our behavior toward making the best choices that contribute to the common good of all. Ethics is what guides us to tell the truth, keep our promises, or help someone in need. There is a framework of ethics underlying our lives daily, helping us make decisions that create positive impacts and steering us away from unjust outcomes. Ethics guides us to make the world a better place through the choices we make (Holland, 2025).

Ethics in business is just as important as ethics in personal life. An ethical framework provides a consistent approach to decision-making, ensuring businesses operate with integrity, build trust, and achieve long-term success. Business leaders have a unique role and a great responsibility in shaping the ethical culture of their businesses and thereby influence their broader communities as well. While doing business is essential to the company, carrying out work correctly is critical. It affects the business's reputation since investors are less likely to buy stock or invest in a company that operates unethically. Therefore, the ethical operation is directly linked to short-term and long-term profitability.

With strong business ethics, a company is sure to work legally, protecting its employees, partners, and clients. These principles preserve company standards, keep businesses honest and fair, and stop misleading or unfounded product claims.

Business leaders may not set out to define the ethical culture of their businesses, but they inevitably do. Here are a few key questions to consider bringing ethics into your business mindset:

- How do leaders identify the common good for the business? What does it mean for customers, employees, the community where the business is located, the investors, and the supporters?
- How do leaders make good ethical decisions? How do they analyze a situation and make decisions that positively contribute to the common good?
- What kinds of structural conditions or company policies does the business need to put in place to create an ethical culture?

DOI: 10.4324/9781042000258-22

- How will the ethical culture of my business be monitored?
- How will unethical behavior in my business be addressed or corrected?

Social Responsibility

Social responsibility is the idea that an individual (or organization) has an obligation to act for the benefit of society at large. Today, social responsibility has become an important part of culture for businesses of all sizes.

TOMS Shoes is an exceptional example of a business that prioritizes social responsibility. Toms' business model is known as the one for one concept model, which refers to the company's promise to deliver a pair of free shoes to a child in need for every sale of their retail product. The countries involved have included Argentina, Ethiopia, Guatemala, Haiti, Mexico, Rwanda, South Africa, and the United States. The business has grown beyond producing shoes and has included eyewear and apparel in Toms product lines. The company uses word-of-mouth advocacy for much of its sales, centering its business focus on corporate social responsibility. Part of this model originally involved a non-profit arm called "Friends of Toms" that recruited volunteers to help in the shoe distributions in foreign countries. The company has now expanded to support other causes such as safe water, mental health, and equality. TOMS Shoes' inspirational tagline "Stand for Tomorrow" communicates its dedication to social responsibility in just three words.

Social responsibility can be practiced in big or small ways every day. Businesses can volunteer with local organizations, donate funds to a chosen cause, sponsor a neighborhood group or sports team, and much more. When businesses give back, they not only contribute to the common good but also engage with their communities in meaningful ways, build morale among employees, and create positive regard for the business.

Another example of business ethics involves the outdoor clothing and gear company **Patagonia**. They announced that they would donate 100% of their Black Friday sales in 2016 to grassroots environmental organizations. This decision was a clear demonstration of their commitment to environmental sustainability, which is one of their core values.

The company's founder, Yvon Chouinard, has been a vocal advocate for protecting the environment and promoting sustainable practices in the business world. By donating their Black Friday sales, Patagonia not only showed their commitment to their values but also encouraged their customers to support environmental causes. After achieving a record-breaking Black Friday in sales, outdoor apparel maker Patagonia was giving the environment an early Christmas present in the form of $10 million. The 100% donation helped the company to strengthen its relationship with its stakeholders and increase brand loyalty. This example showcases how business ethics can be used to promote a positive impact on society while still achieving business success. Patagonia's ethical behavior supported the social responsibility of their business by considering the impact of their actions on the environment and society. By behaving ethically, they contributed to the well-being of the community and the planet, creating a positive impact that benefits everyone.

An organization's approach to business ethics is the foundation upon which its brands are built. This approach can shape business investors and customers' perceptions of a business. Therefore, developing the right set of business ethics is essential for business growth and can be achieved by understanding the fundamentals of the concept.

It is not easy to handle a business crisis. Avoiding it or postponing a response could make it worse. Businesses must think ethically when coming up with a plan to handle an ethical crisis. In other words, they must act in a way that promotes the greatest common good and encourages trust rather than diminishing it. Some situations may warrant the advice of a lawyer and a crisis expert. Here are some general practices that could be followed:

- Be accessible and transparent
- Prioritize those impacted by the situation
- Apologize
- Remedy the problem

Building Foundation on Ethics

Principled leadership is about creating and implementing a focus on ethical practices and culture for business success. Principled leaders motivate their employees to do their best work and consider ethical implications of their decisions and actions. These are unique leaders because they help their organizations be successful by championing and educating employees to consistently engage in ethical practices for the benefit of all stakeholders. An important step for making noble ethical decisions is by accurately identifying and weighing all considerations of an issue. To determine the best course of action, principled leaders must evaluate problems through an ethical perspective as well as a business perspective. Using ethical frameworks can guide decision-makers, and when practiced regularly, the ethical choice becomes an automatic consideration when faced with any dilemma. The following concepts can ensure that negotiations are built on a foundation of ethics: (1) Know what is not negotiable and what is negotiable and what is not; (2) Be honest and ethical even though it costs you something, you gain points; (3) Have multiple options to help all parties achieve their goals. If someone proposes an option you feel is unethical, you will be ready with another, ethical option for accomplishing the same goal; and (4) Be willing to walk away from a deal.

There are several doctrines of business ethics that steer the code of conduct of businesses. These business ethics principles include the following:

- Accountability: This denotes that the businesses take full responsibility for their actions or practices. This includes any faulty decisions taken or unethical business practices followed during business operations.

- Care and respect: Shared respect must be maintained between business owners, employees, and customers.
- Truthfulness: Transparent communication between business owners and employees is much desired. This characteristic helps build trust and establish a relationship between employees and the business.
- Healthy competition: Businesses should encourage healthy competition in their workforce and reduce conflicts of interest to a minimum among employees.
- Information transparency: Important information disseminated among a business's customers, employees, or partners is to be provided comprehensively. This includes both positive and negative information, terms and conditions, or any other crucial information, as it is against business ethics to withhold or hide relevant facts.

The first step in the evolution of ethics is a sense of solidarity with other human beings.

~ Albert Schweitzer

Ethical Concerns

In the fast-fluctuating business world, ethical decision-making has become an obligation. Companies today face growing pressure from consumers, employees, and investors to prioritize values like integrity, transparency, and impartiality. To meet these demands, businesses are turning to structured ethical frameworks to guide their choices. These frameworks provide a consistent approach to resolving dilemmas, ensuring that decisions are not only profitable but also principled.

The significance of an ethical framework in business is that it provides a consistent approach to decision-making, ensuring businesses operate with integrity, build trust, and achieve long-term success. A question of what type ethical framework should businesses choose points to a choice that depends on a company's goals and values. Businesses can implement ethical frameworks effectively by defining core values, training employees on ethical practices, and using frameworks to guide daily operations and strategic decisions.

With many businesses now moving their operations to the digital space through the adoption of e-commerce practices, technology business ethics are necessary. These ethics include customer data protection, customer privacy, customer personal information protection, fair intellectual property practices, etc.

Embedding ethics in tech systems is important to improving or mitigating any challenges to safety, equity, fairness, representation, inclusion and sustainability. To build trust, companies should be aware of technology's challenges, including:

- The potential to displace people from their jobs, while failing to provide meaningful opportunities for them to learn new skills

- Instances where technology unintentionally demeans or harms a group of individuals
- Situations in which biased tech causes people to be denied access to basic needs and meaningful participation in the economy, services or communities
- Cases in which data-hungry practices are fed by ghost labor (people who do task-based, content-driven work on a contractual basis, frequently for low pay).

The human resources professionals and management teams may find it challenging to manage ethical issues effectively. Although there are many laws to hold people accountable, unethical behavior can still occur in the workplace and an organization can also act unethically. Learning about the ethical issues a business can face can help management and others prepare to manage them effectively if they occur. Ethical issues in business arise when decisions or actions conflict with ethical standards, involving both organizational and individual concerns, and can pose risks ranging from legal non-compliance to negative reactions from third parties, highlighting the need for clear policies to guide ethical decision-making. Understanding and addressing ethical issues early helps prevent them from becoming major problems, allowing the company to focus on business success and growth. HR and management professionals can manage ethical issues by evaluating and refining policies, setting and monitoring responsible goals, enforcing a strong code of ethics, and ensuring compliance and transparency.

> *Ethics is knowing the difference between what you have a right to do and what is right to do.*
>
> ~ Potter Stewart

One of the ethical challenges that large organizations face are shaped by its culture. Dimensions that shape an organizational culture (Cartwright and Cooper, 1993) have four definite features: power, bureaucracy, achievement, and support.

✓ Power: This includes implicit rule, as well as control, stability, and loyalty.
✓ Bureaucracy: Hierarchical structure that includes efficiency, predictability, and control.
✓ Achievement and innovation: Focus on creativity, adaptability, risk taking and teamwork.
✓ Support: Characteristics include commitment, consensus and growth.

Ethical concerns are at the core of any reflective leadership model. Three major components are as follows: awareness to recognize legal, economic, and ethical responsibilities; judgment and action to consider arguments, biases, and shared concepts that shape a company's mindset; and reflection on responsibilities and judgments that comprise actions that are gleaned from previous decisions and resolutions.

Contrary to popular belief, ethical decision-making often leads to wealth and success in business. There are many examples of how ethical decision-making can help a business make a profit. Crafting good ethical business decisions can also improve your relationship with employees. **Costco Wholesale** is one of the biggest successes in American retail and much of Costco's success comes from the high level of customer service offered by satisfied employees. One reason Costco can attract high-quality employees is its willingness to pay higher-than-average wages (Moore, 2024)

For example, Fortune reports that Costco raised its base wage from $13 an hour to $14 an hour in 2018 and to $15 per hour in 2019. In contrast, the average retail worker in America makes between $7.25 and $9 an hour. Meanwhile, the average US retail department manager makes $11 to $12 an hour. Costco succeeds because it can attract the best workers. Additionally, Costco avoids labor trouble, high turnover, and conflict because its employees are happier.

In another example, the American drug store and health insurance giant **CVS Health** stopped selling tobacco products in 2014. CVS stopped selling cigarettes and other tobacco products in September 2014. Interestingly, American cigarette sales fell by 1% in states where CVS had a 15% or greater share of the pharmacy market. CVS Health estimates that 95 million packs of cigarettes were sold due to its decision. However, CVS made some money because nicotine patch sales grew by 4% at its stores. Interestingly, CVS has been doing well since it quit selling tobacco. CVS is now one of America's largest grocers, with a 3.9% share of the US grocery market. Consequently, CVS is America's fourth-largest grocer without tobacco (Moore, 2024).

Business Stress Test

Ethical decision-making is critical in the following stress test situations:

- An apparent conflict of interest when an enterprise manager must choose between awarding a contract to a vendor who is a cousin of the manager or a more qualified competitor.
- Eco-friendly trade-off when a manufacturer can cut costs by using cheaper, polluting materials.
- A company is not fully transparent about recalling some minor defective products.
- Realizing that layoffs are bad for business, the company is reticent about reducing its workforce and is simply considering not replacing retiring employees.
- The vice-president of sales notices that one of their high-performing team members is manipulating data to meet targets. She is tempted to let it go

because the employee's overall performance looks strong on paper and punishing them could disrupt output.
- A large enterprise discovers that their largest supplier is using exploitative labor practices.

Ethical decision-making becomes more challenging in high-pressure work environments. Tight deadlines and organizational demands can lead individuals to compromise on values they would typically uphold. However, maintaining integrity under stress is essential for creating a strong workplace culture, building trust, and guaranteeing long-term success. Workplace pressure can weaken judgments, leading teams to take shortcuts to meet expectations. Environments with extreme performance targets or high job insecurity may see a rise in unethical behavior, such as falsifying reports or cutting corners.

Business leaders set the climate for ethical behavior. Team leaders are far less likely to compromise their values when leadership consistently demonstrates integrity and businesses can take proactive steps to ensure ethical decision-making remains strong, even in difficult situations.

Corporate Social Responsibility/CSR

Corporate social responsibility (CSR) is a self-regulating business model that helps a company be socially accountable to itself, its stakeholders, and the public. By practicing corporate social responsibility companies are aware of how they impact aspects of society, including economic, social, and environmental. Engaging in CSR means a company operates in ways that can enhance society and the environment instead of contributing negatively to them.

There are several kinds of CSR. Environmental responsibility is rooted in preserving the environment. An enterprise can pursue environmental stewardship by reducing pollution and emissions in manufacturing, recycling materials, replenishing natural resources like trees, or creating product lines consistent with CSR. Corporate ethical responsibility includes acting fairly and ethically. Instances of ethical responsibility include fair treatment of all clients regardless of age, race, culture, or sexual orientation, favorable pay and benefits for employees, vendor use across demographics, full disclosures, and transparency for investors. Financial responsibility can include supporting plans through financial investments in programs, donations, or product research including research and development for products that encourage sustainability, creating a diverse workforce, or implementing DEI, social awareness, or environmental initiatives. Another kind of CSR is philanthropic responsibility which asks a company to contribute to society, whether a company donates a profit to charities, enters into transactions with suppliers or vendors that align with the company philanthropically, supports employee philanthropic endeavors, or sponsors fundraising events.

In some ways, corporate social responsibility can be seen as a public relations effort. However, corporate social responsibility can also boost a firm's competitiveness. The business benefits of corporate social responsibility may include the following:

- Stronger brand image, appreciation, and reputation
- Increased customer allegiance and sales
- Operational cost savings
- Keeping key and talented workers
- Easier access to funding and financing

While business ethics and corporate social responsibility share similar goals in promoting responsible practices, they are distinct concepts. On the one hand, business ethics focus on the company's internal conduct and daily practices, including compliance with laws and regulations, honesty in communication, and fairness in dealings with stakeholders.

On the other hand, corporate social responsibility refers to an organization's commitment to contributing to social and environmental well-being beyond its legal obligations. This discipline encompasses initiatives such as sustainability, community support, and respect for human rights throughout the supply chain. There are many differences between business ethics and CSR. Doing the right thing, which means engaging in good business ethics, is not the same as corporate social responsibility. CSR is the onus on a business to act in the interest and for the benefit of the community whenever possible, sometimes even at the detriment of a profitable opportunity that may have adverse outcomes for the environment or people.

Some ethical questions that business managers may be faced with might include the following scenarios:

- A new vendor can supply the company with less expensive parts but has a reputation of poor labor practices. Your own margins are stretched. Do you proceed?
- The manager of your marketing department has found a way to use your customer information to increase sales. Although it is not illegal, it might be perceived as invasive. Do you consent?
- A newer employee has approached your human services department complaining about a senior manager's allegedly unethical behavior. What is the response and are there business protocols in place for this type of issue?

Defined by Archie B. Carroll (1991) in the latter part of the 20th century, the pyramid of corporate social responsibility contended that companies had obligations in four key areas: profitability, legality, ethics and philanthropy. In Carroll's model, these obligations were not all equal. Economic drivers were first and foremost, making profitability the pyramid's base.

Business ethics is a broader idea that should govern everything a business and its people do. A company that operates ethically often makes decisions that support strong corporate social responsibility. Built upon it (in decreasing importance) was the need to obey the law, engage in good business ethics and become a moral member of the community making local contributions.

That model does not work for businesses today. Consumers, governments and cultures are looking for more from corporate entities. It is still vital to maintain a profit. Profitable companies can be better contributors to the community than those that don't earn a profit. It is equally necessary for businesses to shepherd social and environmental resources. Thus, the triple bottom line is upending the pyramid, replacing it with a triune obligation toward profits, people and the planet (Bartell, 2022).

Three examples of companies with solid CSR programs are (Goodera, 2024):

- Coca Cola Goals: ESG, Women's Empowerment, Sustainable Packaging, Water Security, DE&I
  Coca-Cola's CSR programs are focused on a "Better Shared Future" with diversity initiatives, community interaction and ESG dedicated to using Coca-Cola's voice and position to support equality, justice, and human rights advocacy across communities. To advance sustainability, 90% of Coca-Cola's product packaging is recyclable, with plans to reach 100% by 2025. They're also committed to water conservation and return 100%+ of water used in their beverages to increase water security.
- Microsoft Goals: Racial Equity, Employee Volunteering, Humanitarian Aid, Digital Literacy, Carbon Negative, Zero Waste, Water Positive.
  Microsoft has consistently ranked high among companies with best CSR programs over the past few years. They're pioneering employees volunteering with a promise of supporting inclusive economic growth and protecting fundamental rights. In 2022, Microsoft and its employees donated $255 million to over 32,000 nonprofits, and over 29,000 Microsoft employees volunteered more than 720,000 hours. They're big on sustainability, have pledged $1 billion to accelerate climate innovations, and aim to be carbon negative by 2030
- Nike Goals: DE&I, Women's Empowerment, Racial and Ethnic Equity, Disaster Relief, Carbon Neutrality, Supply-Chain Sustainability, Waste Reduction, Freshwater Preservation
  Best known for its efforts against racial injustice and for women's rights in sports, Nike has consistently evolved its efforts for DE&I and empowering communities over the past decade and now ranks as a giant in the CSR industry. Their equitable approach begins with coaching kids through their Made to Play program, of which young girls hold 50% of participation.

The fourth company that ranks high in outstanding CSR is **Ben and Jerry's.** Ben and Jerry's ice cream is world-famous, but it's equally well-known for its activism and philanthropy for various social issues. They've supported a lot of social causes that are closely related to their business of making and selling ice cream. Their work for justice comprises that for refugees, the LG-BTQ community, climate action, and more. They also donate some of their pre-tax profits to corporate philanthropic initiatives. This is done through the Ben and Jerry's Foundation and Community Action Teams (CATs) at site locations. The Grassroots Organizing for Social Change Program supports grassroots nonprofits in the US, especially ones that work around social justice, environmental justice, and sustainable food systems (Aquire, 2025).

The primary goal of any business is to generate profit. Profits are necessary to sustain operations, pay employees, reward shareholders, and invest in future growth. Financial performance is typically measured through metrics such as revenue, profit margins, and return on investment. Companies that fail to generate sufficient profits may struggle to survive, leading to layoffs, closures, or takeovers and the pressure to meet financial targets can sometimes drive companies to engage in practices that prioritize short-term gains over long-term sustainability and ethical considerations.

The conflict between profit motives and corporate social responsibility objectives often manifests in various ways. Cost versus benefit initiatives often involve upfront costs, such as investing in eco-friendly technologies or improving labor conditions. While these initiatives can lead to long-term benefits like brand loyalty and operational efficiencies, they may strain financial resources in the short term. Market pressures impact companies that involve pressure from investors to deliver strong financial performance. This may lead to decisions that prioritize short-term profits over long-term sustainability, such as cutting corners on environmental regulations or reducing employee benefits to lower costs.

Finally, corporate social responsibility focusses on the idea that a business has a social obligation above and beyond making a profit. It requires management to be accountable to the full range of stakeholders. CSR is the continuing commitment by enterprises to behave ethically and contribute to the economic development of the country while improving the quality of life of the employees and their families and local community and society at large. CSR is achieving commercial success in ways that honor ethical values and respect people, communities and the natural environment. CSR is a combination of policies, education and practices which extend through a corporation's operations and into the communities in which they operate.

References

Aquire, S. (2025). *14 Best Socially Responsible Companies Making an Impact*. Alexandria, VA: Donor Box.

Bartell, J. (2022). Corporate social responsibility and business ethics. *Forbes*.

Carroll, A. (1991). The pyramid of corporate social responsibility: Toward the moral management of organizational stakeholders. *Business Horizons*, *34*(4), 39–48.

Cartwright, S., and Cooper, C. L. (1993). The role of culture compatibility in successful organizational marriage. *Academy of Management Executive*, 7(2), 62.

Goodera, T. (2024). *Leading Companies Shaping the CSR Landscape with Remarkable Impact. Menlo Park*, CA: Mediabrief.

Holland, P. (2025). *Ethics in Life and Business*. Santa Clara, CA: Leavy School of Business.

Moore, B. (2024). *10 Great Examples of Ethical Decision Making In Business*. Moosinning, Germany: Great Work Life.

22 Enterprise Reinvented

The phrase "enterprise reinvented" refers to the transformation of how businesses operate, compete, and create value—typically driven by new technologies, changing markets, and evolving workforce expectations. It goes beyond digital transformation. It is not only about adopting new tech but also about changing the entire enterprise model to thrive in new realities. An alert workforce is capable of transforming their skills to meet and exceed cultural, conflict-driven, and structural change. Reinvented enterprises can pivot quickly to new market realities where people, technology, and strategy all work together. These enterprises will be capable of anticipating disruptions rather than reacting to them.

To streamline enterprise conflict resolution, organizations should adopt structured, proactive strategies that transform disputes into opportunities for collaboration, innovation, and trust-building. The previous chapters have examined a host of important aspects for organizations to identify and address conflicts, crisis issues, power and leverage, and negotiation and mediation scenarios that may be faced in the course of conducting business.

Workplace conflict is inevitable, but its impact doesn't have to be negative. Unmanaged disagreements cost US businesses an estimated $359 billion annually in lost productivity, with employees spending an average of 2.8 hours per week dealing with disputes. The difference between a minor friction point and a major operational disruption lies in having a robust toolkit of workplace conflict resolution strategies (Jafferi, 2025).

Interest-based negotiation (IBN) is a powerful workplace conflict resolution strategy that focuses on satisfying the underlying needs and concerns of all parties, rather than haggling over rigid positions. This approach fundamentally changes the dynamic from a contest of wills to a search for mutual gain. The core principle is to look past what people say they want (their position) to understand *why* they want it (their interest).

Enterprises that utilize this method have found it to be highly effective because it avoids the zero-sum game where one party's gain is another's loss. For example, in labor-management relations, the type of negotiation has been used to shift from arguments over fixed wage percentages to addressing shared interests like long-term company viability and job security. This

DOI: 10.4324/9781042000258-23

can lead to more creative agreements involving profit-sharing or professional development funding. By uncovering shared or compatible interests, IBN expands the range of possible solutions, fostering more durable and respectful outcomes.

Conflict resolution is a critical competency for leaders in today's business landscape. It influences team dynamics, productivity, and overall organizational success. Here's why it's indispensable (Dsouza, 2025):

- Productivity enhancement: Unresolved conflicts drain productivity. Effective conflict resolution reclaims employee lost time and boosts overall efficiency.
- Employee retention: Workplace conflicts are a leading cause of employee turnover. By fostering a culture of constructive conflict resolution, organizations improve employee satisfaction, loyalty, and retention rates.
- Innovation catalyst: When managed effectively, conflict sparks innovation. Diverse perspectives and constructive disagreements lead to more creative solutions and better decision-making.
- Team cohesion: Successfully navigating conflicts strengthens team bonds, builds trust, and creates a more cohesive and resilient workforce.
- Organizational reputation: How an organization handles internal conflicts impacts its external reputation, attracting top talent and maintaining strong stakeholder relationships.

Business leader should address their own conflicts and also help the company workforce grind through theirs. To streamline the conflict process, leaders should group their basic responsibilities into the following areas:

- Well-being: What's eventually good for the employee.
- Rights: Entitlement to receive certain treatment.
- Duties: An ethical obligation to behave in a specific way.
- Best practices: Aspirational standards not required by law or cultural norms.
- Fairness: Impartial and just treatment.

Fairness and Impartiality

Fairness and impartiality are crucial principles for effectively resolving disputes and maintaining trust among all parties involved. Ensuring that conflicts are managed in a fair and unbiased manner helps achieve equitable outcomes and fosters positive relationships.

Fairness ensures that all parties are treated equitably and that their concerns and interests are considered.

Impartiality involves being neutral and unbiased, without favoring any party or outcome.

Three types of fairness business leaders can use when helping employees solve conflicts:

- Legitimate expectations: Employees reasonably expect certain practices or behaviors to continue based on experiences with the company and explicit promises.
- Bureaucratic fairness: Managers must resolve issues impartially and consistently.
- Distributive fairness: The company equitably allocates opportunities, benefits, and burdens.

Concerning procedural fairness, management must ensure they do not take sides when mediating conflict. Treating both parties equally allow them time to speak and share their perspectives. The focus is to guide the team toward collaboration or compromise and work toward a solution that achieves the goal while maintaining and even strengthening relationships.

The importance of neutrality and fairness in conflict resolution cannot be stressed enough. Neutrality and fairness are essential components of impartiality. A neutral and fair approach ensures that all parties are given equal opportunities to present their perspectives and concerns. This helps to prevent the dominance of one party over others and promotes a more balanced and inclusive resolution process.

Enterprise leaders recognize that personal biases and emotions can significantly impact one's ability to remain impartial. It is essential to recognize and acknowledge our own biases and emotions to manage them effectively. This involves developing self-awareness, emotional intelligence, and a deep understanding of our own values and motivations (Lee, 2025).

Impartiality is essential for building trust and promoting long-term relationships. By remaining neutral and fair, we can create a foundation for constructive dialogue and cooperation. Impartiality promotes trust and credibility with all parties and fosters a culture of cooperation and collaboration that can encourages long-term relationships and sustainable agreements

Causes and Attitudes of Conflict

Conflicts may be thought of as having three dimensions: perception, feeling, and action. Conflict involves the perception that one person's interests, needs, or values are incompatible with those of another person. Conflict also involves feelings, such as anger, fear, or sadness. Conflicts are manifest through the parties' actions, from speech to violence. Each of these dimensions can vary independently of the other, although they usually do affect each other.

Mayer (2012) uses a wheel metaphor to describe the causes of conflict. Human needs are the ultimate causes of conflict—the "hub." However, basic needs are expressed through, and must be addressed through, other proximate causes: history, structure or context, emotions, values, and communication.

These proximate causes make up the "wheel of conflict." Attempts to understand a conflict should start by examining the proximate causes. A better understanding of the conflict's history and its context, and of the parties' feelings, values, and patterns of communication, will reveal their deeper needs. Human needs range from survival to substantive, procedural, and psychological concerns, to identity-based needs for community, meaning intimacy and autonomy.

Individuals exhibit many different cognitive, emotional, and behavioral conflict styles. A person's way of thinking may be analytic or intuitive, linear or holistic, integrative or distributive, reactive or proactive, process-oriented or outcome-oriented. Emotionally people may be enthusiastic or reluctant, feeling or rational, calm or volatile. People can be direct or indirect in their behavior, submissive or dominant, threatening or conciliatory. It is a trained and prudent business manager that can discern these behaviors that may be exhibited at the workplace.

To simplify the conflict resolution process at the business level means to recognize that the conflict exhibited at the workplace can take the form of action. This action is meant to express feelings and to articulate the individual's perceptions. The conflict behavior might involve a direct attempt to make something happen at someone else's expense. It might involve some type of violence or exercise of power. Whatever its tendency, the outward purpose is for the disputant to get their needs met. The nature and strength of the conflict and other issues should be brought out in an orderly conflict resolution session with a trained negotiator or mediator or in a peer review committee. This trained individual should possess emotional control techniques to manage high-stress encounters and have available frameworks for de-escalating tense conversations and exhibit active listening skills that open lines of communication.

Conflict Management in the Workplace

In the workplace, conflict among employees may create a hostile environment and hamper communication and collaboration. It can also affect the reputation of the management and the brand. Throughout the previous chapters, we have examined the benefits of conflict management in the workplace.

In any collaborative work environment, differences in opinions, priorities, and aspirations are inevitable, but these conflicts do not have to lead to dysfunction. Effective conflict resolution can spark meaningful dialogue, foster deeper understanding, and ultimately strengthen teams. However, many employees feel uneasy about addressing conflicts directly and are often unsure how to navigate these difficult conversations. Left unresolved, tensions from workplace conflict can fester, damaging morale, diminishing trust, and ultimately eroding engagement and retention. Ignoring conflict may feel easier in the short term, but over time, it creates a culture of avoidance rather than accountability. Organizations that prioritize healthy conflict resolution empower their teams to communicate more openly, address concerns early, and build stronger, more resilient workplace relationships.

Many may associate conflict with its potential for negative consequences. However, it can be productive when it is managed effectively. Conflict is destructive when:

- Communication breaks down.
- Relationships are impacted.
- Regular activities are disrupted.
- Individuals become fixed in their positions.
- Winning becomes the chosen goal.
- Disengagement occurs.
- It causes unnecessary stress.
- It creates a toxic environment.
- People outside of the conflict are impacted.

Conflict can be productive when:

- There is forward movement in communication, processes, and procedures.
- Those involved are relaxed with the disagreement and agree to disagree.
- It acts as a motivator for change (to do something differently or better as a result).
- It breaks down communication barriers.
- Individuals develop a better understanding of one another.
- The side effects do not create enduring damage for the individuals involved and those around them.

Successful Businesses

Successful business practices incorporate clear goal-setting, customer-centric strategies, and adaptive innovation. It is also wise to understand your market, build a strong team, and prioritize the customer experience. Part of strategic planning is to define SMART goals—Specific, Measurable, Achievable, Relevant, and Time-bound. Setting both short-term and long-term goals proves beneficial. This dual approach helps you recognize immediate financial targets while also developing your brand over time. Keeping detailed records of your progress can significantly enhance the probability of achieving these goals. Successful businesses have clear and well-documented goals, and they are the underpinning of any successful business.

An earlier chapter described and discussed technology issues with respect to enterprise operations. Utilizing technology has been key to streamlining business operations and gaining traction in a competitive landscape. The concept of leveraging technology is crucial for enhancing team communication and productivity. Using instant messaging platforms can enhance team communication by allowing for real-time discussions and file sharing. Video conferencing tools like Zoom facilitate virtual meetings, making it easier for remote teams to collaborate.

Enterprise Resource Planning (ERP) software streamlines daily operations by centralizing data access and reducing redundant tasks. Upgrading outdated workstations and software is vital for enhancing employee productivity and operational efficiency. The core elements of understanding legal requirements will be essential for avoiding potential legal issues and ensuring business compliance. Different types of business structures, such as LLCs and corporations, offer varying levels of personal liability protection. Business structure often requires specific licenses and permits depending on their industry and location (Nelson, 2025).

Successful enterprise practices are the techniques and strategies proven to produce desired results in a particular industry or business niche and implementing best practices can improve both individual productivity and the productivity of the business as a whole. By optimizing the processes, wasted time is reduced and the effort increases overall efficiency. Implementing best practices also means staying up-to-date with the latest technologies and industry advancements, which allows the company to remain competitive and relevant in the industry.

An additional benefit of implementing best practices is the reduction of risks and errors. By following established best practices, businesses can minimize the risk of mistakes, errors, and losses. It's also worth observing that these practices often incorporate quality standards, ethical guidelines, and safety measures that ensure compliance with all relevant regulations and laws.

Almost all successful businesses focus on customers, including what they want, how they feel, and where to find them. They also have a cadre of trained staff to monitor and address conflicts, disputes, and disagreements. It is key to remain flexible and willing to try new things to help the company meet its goals.

One example of a successful company that reinvented their business strategy is **Corning**. Corning, a world leader in glass, ceramics, and industrial material manufacturing, initially found success in the mid- to late 1800s by mass-producing glass for Thomas Edison's lightbulbs. The company continued to innovate and reinvent what it could do with glass. It notably created the Pyrex durable cookware line, as well as the optical fiber that paved the way for internet telecommunication adoption.

In 2010, Corning created its proprietary Synthemax, an animal-free surface that can be used for stem cell cultures. It acquired **Mediatech, Inc.**, the following year, and much of the Discovery Labware business the year after that. However, Corning is perhaps best known for its development of the hard-to-break Gorilla Glass used on technology products, such as the iPhone, iPad, and Apple Watch (Ludwig, 2025). The ongoing partnership between Corning and Apple has led to new advancements like the Ceramic Shield, designed to be stronger than any existing smartphone glass to date.

Most large companies are transforming more and faster than ever before. But an advanced group, reinventors, are embracing a deliberate strategy centered on a strong digital core (Total Enterprise Reinvention). These reinventors realize 10% higher incremental revenue growth, 13% higher cost-reduction improvements, and 17% higher balance-sheet improvements. Total Enterprise Reinvention sets a new performance frontier for companies and, in most cases, the industries in which they operate. Centered around a strong digital core, it helps drive growth and optimize operations. There are five characteristics companies must embrace to succeed at reinvention (Sweet, 2023):

- Reinvention is strategy.
- The digital core becomes a primary source of competitive advantage.
- Reinvention goes beyond benchmarks, embracing the art of the possible.
- Talent strategy and people impact are central to reinvention.
- Reinvention is continuous.

Some of the most fundamental skills objectives that were covered in this book are (1) to effectively distinguish between positions, needs and interests; (2) to be capable of reframing a conflict so it can viewed as a mutual problem to be resolved collaboratively; (3) to create and ask open-ended questions in a way that elicits the needs of the other side; (4) to listen actively and being able to reflect back the other side's needs; and (5) to create a collaborative climate through the use of open and transparent behaviors that are focused at uniting all parties to satisfactory resolutions.

Organizational Failures

In an extensive study of interorganizational relations (Burke and Biggart, 1997 in Druckman, Singer and Van Cott), researchers found that the majority of business failures are primarily due to the following reasons or conditions:

- Insufficient clarity about goals and how to measure progress toward the goals
- Imbalance of power and control among negotiating organizations
- Imbalance of status, expertise
- Unrealistic notions about future success of the relationship between organizations
- Lack of perceived equity

The possible conditions to deal with enterprise relations to accomplish success are as follows:

- Have subordinate goals or issues that can be accomplished.
- Create a balance of power.
- Create and nurture mutual gains.

- Have committed leaders and managers and negotiators.
- Have realistic assumptions about what can be accomplished or resolved and in what time frame.

Successful Business Diagnostics

Enterprises today want a comprehensive evaluation to identify issues and improve them to scale. Business diagnostics help achieve this clarity by revealing a business's strengths and weaknesses. Diagnostics identifies the source of an organization's shortcomings and helps one to fix them. The diagnostics is a structured process of assessing the health and performance of an organization and has recently emerged as a strategic imperative for employees, managers, and subject matter experts looking to pivot, scale, or sustain growth. For a seasoned workforce of professionals, understanding how to conduct effective diagnostics and leverage the right tools is key to making informed decisions that drive value and resilience. A diagnostic tool exploring three vital areas can help teams assess how well they're applying successful business practices.

Once work teams analyze the above three practices, workshops and seminars could ensue that cultivate further discussions by entertaining the following questions:

- What are the strengths and weaknesses of the actions?
- Are there any blind spots in these practices?
- What are some key actionable improvements?
- How can these actions be implemented?
- Are there any vital upgrades that seem to be missing or lacking?

To develop and conduct a business diagnostic involves the following:

- Begin by setting a clear objective.
- Use a structured framework that evaluates internal capabilities, external market alignment, financial health, and digital maturity.
- Engage the key stakeholders (leadership, departmental heads, and project managers).
- Leverage data along qualitative benchmarks.
- Interpret, prioritize, and act on the findings.

Table 22.1 Business practice diagnostic

Indicators	*Actions*
Data-driven indicators	Basic reporting, predictive analytics
Operational excellence	Empowered work teams, sharing best practices
Ethical leadership	Transparent governance, values-based accountability

Key and elemental to any organizational diagnosis is to identify the goal and scope. Following are the four important questions to consider:

- Why do you want to diagnose your organization?
- What specific concerns or obstacles do you want to address?
- What are the predicted results of the diagnosis?
- How will the outcomes influence your decisions and actions?

These questions will help the enterprise define the diagnostic goals and limits. They will also help the company to communicate them to all stakeholders.

Finally, a business diagnostic is a tool that can give a business clarity about how it's positioned to meet its growth aspirations. It looks across the enterprise to identify what's going well and what might be hindering any growth plans. It can help to address those issues you know about and identify those you don't. The main objective is to draw out the information you need to make informed decisions about improvements you can make in the business.

The diagnostic should tell you what's working well in the business, but you also need the mindset that accepts that:

- It's not a failure to discover that some things in your business could be done better or differently for an improved outcome.
- It's not a failure to discover that the workforce does not understand what the business stands for and how they contribute to its success.
- It's also not a failure to know, with certainty, that improvements could be made to basic processes in the business.

Enterprise Reinvention

Despite successive technological revolutions—from the internet boom to generative AI—productivity growth remains disappointingly sluggish. While many firms are already embracing reinvention to some extent, those who succeed in navigating the scale and speed of disruption in the next decade will be called reinventors.

Consider the European Union, where GDP per hour worked has risen by just 0.6% annually in recent decades. This lackluster growth contradicts the widely held expectation that advanced technologies would rapidly boost efficiency and replace human tasks at scale.

The reality is strikingly different: technology's potential to dramatically improve productivity remains largely untapped. Recent BCG (Bellefonds, 2024) research underscores that the GenAI revolution, at least so far, is no exception to this productivity paradox. Among more than 1,000 companies studied, only 4% have developed cutting-edge AI and GenAI capabilities across functions and are using them to consistently generate substantial value.

Organizations face two main barriers to translating technological advancements into substantial productivity gains. First, many companies implement advanced technology within outdated workflows rather than rethinking those processes entirely. Simply put, new technologies demand new, disruptive ways of working; applying innovative tools to old methods severely limits their potential. Second, fragmented governance and departmental silos cause narrow priorities to override broader organizational objectives, amplifying inefficiencies and eroding margins.

To overcome these obstacles, organizations must embrace an end-to-end reinvention strategy, fundamentally transforming ways of working and breaking down organizational and knowledge. Rather than optimizing isolated tasks, this approach rethinks entire workflows and eliminates frictions, conflicts, and inefficiencies, focusing on unmet needs, and seamlessly driving processes across different departments, such as sales and operations.

> *Leaders are not only deploying productivity plays but also reshaping core business processes and inventing new revenue streams.*

Enterprise reinvention and conflict resolution are deeply intertwined because reinvention disrupts the status quo, and conflict, if managed capably, can become a catalyst for innovation, alignment, and cultural transformation.

The redesigning of workflows and employee roles coupled with a shifting power dynamic can inevitably trigger conflict between departments, work teams, and leadership styles. However, if the changes are managed well, it can surface hidden assumptions, challenge outdated norms, and force clarity on what actually matters.

To transform conflict into a reinvention asset, businesses should adopt strategic conflict resolution frameworks that align with reinvention goals. The key component is the five modes Thomas–Kilmann Conflict Mode Instrument (TKI)—Competing, Collaborating, Compromising, Avoiding, Accommodating. Another component—the Interest-Based Relational Approach—is a framework that focuses on finding a win–win solution for both parties in a conflict. It emphasizes the importance of maintaining a positive relationship, respecting each other's interests and needs, and communicating openly and honestly. The approach involves four steps: separating the people from the problem, focusing on interests rather than positions, generating creative options, and using objective criteria to evaluate solutions. The approach helps you avoid getting stuck in a positional bargaining, where each party tries to defend their own position and make concessions, and instead look for a mutually beneficial outcome.

In April 2025, leaders from 38 countries and countless industries gathered in Dublin for the Reinvention Summit 2025. Three focused questions were posed: (1) Why are enterprise old tools no longer working? (2) What does a successful leader look like in an age of permanent disruption? (3) How do companies prepare for a future that can't be predicted? Some of the discussions centered around the following concepts (Zhexembayeva, 2025):

- The average lifecycle of a business model has dropped from 75 years to just 6.
- Success today depends on bridging the gap between strategy, innovation, and change.

Table 22.2 Enterprise reinvention/renegotiation triggers

Material changes in conditions	Shifts in market, trends, regulations
Operational breakdowns	Quality issues, delivery failures
Strategic realignment	Restructuring, outsourcing, mergers
Uneven risk allocation	Some carrying more risk than anticipated
Relationship maintenance	Litigation and other factors damage value

- Enterprises stop managing only change and start managing continuity.
- Instead of top-down control, companies need leadership that is cross-functional and cross-generational that can address problems quickly and collaboratively, then disperse.
- True reinvention is not about changing everything. It's about knowing what to protect at all costs.

The central hypothesis that frames reinvention is that reinvention is the strategy. Change isn't an initiative on the side; it is the strategy. Every part of the business is in scope for reinvention, and leadership mindset shifts from "How much can we change?" to "We're all about change, continuously." This means no area is off-limits; from business models to internal processes, everything can be reimagined to pursue new value.

Summary and Final Word

The emphasis of this book was to explore that in any enterprise environment, conflicts are inevitable. Differences in opinions, goals, and personalities can lead to disputes that, if not managed properly, can harm relationships and impact productivity. Understanding how to navigate these challenges effectively, both on an individual and company basis, is crucial for maintaining a healthy workplace and achieving long-term success. Discussed at length in previous chapters is an exploration of how work team disagreements over project priorities can be resolved by encouraging open dialogue and finding common ground. This not only solves the immediate issue but also builds trust amid team members. Companies that prioritize resolving disputes quickly and fairly often see improved employee satisfaction and better overall performance. Proactive and reactive management directly influence how organizations handle challenges related to conflict, risk, and deadlines. Proactive leadership strategies prevent and resolve conflicts more efficiently, mitigate risks, and enhance overall team cohesion.

Being proactive rather than reactive to enterprise conflict issues is the desired approach and prevention is often better than cure. Some tips to minimize the occurrence of disputes:

- Establish clear policies.
- Define roles, responsibilities, and procedures to reduce ambiguity.

- Promote a positive culture.
- Encourage respect, inclusivity, and open communication.
- Seek out strategies to diffuse tensions.
- Provide training.
- Equip employees with conflict resolution skills through workshops and seminars.
- Encourage feedback and develop trust within teams.
- Foster an open communication culture.
- Create channels for employees to express concerns early.
- Monitor and address possible conflict issues quickly.
- Don't let small problems worsen; address them before they escalate.
- Think about enterprise growth.
- Be prepared for anything.

By fostering an environment where conflicts are less likely to arise, businesses can save time and resources while maintaining a friendly and balanced workplace. Conflict resolution is an essential tool enterprise leaders can use to help maintain a positive and productive environment. Workplace disagreements typically exist to one degree or another and it is important to understand the best strategies to create resolution and agreement and to improve communication and collaboration skills among management, employees, and other stakeholders.

Everyone in a business setting is different. Therefore, it's not uncommon for people to have differences in opinions and points of view. These differences are what make collaborating successful, but also why problems happen once in a while. This is why conflict resolution skills are essential. When employees are unable to work together, conflicts can arise. This can lead to company's being unable to achieve their goals and have a high employee turnaround. A few consequences of opinion differences and improper conflict management are as follows:

- Low team confidence
- Negative impact on the project manager's authority
- Increased number of personal battles
- Low productivity and efficiency
- Low-quality work

No conflict resolution skill is more valuable than learning how to be okay with not having the perfect solution, especially when it comes down to working together as a team.

A beneficial way to resolve conflict in the workplace is to ask the question, "Does your behavior violate our core values?" Using the business's core values as the ultimate truth for what is acceptable behavior is a good way of preventing conflicts.

Structuring conflict/dispute resolution strategies requires a proactive and systematized approach to identify and mitigate potential risks. Alternative dispute resolution mechanisms, such as mediation, arbitration, and negotiation, can facilitate more efficient and cost-effective conflict resolution. Effective communication and collaboration approaches, including clear expectations, active listening, and cultural alignment, are essential for resolving disputes efficiently. Technology-driven solutions, like digital forensics can further enhance the dispute resolution process. By implementing a thorough strategy that integrates these elements, parties can reduce cycle time, increase resolution rates, and improve customer satisfaction.

A collaborative approach to dispute resolution can substantially improve outcomes by fostering an environment of mutual trust, respect, and open communication among parties. This collaborative approach involves active trust building measures, such as establishing clear goals and expectations, encouraging transparency, and promoting empathy and understanding. By doing so, parties can create a foundation for constructive dialogue, facilitating the exchange of information and ideas that benefit the entire community.

References

Bellefonds, N. (2024). *Where's the Value in AI?* Boston: Boston Consulting Group.

Burke, W. W., and Biggart, N. W. (1997). Interorganizational relations. In D. Druckman, J. Singer and H. Van Cott (eds.), *Enhancing Organizational Performance*. Washington, DC: National Academy Press.

Dsouza, M. (2025). *From Clashes to Collaboration: Practical Conflict Resolution Strategies for Leaders in 2025*. India: Eubrics Digital.

Jafferi, T. (2025). *Top 8 Workplace Conflict Resolution Strategies for 2025*. Myculture.ai

Lee, S. (2025). *The Art of Impartiality: A Guide to Conflict Resolution: Effective Strategies for Fair and Successful Dispute Resolution Outcomes*. New York: Number Analytics.

Ludwig, S. (2025). *13 Hugely Successful Companies That Reinvented Their Business*. Washington, DC: U.S. Chamber of Commerce.

Mayer, B. (2012). *The Dynamics of Conflict: A Guide to Engagement and Intervention* (2nd ed.). San Francisco, CA: Jossey-Bass.

Nelson, L. (2025). *15 Best Practices on How Do You Run a Successful Business*. AFA Education. Afaeducation.org.

Sweet, J. (2023). *Total Enterprise Reinvention: Setting a New Performance Frontier*. New York: Accenture.

Zhexembayeva, N. (2025). *Reinvent or Fall Behind: 5 Hard Truths from the Frontlines of Business*. Jersey City, NJ: Forbes.

23 PowerPoint Media Presentations

Negotiation Essentials PowerPoint—24 slides
Perception, Cognition, and Emotion PowerPoint—28 slides
Cross-Cultural International Negotiations PowerPoint—12 slides
Conflict, Power, Trust, and Culture PowerPoint—26 slides
Ethics in Negotiation PowerPoint—26 slides
Managing Disputes through Mediation—14 slides

DOI: 10.4324/9781042000258-24

Appendix

Sample Enterprise Exercises

Encouraging creative thinking allows teams to come up with innovative solutions to challenges. Teams that foster a culture of creativity can think outside the box and approach problems from different angles. Cohesive teams are those that work well together, have a strong sense of unity, and align with shared values and goals. Cohesion ensures that the individuals can function smoothly and efficiently, even in challenging situations.

The Dozen Question Work Relationship Exercise

Goals: To enhance work relationships in teams or groups. To stimulate group discussion about work-related topics. To clarify assumptions that team members make about each other.

Directions: Take turns asking questions. You must be willing to answer any question that you ask. Any member may decline to answer any question that someone else asks. All answers remain confidential within the group.

Questions Can Be Asked in Any Order

- How do you feel about yourself in your present job?
- What do you see as the next step in your career development?
- What personal characteristics do you have that get in the way of your work?
- What are you doing right now?
- Where do you see yourself five years from now?
- What was your first impression of me?
- How many different hats do you wear?
- What things do you do best?
- To whom are you closest with in your work situation?
- How do you want to receive feedback?
- What puzzles you about me?
- What personal growth are you making?

After 20–30 minutes, the facilitator assists members in discussing how the exercise is progressing. They may be alerted to the following considerations:

- Who questions whom?
- How open are we being?
- What risks are present in this exercise?
- To what degree is trust being generated?
- What are we learning about ourselves?
- What are we learning about each other?
- Whom might you want to do this with privately?
- How might we improve the exercise in the next round?

Work Supervisor Worksheet

Directions: Below is a list of characteristics that might be used to describe a work supervisor or administrator. Select the five characteristics that you feel are the most important for a supervisor or administrator and rank them in order of importance (1 is the most important; 5 is the least important).

Which of the five following characteristics are most important for a work supervisor or administrator?

________	initiative	________	generalized experience
________	interest in all employees	________	specialized experience
________	well organized	________	sense of humility
________	intelligence	________	good socializer
________	emotional stability	________	sense of humor
________	loyalty to the company	________	grasp of work issues
________	awareness of office politics	________	forward, progressive thinker

Life Crisis Consensus-Seeking Survey

Directions: Some events in our lives require significant personal and social readjustments. Rate the life crisis as to the amount of readjustment they require. MAJOR, MODERATE, MILD.

Crisis events to be ranked under the three levels:

A. Foreclose of loan/mortgage	G. Personal illness
B. Divorce	H. Pregnancy
C. Personal sex problems	I. Fired at work
D. Vacation	J. Change in residence
E. Death of a close friend	K. Death of relative/spouse
F. Child leaving home	L. Marriage

First Level: MAJOR	*Second Level: MODERATE*	*Third Level: MILD*
1.	4.	10.
2.	5.	11.
3.	6.	12.
	7.	
	8.	
	9.	

Growth Group Values Worksheet

Directions: Place a "+" in front of those values that correspond to your own and place an "x" in front of those that you personally reject. When completed, form groups of two to four and discuss your choices.

________ Active	________ Explorative	________ Sensitive
________ Ambitious	________ Good	________ Spontaneous
________ Aware	________ Helpful	________ Superior
________ Better	________ Honest	________ Supportive
________ Careful	________ Influential	________ Sure
________ Competitive	________ Loyal	________ Thoughtful
________ Considerate	________ Open	________ Tolerant
________ Creative	________ Productive	________ Trusting
________ Critical	________ Right	________ Unique
________ Different	________ Risky	________ Warm

After small group discussions are over, reconvene as a larger group and brainstorm which values are significant and important.

Characteristics of a Good Negotiator

Directions: Rank the items below as you perceive them in the order of importance from 1 to 10, 1 being the most important characteristic. After you have made a ranking, you will be asked to form into designated groups and discuss the items below until you arrive at consensus about the importance of the items as you see them.

Your ranking	*Ranking by group consensus*	
____	____	The negotiator is well disciplined and orderly.
____	____	The negotiator uses many methods to present the issues.
____	____	The negotiator sets high standards with sloppy work.

(Continued)

(Continued)

Your ranking	*Ranking by group consensus*	
_____	_____	The negotiator admits own faults/ errors to the other parties.
_____	_____	The negotiator makes outstanding use of time and space.
_____	_____	The negotiator is helpful and cooperative to other parties.
_____	_____	The negotiator keeps up to date on all aspects of company policies.
_____	_____	The negotiator places great emphasis on active listening
_____	_____	The negotiator sticks to a plan and does not concede easily.
_____	_____	The negotiator employs tactics/ strategies that may confuse or befuddle the other side.

Connect the Dots

Directions: Connect all nine dots with four straight lines. Do not lift the pen off the paper or retrace any line.

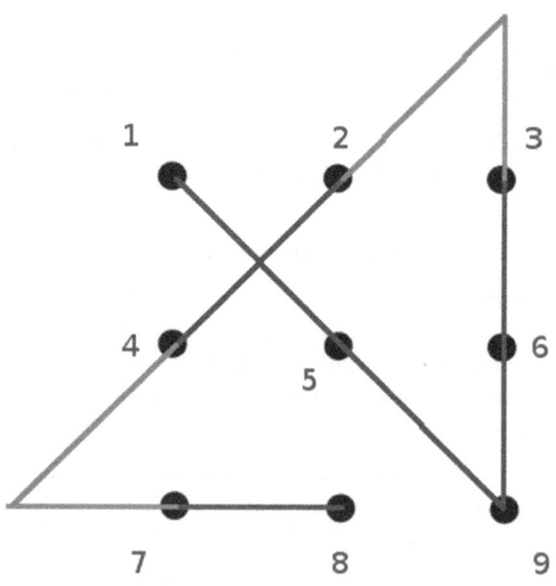

Figure A1 Possible solution.

Cultures in Conflict Research Project

Directions: This exercise is meant for groups of four. Select two countries or cultural groups that are currently in conflict or that have historically been in conflict.

In the group, form two pairs. One pair will research the conflict from the perspective of one of the two cultural groups or countries; the other pair will research the conflict from the perspective of the other group or country.

Outline the major issues and arguments. Explore the role of cultural values and political, economic, and historical contexts that may contribute to the conflict.

What about your team's reactions to conflict is useful? What is the cost of these reactions (is there a negative consequence to them)?

How do these reactions support or hinder the culture or country's place in the world?

Two Truths and a Lie

Goals: This activity encourages personal sharing in a light-hearted manner. In just several minutes, team members reveal interesting and often unexpected facts about themselves, breaking down formal barriers and promoting a culture of openness. As team members engage in guessing the lie, they pay close attention to each other's expressions and stories, enhancing their ability to understand and connect with each other.

The exercise also allows participants to get to know and appreciate one another better, through discovering both common and unique interests and experiences.

Directions: Break up into groups of three people. Each team member shares two true statements and one false statement about themselves. The rest of the team tries to guess which statement is a lie. The more memorable the facts (e.g., I went skydiving in Mexico) and the more believable the lies (e.g., I have three cats), the more fun the game will be!

Stranded

Goals: This group exercise activity helps employees learn about each other's values and problem-solving styles and promotes teamwork.

Directions: This exercise is ideal for groups of five people. Have available a flip chart and markers.

You are stranded on a remote island. What six items would you have brought with you if you knew there was a chance that you might be marooned? Note that they are only allowed six items per team, not per person.

Discuss and defend the choices with the whole group.

What Would "X" do?

Goals: Getting stuck in your own head can often keep you from solving a problem efficiently and effectively. By stepping into the shoes of someone else, you may uncover new solutions. And more, it's fun pretending to be someone else for a little while!

Directions: Team size: 5–10 people; Time: 45–60 minutes

Present your team with a problem and ask everyone to come up with a famous person or leader they admire. This can be a celebrity, a businessperson, or a relative. Challenge your teammates to approach the problem as if they were that person and present their solution (extra points for playing in character).

Sample problems/issues:

- Electrical power in the office is knocked out for two hours.
- Your personal computer has been hacked.
- A massive rainstorm has stranded every in the office for hours.
- Corporate management has introduced a company product you hate.
- Strict dress code policy mandated starting in a week.

Turning Back the Clock

Goals: This activity is an outstanding way to help team members remember their priorities and bond on a deeper level. In a team that's facing disconnection or stress, sharing personal highlights that aren't work-related can help create a sense of togetherness. Although the exercise doesn't take too long, it's best to do it toward the end of the day so your team has a chance to reflect on what's been said

Directions: Team size: 5–10 people; Time: 20–30 minutes

This team-building exercise works best in a quiet environment with everyone sitting in a circle.

Ask individuals to silently think of a unique memory in their lives. Allow everyone a few minutes to collect their thoughts. Then, everyone shares the one memory they'd like to relive if they could turn back time.

NOTE: Not everyone may be comfortable opening at first, so lead with vulnerability and make everyone in the room feel safe about sharing their moment.

Back-to-Back Drawing

Directions: Team size: 4+ people; Time: 5–10 minutes

> *Split your team into groups of two and make them sit back-to-back. Hand one person a pen and piece of paper and show the other person a picture of something that's fairly simple to draw (e.g., a car, a flower, a house).*
>
> *This person now must describe the picture to their teammate without actually saying what the item is so they can draw it. They're allowed to describe shapes, sizes, and textures but can't say, "Draw a rose." Once the blind drawing is finished, compare it with the original to see how well you communicated.*

This activity is a fun way to polish communication skills, especially listening skills. It also gives a team a chance to get creative and innovative by thinking outside the box to describe the image to their teammate.

Moon Survival

Goal: This activity shows the importance of teamwork by first having individuals try to complete the task alone. They will learn that after they're able to get in groups, it will be a lot easier (and more fun) determining the most logical ranking system for survival items on the moon.

Copy and distribute the following three pages (print enough copies of page one for each individual, plus one per team):

Directions: 1. Read the scenario out loud to the group. Give everyone 2–3 minutes to fill out their individual rankings. 2. Then, divide them into groups of three to six people and have them talk to each other and compare rankings. Have each team create a team ranking. 3. Then, read the real rankings out loud and give an explanation. Have each group calculate the absolute difference (positive or negative doesn't matter) between their ranking and the real ranking. Do the same for each team. 4. Then on the front whiteboard, have each team come up and write their average individual score, their team score, the difference between their individual average and their team score, and the number of people in their group who scored lower than the team score.

Scenario: You are a member of a space crew originally scheduled to rendezvous with a mother ship on the lighted surface of the moon. However, due to mechanical difficulties, your ship was forced to land at a spot some 200 miles from the rendezvous point. During reentry and landing, much of the equipment aboard was damaged and, since survival depends on reaching the mother ship, the most critical items available must be chosen for the

200-mile trip. Below are listed the 15 items left intact and undamaged after landing. Your task is to rank order them in terms of their importance for your crew in allowing them to reach the rendezvous point. Place the number 1 by the most important item, the number 2 by the second most important, and so on through number 15 for the least important.

Your ranking		*NASA ranking*
____	Box of matches	____
____	Food concentrate	____
____	50 feet of nylon rope	____
____	Parachute silk	____
____	Portable heating unit	____
____	Two .45 caliber pistols	____
____	One case of dehydrated milk	____
____	Two 100 lb tanks of oxygen	____
____	Stellar map	____
____	Self-inflating life raft	____
____	Magnetic compass	____
____	20 liters of water	____
____	Signal flares	____
____	First aid kit, including injection needle	____
____	Solar-powered FM receiver–transmitter	____

Answers

Item	*Ranking*	*NASA's reasoning*
Box of matches	15	Virtually worthless—there's no oxygen on the moon to sustain combustion
Food concentrate	4	Efficient means of supplying energy requirements
50 feet of nylon rope	6	Useful in scaling cliffs and tying injured together
Parachute silk	8	Protection from the sun's rays
Portable heating unit	13	Not needed unless on the dark side
Two .45 caliber pistols	11	Possible means of self-propulsion
One case of dehydrated milk	12	Bulkier duplication of food concentrate
Two 100 lb tanks of oxygen	1	Most pressing survival need (weight is not a factor since gravity is one-sixth of the Earth's—each tank would weigh only about 17 lbs. on the moon)
Stellar map	3	Primary means of navigation—star patterns appear essentially identical on the moon as on Earth
Self-inflating life raft	9	CO_2 bottle in military raft may be used for propulsion
Magnetic compass	14	The magnetic field on the moon is not polarized, so it's worthless for navigation

(Continued)

(Continued)

Answers

Item	*Ranking*	*NASA's reasoning*
20 liters of water	2	Needed for replacement of tremendous liquid loss on the light side
Signal flares	10	Use as distress signal when the mother ship is sighted
First aid kit, injection needle	7	Needles connected to vials of vitamins, medicines, etc. will fit special aperture in NASA space suit
Solar-powered FM receiver	5	For communication with mother ship (but FM requires line-of-sight transmission and can only be used over short ranges)

Scoring: For each item, mark the number of points that your score differs from the NASA ranking, then add up all the points. Disregard plus or minus differences. The lower the total, the better your score.

0–25 excellent
26–32 good
33–45 average
46–55 fair
56–70 poor—suggests use of Earth-bound logic
71–112 very poor—you're one of the casualties of the space program

Team Conflict Building and Assessment Survey

Do you want to maximize your participation in conflict discussions?	Y	N	Not sure
Will members share information candidly?	Y	N	Not sure
Can you work together to resolve conflicts?	Y	N	Not sure
Do you feel you know enough about conflict resolution techniques?	Y	N	Not sure
Are you confident in your manager/leader to resolve issues?	Y	N	Not sure
Are there long-standing conflict issues in your team?	Y	N	Not sure
Can your team work together successfully to address conflicts?	Y	N	Not sure
Are you or the team apprehensive about conflict resolution?	Y	N	Not sure
Will team members feel comfortable discussing conflict issues?	Y	N	Not sure

Scoring: If there are three or more NO responses, the team may need a trainer's help to discuss the results and plan for a conflict resolution training or workshop session.

Cited Enterprise Examples

Agrokor
Amazon Web Service
Ben & Jerry's Ice Cream
BMW
Boeing
British Aerospace
British Petroleum
Capital One
Chipolte
Coca Cola
Corning Glass
COSTCO Wholesale
CVS Health
Delta Airlines
Disney
eBay
Enron
Equifax
Honda Motors
Image retention theory
International Business Machines
Johnson & Johnson
Lucas Films
McDonald's
Meta
Microsoft
Netflix
Nike
Nokia
Patagonia
PayPal
Pepsi Cola
Rover

Samsung
SoftBank
Southwest Airlines
Starbucks
Target
TD Bank
Theranos
Ticketmaster
Tylenol
TOMS Shoes
United Airlines
WeWork
WorldCom

References

Abbas, T. (2023). *12 Important Steps in Crisis Communication*. Change Management Insight. changemanagementinsight.com.

Adams, B. (2024). *The Top 6 Tech Challenges Facing Businesses Today*. Mesa, Arizona: AZComp Technologies.

Agnes, M. (2024). *How to Create a Crisis Management Plan: A Step-By-Step Guide*. Austin, TX: Alert Media.

Allen, P. (2025). *7 Strategic Alliance Examples That Master Business Leverage*. ThinkinLeverage.com.

Altomonte, L. (2025). *What Is Risk Mitigation?* Sydney, Australia: SafetyCulture.

Ansler, L. B., Martinez, J. K., and Smith, S. E. (2020). *Dispute System Design: Preventing, Managing, and Resolving Conflict*. Menlo Park, CA: Stanford University Press.

Aquire, S. (2025). *14 Best Socially Responsible Companies Making an Impact*. Alexandria, VA: Donor Box.

Augsburger, D. (1992). *Conflict Mediation Across Cultures*. Louisville, KY: Westminster/John Knox Press.

Avgar, A. (2022). *Streamlining Conflict Resolution Through Technology*. Alexandria, VA: HRCI.

Barkacs, C. B. (2021). *The Top 7 Mistakes You Might Make That Squander Your Power*. Psychology Today.

Bartell, J. (2022). Corporate social responsibility and business ethics. *Forbes*.

Bazerman, M. H., and Neale, M. A. (1992). *Negotiating Rationally*. Free Press.

Belczyk, J. (2023). *Corporate Compliance Laws and Regulations You Should Know*. PA: University of Pittsburgh School of Law.

Bellefonds, N., and others. (2023). *Where's the Value in AI?* Boston: Boston Consulting Group.

Benoit, W. L. (1995). *Accounts, Excuses and Apologies: A Theory of Image Restoration*. Albany, NY: State University of New York Press.

Bensla, A. (2023). *Cultural Sensitivity in the Workplace*. Lewes, Delaware: Risely.

Bercovitch, J., Kremenyuk, V., and Zartman, I. W. (2009). *The Sage Handbook of Conflict Resolution*. Thousand Oaks, CA: Sage.

Berger, C. R. (2002). Goals and knowledge structures in social interaction. In M. Knapp and J. Daly (Eds.), *Handbook of Interpersonal Communication* (3rd ed.). Thousand Oaks, CA: Sage.

Bigham, L. B., Kim, K., and Raines, S. (2002). Exploring the role of representation in employment mediation. *Ohio State Journal of Dispute Resolution*, *17*, 341–378.

Birke, R. (2024). *Seven Tips for Interpersonal Conflict Resolution at Work*. Irvine, CA: Jams Pathways.

Blank, S. (2020). *Managing Organizational Conflict.* Jefferson, NC: McFarland & Company.
Blankenburgh, M. (2022). *The Four Pillars of Successful International Negotiations: Best Practices.* Dubai, UAE: Knowledge Workx.
Block, J. (2023). *After a Breach of Trust Don't Make It Worse.* New York: Psychology Today.
Bourque, S. (2025). *Power Must Be Balanced by Responsibility and Accountability.* Sambourque.com.
Broom, M. (2023). *Two Perspectives of Power & Conflict in Teams and Organizations.* Baltimore, MD: Cenor Human Systems.
Bryant, A. (2001). The quest to build a better boss. *The New York Times*, March 13.
Burke, W. W., and Biggart, N. W. (1997). Interorganizational relations. In D. Druckman, J. Singer and H. Van Cott (eds.), *Enhancing Organizational Performance.* Washington, DC: National Academy Press.
Burton, J. (1998). Conflict resolution: The human dimensions. *The International Journal of Peace Studies*, *3*(1).
Caburao, E. A. (2025). *What Is Compliance Management?* Sydney, Australia: Safety Culture.
Cai, J. (2025). *How to Successfully Negotiate with People in Cross-Cultural Settings.* Las Vegas, Nevada: The Black Swan Group.
Caplan, G. (1961). *An Approach to Community Mental Health.* New York: Grune & Stratton.
Carmeli, A., and Schaubroeck, J. (2008). Organizational crisis-preparedness: The importance of learning from failures. *Long Range Planning*, *41*, 177–196.
Carroll, A. (1991). The pyramid of corporate social responsibility: Toward the moral management of organizational stakeholders. *Business Horizons*, *34*(4), 39–48.
Cartwright, S., and Cooper, C. L. (1993). The role of culture compatibility in successful organizational marriage. *Academy of Management Executive*, *7*(2), 62.
Carvajal, A. (2024). *How to Optimize the Internal Negotiation of Contracts.* Munich, Germany: Top Legal.
Chaddock, L. (2023). *Bad Crisis Management Examples in Companies.* Salt Lake City, Utah: Sentiment.
Chen, F. (2023). *An Evaluation of Ticketmaster's Crisis Management During the Taylor Swift Ticket Fiasco.* San Francisco, CA: Medium.
Cheng, H. (2023). *Best Secrets for Leveraging Resources to Grow Your Business.* https://www.freedomtoascend.com.
Chladek, N. (2019). *Why You Need Sustainability in Your Business Strategy.* Harvard Business School Online.
Coleman, P., Chen-Carrel, A., and Regan, B. (2022). A new conflict-resolution model to advance DEI. *MIT Sloan Management Review*, Winter 2023.
Coleman, P., and Deutsch, M. (2000). *The Handbook of Conflict Resolution.* San Francisco, CA: Jossy-Bass.
Coombs, W. T. (2014). *Applied Crisis Communication and Crisis Management.* Thousand Oaks, CA: Sage.
Correa, M. (2024). Organizational harmony: A fresh framework to navigate tensions. In *The Leadership & Happiness Laboratory.* Cambridge, MA: Harvard Kennedy School.
Covey, S. (2004). *The 7 Habits of Highly Effective People.* New York: Simon & Schuster.
Crandell, S. (2022). *Integrative Thinking: Step Away from the Vantage Point.* Atlanta, Georgia: Korn Ferry.
Creswell, J., and Mahenswari, S. (2017). United grapples with PR crisis over videos of man being dragged off plane. *The New York Times*, April 11.
Cullington, N. (2023). *Not Just Another Vendor.* Cork, Ireland: Oak Tree Press.

Dana, D. (2006). *Managing Differences: How to Build Better Relationships at Home and Work*. St. Louis, MO: MTI Publications.
Dantas, R. G., Silva, V., Gomes, J., Vieira, M., and Amaral, J. C. (2024). Competitiveness, competitive intelligence, and strategic positioning: An integrated approach for organizational success. *IOSR Journal of Business and Management*. www.iosjournals.org.
Desimone, R. (2024). *Improve Work Performance with a Focus on Employee Development*. Gallup Workplace.
Dimitrov, P. (2025). *Agrokor's Legacy: How Ivica Todorić Became Croatia's Most Controversial Businessman*. Research Initiative. support@researchinitiative.org.
Doran, C. (2017). *Mediation Techniques for Managing Emotions*. Boston, MA: MWI.
Douglas, A. (1962). *Industrial Peacemaking*. New York: Columbia University Press.
Dsouza, M. (2025). *From Clashes to Collaboration: Practical Conflict Resolution Strategies for Leaders in 2025*. India: Eubrics Digital.
Economy, P. (2025). *Adaptability Is the Key to Success in an Evolving Market*. New York: About Inc.com.
Eichler, R. (2024). *Risk Management Framework (RMF): Definition and Components*. New York: Investopedia.
Falcao, H. (2017). *Four Reasons Why Internal Negotiations Are Harder Than External Ones*. San Francisco, CA: Insead.
Festinger, L. (1957). *A Theory of Cognitive Dissonance*. Stanford University Press.
Filley, A. (1975). *Interpersonal Conflict Resolution*. Glenview, IL: Scott, Foresman.
Folger, J., Poole, M., and Stutman, R. (2013). *Working Through Conflict: Strategies for Relationships, Groups, and Organizations*. Boston: Pearson.
Fruhlinger, J. (2020). *The Sarbanes-Oxley Act Explained: Definition, Purpose, and Provisions*. San Francisco, CA: CSO.
Garmston, R. J., and Wellman, B. M. (2013). *The Adaptive School: A Sourcebook for Developing Collaborative Groups*. Lanham, MA: Rowman & Littlefield Inc.
Garton, E. (2025). *Your Organization Wastes Time: Here's How to Fix It*. Boston, MA: Bain and Company.
Gentner, J., Lowenstein, J., and Thompson, L. (2003). Learning and transfer: A general role for analogical encoding. *Journal of Educational Psychology*, *95*(2).
Gerardi, D. (2001). Developing creativity and intuition for resolving conflicts: The magic of improvisation. *Mediate.com*.
Golbin, I. (2023). *Best Practices to Achieve Purpose-Led Tech*. New York: Price Waterhouse Coopers.
Goodera, T. (2024). *Leading Companies Shaping the CSR Landscape with Remarkable Impact*. Menlo Park, CA: Mediabrief.
Gosselin, T. (2007). *Practical Negotiating: Tools, Tactics & Techniques*. Santa Rosa, CA: O'Reilly Media.
Gotian, R. (2025). *4 Steps to Successfully Navigate Power Dynamics at Work*. Psychology Today.
Gottlieb, M., and Healy, W. J. (1998). *Making Deals: The Business of Negotiating* (2nd ed.). Albuquerque: The Communication Project.
Greer, L. (2014). *How Power Struggles Escalate*. CA: Standford Business.
Griffith, D. B., and Goodwin, C. (2016a). *Conflict Survival Kit: Tools for Resolving Conflict at Work*. Upper Saddle River, NJ: Pearson.
Griffith, D. B., and Goodwin, C. (2016b). *Conflict Survival Kit: Tools for Resolving Conflict at Work*. Boston, MA: Pearson.
Guevara, P. (2023). What is construction risk management? *Safety Culture*. Kansas City, MO.
Hayes, J. (2008). *Workplace Conflict and How Businesses Can Harness It to Thrive*. CPP: Global Human Capital Report Workplace.
Hedlund, W. (2019). *The Five Styles of Conflict*. Rochester, NY: Transforming Leader.

Hendon, D., Hendon, R., and Herbig, P. (1996). *Cross-Cultural Business Negotiations*. Westport, CT: Quorum Books.
Herbert, L. (2023). *The Power of Proactive Conflict Management*. Sunnyvale, CA: LinkedIn.
Herrity, J. (2024). *5 Conflict Resolution Strategies: Steps, Benefits and Tips*. New York: Indeed.
Holland, P. (2025). *Ethics in Life and Business*. Santa Clara, CA: Leavy School of Business.
Howe, D. (2023). *Understanding Interests, Rights, and Power in Negotiation*. Canyon, TX: ProfSpeak.com.
Jacquet, P. (2024). *The Jungian Confrerie*. London: Jungian Analysis & Psychotherapy.
Jafferi, T. (2025). *Top 8 Workplace Conflict Resolution Strategies for 2025*. Myculture.ai.
Jain, S. (2025). *Top 25 New Technology Trends in 2025*. Noida, Uttar Pradesh: Geeks for Geeks.
Johnson, E. (2020). *Boeing's 737 MAX Crisis*. Vancouver, BC: Wall Street Star.
Jones, T. (2001). Mediating with heart in mind: Addressing emotions in mediation practices. *Negotiation Journal*, *17*(3), 217–244.
Kahneman, D., and Tversky, A. (1979). Prospect theory in psychology: Loss aversion bias. *Econometrica*, *47*(2), 263–291.
Kanter, R. M. (1977). *Men and Women of the Corporation*. New York: Basic Books.
Kaplan, R., and Mikes, A. (2012). *Managing Risks: A New Framework*. Boston, MA: Harvard Business Review.
Kaplan, S. (2024). *How to Manage Team Conflict in Your Workplace*. New York: Psychology Today.
Karrass, C. L. (2020). *Effective Negotiating*. Los Angeles, CA: Karrass.com.
Katwala, J. (2024). *What to Avoid When Reporting Conflict*. Mountain View, CA: Creative Commons.
Katz, N. H. (2006). Interest-based negotiation: Increasing satisfaction levels among critical stakeholders. *Government Finance Review*, *22*. Nova Southeastern University.
Kaufmann, K. (2024). *Maximizing Impact: The Power of Leverage in Business*. San Diego, CA: Action Coach.
Kauth, K. (2020). *Cost of Workplace Conflict*. Mediate.com. www.mediate.com/articles/kauth-cost-workplace.cfm.
Kelley, H. H., and Schenitzki, D. (1972). Bargaining. In C. G. McClintock (ed.), *Experimental Social Psychology*. New York: Holt, Rinehart & Wilson.
Khonko, A. (2025). *How to Write a Report on Conflict Resolution: Win Trust, Share Leadership, Document Right*. San Francisco, CA: DART.
Kispert, P. (2023). *Integrative Thinking Success Stories: Real-world Examples of Innovation*. Boston, MA: Think Better Academy.
Klapper, M. (2011). *Defensive Creative Impasse-Breaking Techniques in Mediation*. New York State Bar Association.
Kleinfield, N. (1983). Tylenol's rapid comeback. *The New York Times*, *132*(45804).
Knapp, M., Vangelisti, A., and Caughlin, J. (2014). *Interpersonal al Communication and Human Relationships*. Boston, MA: Pearson.
Krantz, T. (2024). *What Is Environmental, Social and Governance (ESG)?* Armonk, NY: IBM.
Kressel, K. (1972). Practice-relevant research in mediation: Toward a reflective research paradigm. *Negotiation Journal*, 143–160.
Kurtz, C., and Snowden, D. (2003). The new dynamics of strategy: Sense-making in a complex and complicated world. *Armonk, NY: Systems Journal*, *42*.
Laksama, E. (2020). *Global Expert Survey 2020: Global and Regional Dynamics After COVID-19*. Jakarta, Indonesia: Center for Strategic and International Studies.

Laymon, R. (2024). *What Are Some Common Barriers to Effective Critical Thinking and Problem-Solving?* New York: Strategic Leaders Consulting.
Lee, S. (2015). Conflict is good for creativity. *INSEAD Knowledge*. Daejeon, South Korea Association to Advance Collegiate Schools of Business.
Lee, S. (2025). *The Art of Impartiality: A Guide to Conflict Resolution: Effective Strategies for Fair and Successful Dispute Resolution Outcomes*. New York: Number Analytics.
Leighton, N. (2023). *Top Five 2022 Corporate Crises and the Lessons Learned*. Phoenix, AZ: Public Relations Global Network.
Leonard, K. (2025). *Differences Between Destructive & Constructive Conflict*. Houston, TX: Chron.
Levine, S. (2002). *The Book of Agreement: 10 Essential Elements for Getting the Results You Want*. San Francisco: Berrett-Koehler Publishers.
Lewicki, R., Saunders, D., and Barry, B. (2007). *Essentials of Negotiation*. New York: McGraw-Hill.
Lewis, G. (2006). *Organizational Crisis Management: The Human Factor*. Boca Raton, FL: Auerbach Publications.
Lim, T. (2024). *Harnessing Creative Tension to Lead Organizational Change*. Jersey City, NJ: Forbes Coaches Council.
Ludwig, S. (2025). *13 Hugely Successful Companies That Reinvented Their Business*. Washington, DC: U.S. Chamber of Commerce.
Mahna, R. (2024). *Top 10 Common Cybersecurity Mistakes to Avoid*. New York: Eisner Amper.
Mancini, M. (2003). *Selling Destinations: Geography for the Travel Professional* (4th ed.). Clifton Park, NY: Thomson Delmar Learning.
Marino, R. D. (2024). *Strategies for Successful Cross-Border Negotiation*. Bala Cywyd, PA: Global Link Law.
Marker, A. (2020). *Models and Theories to Improve Crisis Management*. Bellevue, WA: Smart Sheet.
Marklein, M. B. (2014). Cantaloupe farmers get no prison time in disease outbreak. *USA Today*, January 28.
Martin, J. N., and Nakayama, T. K. (2022). *Intercultural Communication in Contexts*. New York: McGraw Hill.
Martin, R. (2007). *The Opposable Mind: How Successful Leaders Win Through Integrative Thinking*. Boston, MA: Harvard Business Press.
Martins, J. (2025). *6 Ways to Build Rapport and Develop Meaningful Relationships*. San Francisco, CA: Asana.
May, D. E. (2024). *The Role of Emotional Intelligence in Conflict Resolution*. Law Offices of Hayward, CA: Denise May.
Mayer, B. (2012). *The Dynamics of Conflict: A Guide to Engagement and Intervention* (2nd ed.). San Francisco, CA: Jossey-Bass.
McGinn, K., and Keros, A. (2003). *Improvisation and the Logic of Exchange in Socially Embedded Transactions*. Thousand Oaks, CA: Sage.
McGrath, A., and Jonker, A. (2025). *What Is SCRM?* Armonk, NY: IBM.
McLain, D., and Pendell, R. (2023). *Why Trust in Leaders Is Faltering and How to Gain It Back*. Gallup. www.gallup.com/workplace.
McLeod, S. (2023). *Social Identity Theory In Psychology*. SimplyPsychology.org. London.
Meers, T. (2024). *Incident Response Tabletop Exercise and Scenarios*. Little Chute, WI: Heartland Business Systems.
Mendiratta, A. (2024). *Bridging the Gap: How to Overcome Cultural Barriers in Negotiation*. New York: Negotiation Academy.
Michels, R. (1911). *Political Parties: A Sociological Study of Oligarchical Tendencies in Modern Democracy*. New York: Dover.

Miles, M. (2024). *How to Build Rapport with Someone and Find Common Ground*. San Francisco, CA: Better Up.
Mintz, S., and Miller, W. (2025). *The Story of Boeing's Failed Corporate Culture*. New York: The CPA Journal.
Mintzberg, H. (1998). *Strategy Safari: A Guided Tour Through the Wilds of Strategic Management*. Upper Saddle River, NJ: Prentice Hall.
Mirra, M. (2024). *Understanding Cross-Cultural Communication and Negotiation Around the World*. Brooklyn, NY: Aligned.
Mnookin, R., Peppet, S., and Tulumello, A. (2000). *Beyond Winning: Negotiating to Create Value in Deals and Disputes*. Boston, MA: Harvard University Press.
Mollah, S. (2024). *The Art of Compromise: External Versus Internal Negotiation*. The Vex Mind.
Moore, B. (2024). *10 Great Examples of Ethical Decision Making in Business*. Moosinning, Germany: Great Work Life.
Moosa, I. (2007). *Operational Risk Management*. New York: Macmillan.
Morrison, T., and Conaway, W. W. (2006). *Kiss, Bow, or Shake Hands*. Avon, MA: Adams Media.
Nelson, L. (2025). *15 Best Practices on How Do You Run a Successful Business*. AFA Education. Afaeducation.org.
Newman, S. (2025). *Embracing Cultural and Behavioral Differences for Global Negotiation Success*. Sydney, Australia: ENS.
Nicodemus, A. (2024). *Top Ethics and Compliance Failures of 2024*. Boston, MA: Compliance Week.
Nunn, J. (2026). *What Is Incident Reporting?* Perth, Australia: Work Metrics.
Overvest, M. (2024). *International Negotiation: The Ultimate Guide of 2025*. Wichita, KS: Procurement Tactics.
Overvest, M. (2025). *13 Negotiation Principles: A Guide to Crush Your Next Deal*. Wichita, KS: Procurement Tactics.
Palmer, A. (2019). *The Strangest and Most Alarming Things in WeWork's IPO Filing*. Englewood Cliffs, NJ: CNBC.
Park, J., Mukhi, R., and Doyno, A. (2023). *Best Practices for Crisis Management Preparation*. Reuters.
Pathak, R. (2020). *The Prophet's New Prediction*. Analytics Steps.
Paton, E. (2021). Fears for Bangladesh garment workers as safety agreement nears an end. *The New York Times*, May 28.
Payne, V. (2001). *The Team-Building Workshop: A Trainer's Guide*. New York: Amacom.
Pederson, P. (2001). The cultural context of peacemaking. In D. J. Christie, R. V. Wagner and D. D. White (eds.), *Peace Conflict and Violence Peace Psychology for the 21st Century*. Upper Saddle River, NJ: Prentice Hall.
Peltier, B. (2010). *The Psychology of Executive Coaching: Theory and Application* (2nd ed.). New York: Routledge.
Phelps, R. (2018). *Crisis Management: How to Develop a Powerful Program*. San Francisco, CA: ChandiMedia.
Picinu, A. (2019). *The Effects of Workplace Conflict*. Bizfluent.com.
Pinger, Y. (2025). *Embracing Cultural and Behavioral Differences for Global Negotiation Success*. Sydney, Australia: Negotiation Skills Training International.
Pinto, P. (2025). *7 Powerful Conflict Management Strategies That Transform Technology Teams*. Miami, FL: Coachpedropinto.com.
Pollack, J. (2025). *What Is Organizational Conflict and 5 Strategies for Managing It*. Los Angeles, CA: Peacebuilding Systems.
Pollack, J., Park-Stamm, E., Shaw, N., and Weiner, A. (2022). Negotiating with those like me: Similarity salience increases positive attitudes in imagined negotiation with an out-group member. *Peace and Conflict: Journal of Peace Psychology*, *28*(4), 512–527. Stanford, CA: Crown.

PON Staff. (2024). How to negotiate in cross-cultural situations. In *Program on Negotiation at Harvard Law School*. Cambridge, MA: Harvard Negotiation Law Review.

Pruitt, D. G. (1981). *Strategic Choices in Negotiation*. Negotiation Behavior. New York: Academic Press.

Quoidbach, J. (2024). *Navigating Time Pressure in Negotiations: A Double-Edged Sword By*. Jersey City, NJ: Forbes.

Raines, S. (2024). *Conflict Management and Leadership for Managers*. Lanham, MD: Rowman and Littlefield Publishing.

Randel, M. (2025). *Rebuilding Trust After Difficult Decisions: A Relationship-Based Approach*. San Francisco, CA: Simpler Media Group.

Ré, E. (2003). *101 Secrets to Negotiating Success*. Albuquerque, NM: Canyon Crest Publishing.

Reddington, R. (2023). *How Leadership Trust Guides High-Performing Teams*. San Francisco, CA: Better Up.

Riel, J., and Martin, R. (2017). *Creating Great Choices*. Boston, MA: Harvard Business Review Press.

Rifenburgh, E. (2024). *Protecting Leverage in Negotiations: The Key to Achieving Your Goals*. Denver, CO: The Negotiation Experience.

Roberts, J. (2024). *20 Pros and Cons of Brainstorming*. https://prospluscons.com.

Rock, T. (2025). *7 Real-Life Business Continuity Plan Examples You'll Want to Read*. Invenio IT.com.

Roff, C. (2024). *Everything you Need to Know About the Theranos Scandal*. Hampshire, England: Pan Macmillan.

Roger, G. (2006). *Theory and Practice of Leadership*. New York: Sage.

Rogers, N., Bordone, R., Sander, F., and McEwen, C. (2019). *Designing Systems and Processes for Managing Disputes*. New York: Wolters Kluwer.

Rogula, J. (2025). Optimizing your enterprise risk management strategy. *Risk Management Magazine*. New York.

Rotenberg, M. (2018). *Testimony before the House Committee on Financial Services, Hearing on Examining the Current Data Security and Breach Notification Regulatory Regime*, February 14). https://archive.epic.org.

Rummel, R. J. (1981). *Understanding Conflict and War*. Beverly Hills, CA: Sage Publications.

Rus, D., Knippenburg, D., and Wisse, B. (2013). Leader power and self-serving behavior: The moderating role of Accountability. *The Leadership Quarterly*, *2*(13–26).

Sada, J. (2024). *Comprehensive Guide to Collaborative Risk Management*. Sunnyvale, CA: LinkedIn.

Salacuse, J. (1991). *Making Global Deals: What Every Executive Should Know About Negotiating Abroad*. New York: Times Books.

Schaller, J. (2010). Almost ten years after the Enron meltdown. In *The Hidden Challenge of Cross-Border Negotiations*. Boston, MA: The Magazine HBR.

Schwenk, C. R. (1988). *The Essence of Strategic Decision Making*. MA: Lexington Books.

Scottwork. (2024). *How to Overcome Cultural Barriers in Negotiation*. London, UK: info@scotwork.com.

Senge, P. (1990). *The Fifth Discipline: The Art and Practice of the Learning Organization*. New York: Currency/Doubleday.

Shalimov, A. (2024). *6 Tech Trends (and 4 Challenges) for Enterprises in 2024*. Herzliya, Israel: Eastern Peak.

Shapiro, D. L. (2010). Relational identity theory. *American Psychologist*, *65*(7).

Sharma, K., Schoorman, F. D., and Ballinger, G. A. (2023). How can it be made right again? A review of trust repair research. *Journal of Management*, *49*(1), 363–399.

Shonk, K. (2025). *How to Deal with Cultural Differences in Negotiation*. Program on Negotiation. Harvard Law School.

Silberman, M. (2006). *Active Training* (3rd ed.). San Francisco, CA: Pfeiffer.

Sloane, P. (2023). *Lateral Thinking for Every Day: Extraordinary Solutions to Ordinary Problems*. London: Kogan Page Limited.

Small, J., and McDonald, M. (2024). *7 Surprising Steps to Grow Your Practice Through Leadership*. Dallas, TX: Line of Sight Coaching.

Smith, B. (2023). *The Ethics of Technology: What Businesses Need to Consider When Adopting New Technologies*. Herdon, VA: Centurion Consulting Group.

Srivastav, A. K. (2021). *What Is Compliance Officer?* Mumbai, India: Wall Street Mojo.

Stabell, K. P. (2022). *Negotiating Under Pressure—Conflict Resolution in Crisis Situations*. Ann Arbor, MI: Center for Conversational Conflict Resolution.

Sturges, D. L. (1994). Communicating through a crisis: A strategy for organizational survival. *Management Communication Quarterly*, 7(3), 297–316.

Sur and Anand. (2019). *Cross-Cultural Conflict: Its Evidences And Impact*. Bangalore, India: Christ University.

Swann, W. B., and Bosson, J. K. (2008). Identity negotiation: A theory of self and social interaction. In *Handbook of Personality: Theory and Research*. New York: The Guilford Press.

Sweet, J. (2023). *Total Enterprise Reinvention: Setting a New Performance Frontier*. New York: Accenture.

Tetrick, L. E., and Winslow, C. J. (2015). Workplace stress management interventions and health promotion. *Annual Review of Organizational Psychology and Organizational Behavior*, 2(1), 583–603.

Thomas, K. W., and Kilmann, R. H. (1974). *The Thomas-Kilmann Conflict Mode Instrument*. Mountain View, CA: CPP, Inc.

Thompson, J. (2025). *6 Effective Strategies for Communication in a Crisis*. Los Angeles, CA: Business.com.

Ting-Toomey, S. (2013). Face negotiation conflict theory. In K. Keith (ed.), *The Encyclopedia of Cross-Cultural Psychology*. Hoboken, NJ: Wiley-Blackwell Publishers.

Tristancho, C. (2024). *Project Time Management: Strategies, Tips & Tools*. Austin, TX: Project Manager.

Turanevya, K. M. (2024). Diplomatic negotiations and conflict resolution in international relations. *Ethiopia: International Research Journal of Nature Science and Technology*, *5*(11), 7661–7671.

Ugalde, J. (2023). *15 Technology Challenges Businesses May Face in 2023*. Chesterfield, MI: Systems X.

Villanueva, E. (2023). *Risk Management 101: Process, Examples, Strategies*. Cerritos, CA: Audit Board.

Voss, C. (2016). *Never Split the Difference: Negotiating as If Your Life Depends on It*. Harper Collins.

Weber, R. A., and Camerer, C. F. (2003). Cultural conflict and merger failure: An experimental approach. *Management Science*, *49*(4).

Whitmore, E. (2024). *Cross Cultural Negotiations*. North York, ON: Stitt Feld Handy Group.

Wilkins, A. L., and Ouchi, W. G. (1983). Efficient cultures: Exploring the relationship between culture and organizational performance. *Organizational Culture*, *28*, 468–481.

Wilson, C. (2022). *14 Conflict Resolution Strategies for the Workplace*. PositivePsychology.com. Amsterdam.

Winkler, C. (2024). *Negotiation Skills: Building Trust in Negotiations and Why It's Important*. New York: The Negotiation Academy,

Wish, M., Deutsch, M., and Kaplan, S. J. (1976). Perceived dimensions of interpersonal relations. *Journal of Personality and Social Psychology*, *33*, 409–420.

Wooll, M. (2022). How to build trust in the workplace: 10 effective solutions. *Better Up*. San Francisco, CA.
Zak, P. (2017). *Trust Factor: The Science of Creating High-Performance Companies*. Grand Haven, MI: Brilliance Audio.
Zaki, M. (2025). *Breaking Cultural Barriers: A Guide To Building Trust Across Borders*. Jersey City, NJ: Forbes Media.
Zhang, S. (2022). *How to Embrace Creative Tension and Do Your Best Work*. San Franciso, CA: Dropbox.
Zhexembayeva, N. (2025). *Reinvent Or Fall Behind: 5 Hard Truths from the Frontlines of Business*. Jersey City, NJ: Forbes.

Index

Note: Page numbers in *italics* indicate a figure and page numbers in **bold** indicate a table on the corresponding page.

For Product Safety Concerns and Information please contact our
EU representative GPSR@taylorandfrancis.com Taylor & Francis
Verlag GmbH, Kaufingerstraße 24, 80331 München, Germany